CORRESPONDENCE

OF

WAGNER AND LISZT.

Richard Wagner

Taken from a portrait
painted in 1853.

CORRESPONDENCE

OF

WAGNER AND LISZT.

TRANSLATED INTO ENGLISH,

WITH A PREFACE,

BY

FRANCIS HUEFFER.

New Edition Revised,

AND FURNISHED WITH AN INDEX, BY

W. ASHTON ELLIS.

VOL. 1.

1841–1853.

GREENWOOD PRESS, PUBLISHERS
NEW YORK

Originally published in 1897
by Charles Scribner's Sons

First Greenwood Reprinting 1969

Set SBN 8371-2743-2
Vol. 1 SBN 8371-2744-0

PRINTED IN UNITED STATES OF AMERICA

NOTE TO THE SECOND EDITION.

THIS new edition of the *Correspondence of Wagner and Liszt* is substantially identical with the first, as translated by the late Dr. Hueffer. In view of the admirable nature of Dr. Hueffer's work, revision was unnecessary save in the case of a few misprinted words and dates. These misprints have been corrected in the present edition, so far as they have come or been brought to my knowledge ; as regards the dates of the letters themselves, I may add that I have carefully collated them all with those given in the original German edition.

It was Dr. Hueffer's wish " to supply notes and a serviceable index, to give a clue to the various persons who are hidden under

initials," in a second edition; but alas! a few
months after the writing of that sentence he
himself was taken by death, and the "notes"
remain unwritten. Since then, however, another
large collection of Wagner's letters (the *Letters
to Uhlig*, *etc.*) has appeared, and to a great
extent has removed the necessity of throwing
further light upon the few, the very few
passages in these volumes that formerly required it. One reference alone to me appears
to still demand elucidation — namely, the
mention of "Heine" on pages 161 and 163 of
Volume I. Here it is undoubtedly the poet
Heinrich Heine who is meant, not Ferdinand
Heine, the intimate friend of Wagner to
whom allusion is made in later letters. Nor
would it be necessary to clear up even this
point, had not Liszt mistaken the date of appearance of Heine's skit upon himself; actually,
it was printed in the *Deutsche Monatsschrift*
for September 1850—not in 1851—and
therefore the present intimation may assist the
curious in such matters. The verses, however,

are of little account : merely a splenetic attack
on Liszt for sticking to his work at Weimar
and celebrating Goethe's Centenary in 1849,
while Hungary was in rebellion ; for Heine
seems to have forgotten that he himself lay
idle in Paris—though ill, 'tis true—while Germany was convulsed by the throes of revolt.

As to the two other unfulfilled proposals
of the late Dr. Hueffer, I trust the accompanying index may in some sort fill the gap.
Originally I prepared it simply for my private
use, upon the first appearance of the book,
and all that I now have done is to check
the references.   An index to a work of this
kind must necessarily be more or less imperfect, for as soon as one goes beyond the
proper names—in truth, the *least* essential
thing in such a Correspondence—one is faced
with the difficulty of choosing suitable cate-
gories in which to range the subjects dealt
with.   Such an index must therefore be largely
regulated by one's own personal point of view
as to what is, and what is not important,

and can scarce do more than furnish the rough framework for the individual reader himself to fill in.

Of the "initials" very few are difficult to decipher, though my interpretation of them must be taken as purely personal and without the smallest pretence to an authoritative statement. Some half-dozen, however, are inexplicable by any but the persons directly concerned; these cases, on the other hand, are of quite subsidiary importance.

With regard to the details of enumeration in the Index: in view of the large number of citations, and therefore to economise space, I have adopted a plan which I believe is unusual, though I have found it answer fairly well in the different volumes of my translations of "Richard Wagner's Prose Works." It is this: the figures denoting the *same* tens and hundreds are not repeated for one and the same heading, or sub-heading, saving where a fresh line of type is commenced; thus "16, 19, 107, 108, 125" would be found set up as "16, 9,

107, 8, 25," for instance. I hardly think that any greater difficulty will be experienced in following this indication than in remembering that all references after "ii." pertain to the second volume, without the repetition of that "ii." for every quoted page.

I have only further to commend to the reader a book whose fascination grows with every fresh perusal.

WILLIAM ASHTON ELLIS.

September, 1896.

TRANSLATOR'S PREFACE.

THE best introduction to this important correspondence of the two great musicians will be found in the following extract from an autobiographical sketch written by Wagner in 1851. It has been frequently quoted, but cannot be quoted too often, describing, as it does, the beginning and the development of a friendship which is unique in the history of art.

"Again I was thoroughly disheartened from undertaking any new artistic scheme. Only recently I had had proofs of the impossibility of making my art intelligible to the public, and all this deterred me from beginning new dramatic works. Indeed, I thought everything was at an end with my artistic creativeness. From this state of mental dejection I was raised by a friend. By the most evident and undeniable proofs he made me feel that I was not deserted, but, on the contrary, understood deeply by those even who were otherwise most distant from me ; in this way he gave me back my full artistic confidence.

" This wonderful friend has been to me Franz Liszt. I must enter a little more deeply into the character of this friendship, which, to many, has seemed paradoxical.

" I met Liszt for the first time during my earliest stay in Paris, and at a period when I had renounced the hope, nay, even the wish of a Paris reputation, and, indeed, was in a state of internal revolt against the artistic life I found there. At our meeting Liszt appeared to me the most perfect contrast to my own being and situation. In this world, to which it had been my desire to fly from my narrow circumstances, Liszt had grown up from his earliest age, so as to be the object of general love and admiration at a time when I was repulsed by general coldness and want of sympathy. In consequence, I looked upon him with suspicion. I had no opportunity of disclosing my being and working to him, and, therefore, the reception I met with on his part was altogether of a superficial kind, as was indeed quite natural in a man to whom every day the most divergent impressions claimed access. My repeated expression of this feeling was afterwards reported to Liszt, just at the time when my *Rienzi* at Dresden attracted general attention. He was surprised to find himself misunderstood with such violence by a man whom he had scarcely known, and whose acquaintance now seemed not without value to him. I am still touched at recollecting the repeated and eager attempts he made to change my opinion of him, even before he knew any of my works. He acted not from any artistic sympathy, but was led by the purely human wish of discontinuing a casual disharmony between himself and another being ; perhaps he also felt an infinitely tender misgiving of having really hurt me unconsciously. He who knows the terrible selfishness and insensibility in our social life, and especially in the relations of modern artists to each other, cannot but be struck with wonder, nay, delight, by the treatment I experienced from this extraordinary man.

" This happened at a time when it became more and more evident that my dramatic works

would have no outward success. But just
when the case seemed desperate Liszt succeeded by his own energy in opening a
hopeful refuge to my art. He ceased his
wanderings, settled down at the small, modest
Weimar, and took up the conductor's *bâton*,
after having been at home so long in the
splendour of the greatest cities of Europe.
At Weimar I saw him for the last time,
when I rested a few days in Thuringia, not
yet certain whether the threatening prosecution would compel me to continue my flight
from Germany. The very day when my
personal danger became a certainty, I saw
Liszt conduct a rehearsal of my *Tannhäuser*,
and was astonished at recognizing my second-
self in his achievement. What I had felt in
inventing this music he felt in performing it ;
what I wanted to express in writing it down
he proclaimed in making it sound. Strange
to say, through the love of this rarest friend,
I gained, at the moment of becoming homeless,
the real home for my art, which I had longed
for and sought for always in the wrong place.

"At the end of my last stay in Paris, when ill,
miserable, and despairing, I sat brooding over

my fate, my eye fell on the score of my
Lohengrin, totally forgotten by me. Suddenly
I felt something like compassion that this music
should never sound from off the death-pale
paper. Two words I wrote to Liszt ; his
answer was the news that preparations for the
performance were being made on the largest
scale the limited means of Weimar would
permit. Everything that men and circumstances could do was done in order to make
the work understood. Success was his reward,
and with this success he now approaches me,
saying, ' Behold we have come so far ; now
create us a new work that we may go still
further.' "

Wagner's words, as above quoted, may have
seemed an exaggerated tribute of gratitude to
many. After reading these letters one comes
to the conclusion that they are the expression
of a plain fact. It is a well-known French
saying that in every love affair there is one
person who adores while the other allows
himself to be adored, and that saying may,
with equal justice, be applied to the many
literary and artistic friendships of which, *pace*
the elder D'Israeli, history knows so many

examples. Petrarch and Boccaccio, Schiller and Goethe, Byron and Shelley immediately occur to the mind in such a connection; but in none of these is the mutual position of giver and receiver of worshipper and worshipped so distinctly marked as in the case under discussion.

Nature itself, or, at least, external circumstances, had indeed almost settled the matter. In the earlier stages of this friendship the worldly position of the two men was a widely different one. Liszt was at the time perhaps the most famous musician alive, and although he had voluntarily abandoned an active career, he remained the friend of kings and ecclesiastic potentates, and the head and centre of an admiring school of disciples.

Wagner at the same period was, in familiar language—nobody. He had lost his position at the Royal Opera at Dresden through his participation in the revolutionary rising of 1849, and he was an exile from his country. As an artist his antecedents were not very glorious. He had written three operas, all of which had met with fair success, but none of which had taken real hold of the public, and the Court theatres of Germany were naturally not very prone to favour the interests of an outlawed rebel. In spite of this disparity of fortune, it is curious to see how the two men, almost from the first, assume the mutual position already indicated. Liszt, from the beginning, realises, with a self-abnegation and a freedom from vanity almost unique in history, that he is dealing with a man infinitely greater than himself, and to serve the artistic and personal purposes of that man he regards as a sacred duty.

Wagner's attitude in the matter will be judged differently by different people, according to the opinion they have of the permanent and supreme value of his work. He simply accepts the position as he finds it. "Here am I," he may have said to himself, "with a brain teeming with art work of a high and lasting kind; my resources are *nil*, and if the world, or at least the friends who believe in me, wish me to do my allotted task, they must free me from the sordid anxieties of existence." The words, here placed in quotation marks, do not actually occur in any of the letters, but they may be read between the lines of many of them. The *naïveté* with which Wagner expresses himself on this subject is indeed almost touching, and it must be owned that his demands for help are, according to English notions at least, extremely modest. A pension of 300 thalers, or about £45 of our money, which he expects from the Grand Duke of Weimar for the performing right of his operas, is mentioned on one occasion as the summit of his desire. Unfortunately, even this small sum was not forthcoming, and Wagner accordingly for a long time depended upon the kindness of his friends and the stray sums which the royalties on his operas brought him as his sole support. He for himself, as he more than once declares, would not have feared poverty, and with the touch of the dramatic element in his nature, which was peculiar to him, would perhaps have found a certain pleasure in going through the world, an artistic Belisarius asking the lovers of his art for their obolus. But he had a wife (his first wife), weak in health, and anxious of mind, and to protect her from every care is his chief desire—a desire which has something beautiful and pathetic in it, and is the redeeming feature of the many appeals for a loan, and sometimes for a present, which occur in these letters.

Liszt was only too willing to give, but his means were extremely limited. He had realised large sums during his artistic career; but he was liberal almost to a fault, and poor artists, inundated Hungarian peasants, and the Beethoven monument at Bonn profited a great deal more by his successes than he did himself. What little remained of his savings had been settled upon his aged mother and his three children, and at the time here alluded to his only fixed income was the salary of less than £200, which he derived from the Weimar Theatre. This explanation he himself gives to Wagner, in answer to the following remarkable sentence in one of that master's letters :—" I once more return to the question, can you let me have the 1,000 francs as a gift, and would it be possible for you to guarantee me the same annual sum for the next two years?" The 1,000 francs was forthcoming soon afterwards, but poor Liszt had to decline the additional obligation for two other years.

The above passage is quoted as an instance of many others, and one must admire the

candour of Wagner's widow, who has not
suppressed a single touch in the picture of this
beautiful friendship. But Liszt's help was not
limited to material things. What was infinitely
more valuable to Wagner, and what excited his
gratitude to even more superlative utterance,
was the confidence which Liszt showed in his
genius, and without which, it is no exaggeration to say, Wagner's greatest works would
probably have remained unwritten.

The first performance of *Lohengrin* at
Weimar, which was really the starting-point of
his fame, has already been alluded to. Every
further step in his career was watched and
encouraged by the loving sympathy of Liszt,
and when Wagner, overpowered by the
grandeur and difficulties of his *Nibelungen*
scheme, was on the point of laying down
the pen, it was Liszt who urged him to
continue in his arduous task, and to go on
in spite of all discouragement.

It must not, however, be thought that
Wagner alone derived benefits from this remarkable friendship. Not only did he in his turn
encourage Liszt in the career of a composer of
great and novel works, but he distinctly raised

the intellectual and artistic level of his friend.
Liszt's nature was of a noble, one may say,
ideal kind, but he had lived in dangerous surroundings, and the influence of the great world
and of the glaring publicity in which a virtuoso
moves, had left its trace on his individuality.
Here, then, the uncompromising idealism, the
world-defying artistic conviction of Wagner,
served as a tonic to his character. If the reader
will refer to Letter 21, or at least to that portion
of it which has been vouchsafed by Madame
Wagner, he will see how necessary the admini-
stration of such a tonic was to a man who even
at that time could think it necessary to deprecate
the "superideal" character of *Lohengrin*, and to
advise in a scarcely disguised manner that the
Knight of the Grail should be brought a little
more within the comprehension of ordinary people.
All the more beautiful is it to see how Liszt is
ultimately carried away by the enthusiasm of his
great friend, how he also defies the world, and
adopts the device *L'art pour l'art* as his guiding
principle. Altogether the two friends might
have said to each other in the words of Juliet :—

> " My bounty is as boundless as the sea,
> My love as deep ; the more I give to thee,
> The more I have, for both are infinite."

A few words should be said of the spirit in which the translator has undertaken his extremely difficult task. There are in these pages many things which are of comparatively little interest to the English reader,—allusions to circumstances and persons with which he cannot be expected to be familiar, especially as the latter are frequently veiled by initials. There is no doubt that judicious omissions might have made these pages more readable and more amusing. But then such a book as this is not meant to amuse. It is almost of a monumental character, and his deep respect for that character has induced the translator to produce its every feature,—a remark which applies to manner no less than to matter. In consequence, not a line has been omitted, and the manners and mannerisms of the writers have been preserved as far as the difference of the two languages would allow. Such effusions of German enthusiasm as "dearest, best, most unique of friends," "glorious, great man," and the italics which both Wagner and Liszt employ with a profusion of which any lady might be proud, have been scrupulously preserved. These slight touches give a racy flavour to the

letters; and although they may occasionally call
forth a smile, they will, no doubt, be appreciated
by those who with Sterne "can see the precise
and distinguishing marks of national character
more in these nonsensical *minutiæ* than in the
most important matters of state."

That the task of reproducing these *minutiæ*
without doing too much violence to the English
idiom was an extremely difficult one, the experienced reader need not be told. Liszt, it is
true, writes generally in a simple and straight-
forward manner, and his letters, especially those
written in French, present no very great obstacles; but with Wagner the case is different.
He also is plain and lucid enough where the
ordinary affairs of life are concerned, but as
soon as he comes upon a topic that really interests him, be it music or Buddhism, meta-
physics or the iniquities of the Jews, his brain
gets on fire, and his pen courses over the paper
with the swiftness and recklessness of a race-
horse, regardless of the obstacles of style and
construction, and sometimes of grammar. His
meaning is always deep, but to arrive at that
meaning in such terrible letters, for example, as
those numbered 27, 35, 107, 255, and many

others, sometimes seems to set human ingenuity at defiance. It would of course have been possible, by disentangling dove-tailed sentences and by giving the approximate meaning where the literal was impossible, to turn all this into fairly smooth English. But in such a process all the strength and individual character of the original would inevitably have been lost. What I have endeavoured to do is to indicate the diction which a man of Wagner's peculiar turn of mind would have used, if he had written in English instead of in German.

To sum up, this translation of the correspondence is intended to be an exact facsimile of the German original. To supply notes and a serviceable index, to give a clue to the various persons who are hidden under initials—all this must be left to another occasion, provided always that the Wagner family consents to such a course, and that the interest shown by English readers in the work as it stands holds out sufficient inducement to so toilsome a piece of work.

FRANCIS HUEFFER.

CORRESPONDENCE OF
WAGNER AND LISZT.

I.

DEAR SIR,

If I take the liberty to trouble you with these lines, I must in the first instance rely solely on the great kindness with which you received me during your last short stay in Paris in the late autumn of last year, when Herr Schlesinger casually introduced me to you. There is, however, still another circumstance which encourages me to this step: My friend Heinrich Laube, the author, wrote to me last summer from Carlsbad that he had there made the acquaintance of one of your countrymen, who boasted of being your friend; that he had spoken to that gentleman of me and my plans, and engaged his interest in me to such an extent that he (the gentleman) of his own accord promised to introduce me to *you*, as he was on the point of starting for another watering-place, where he would be sure to meet you.

You observe, dear sir, with what remote and uncertain contingencies I am obliged to connect my great hope; you observe how anxiously I cling to feeble possibilities to attain a priceless boon. Was that promise ever fulfilled, and could it have been? My eternally unlucky

I

star almost forbids me to believe it. The question, however, I owed to myself, and all I ask for at present is the honour of a Yes or a No!

With full admiration, your most devoted

RICHARD WAGNER.

25, RUE DU HELDER, PARIS,
March 24th, 1841.

2.

DEAR SIR,

At last you are within safe reach of me, and I take this long-desired opportunity to gain you, as far as is in my power, for our scheme of celebrating Weber's memory by a worthy monument to be erected in Dresden. You are just on the point of crowning your important participation in the erection of the Beethoven monument; you are for that purpose surrounded by the most important musicians of our time, and in consequence are in the very element most favourable to the enterprise which of late has been resumed chiefly through my means. As no doubt you heard at the time, we have transferred Weber's remains to the earth of his German home. We have had a site for the intended monument assigned to us close to our beautiful Dresden theatre, and a commencement towards the necessary funds has been made by the benefit performances at the Dresden, Berlin, and Munich theatres. These funds, however, I need scarcely mention, have to be increased considerably if something worthy is to be achieved, and we must work with all our strength to rouse enthusiasm wherever something may still be done. A good deal of this care I should like to leave to you, not, you may believe me, from idleness, but because I feel convinced that the voice of a poor German composer of operas, compelled to devote his lifelong labour to the spreading of his works a little beyond the limits of his province, is much too feeble to be counted of importance for anything in the world. Dear Herr Liszt, take it well to heart when I ask you to relieve me of the load which would probably be heaped on me by the reproach that I had compromised our dear Weber's memory, because it was none other than I, weak and unimportant as I am, who had first mooted this celebration. Pray, do what you can in order to be helpful to our enterprise, for gradually, as I observe the vulgar indifference of our theatres, which owe so much to Weber, I begin to fear that our fund might easily *remain* such as it is at present, and that would be tantamount to our having to commence with very inadequate means the erection of a monument which doubtless would have turned out better if a more important personality had started the idea.

I add no more words, for to you I have probably said enough. The committee of which I am a member will apply to you with proper formality. Would that you could let us have a gratifying answer, and that my application might have contributed a little towards it !

With true esteem and devotion, I am yours,

RICHARD WAGNER.

MARIENBAD, *August 5th*, 1845.

3.

MOST ESTEEMED FRIEND,

On and off I hear that you remember me very kindly and are intent upon gaining friends for me ; and

I could have wished that, by staying ın Dresden a little longer, you had given me an opportunity of thanking you personally and enjoying your company. As I perceive more and more that I and my works, which as yet have scarcely begun to spread abroad, are not likely to prosper very much, I slowly familiarise myself with the thought of turning to account your friendly feeling towards me a little, and, much as I generally detest the seeking and making of opportunities, I proceed with perfect openness to rouse *you* up in my favour. There is at Vienna, where you happen to be staying, a theatrical manager, P.; the man came to me a year ago, and invited me to produce *Rienzi* at his theatre in the present spring. Since then I have not been able to hear again from him, but as our Tichatschek goes to his theatre in May for an extensive starring engagement, and thereby the possibility of a good representation of *Rienzi* would be given, the backing out on the part of this P. begins to make me angry. I presume that he, who is personally stupid, has been subsequently set against my opera by his conductor, N. For this Capellmeister N. has himself written an opera, which, because our King had heard it and disliked it elsewhere, was not produced at Dresden, and the wretched man probably thinks he owes *me* a grudge for it, although I had no influence whatever in the matter. However trivial such considerations may be in themselves, they and similar ones largely furnish the real cause why works like mine occasionally die in Germany; and as Vienna for pecuniary reasons, apart from anything else, is of importance to me, I go straight to you, most esteemed friend, to ask that you will set Manager P.'s head right, in favour of an early performance of my *Rienzi* at his theatre. Pray do not be angry with me.

I have ventured to send you through Meser the scores of my *Rienzi* and *Tannhäuser*, and wish and hope that the latter will please you better than the former.

Let me thank you sincerely for the great kindnesses you have shown me. May your sentiments remain always the same towards

Your faithfully devoted

RICHARD WAGNER.

DRESDEN, *March 22nd*, 1846.

4.

DEAR FRIEND,

Herr Halbert tells me you want my overture to Goethe's *Faust*. As I know of no reason to withhold it from you except that it does not please me any longer, I send it to you, because I think that in this matter the only important question is whether the overture pleases you. If the latter should be the case, dispose of my work; only I should like occasionally to have the manuscript back again.

You will now have to go through capellmeister agonies of the first quality; so I can imagine, and my opera is just the kind of thing for that to one who takes a loving interest in it. Learn to know these sufferings; they are the daily bread I eat. May God give you strength and joy in your hard work.

From my heart yours,

RICHARD WAGNER.

DRESDEN *January 30th*, 1848.

5.

MOST EXCELLENT FRIEND,

You told me lately that you had closed your
piano for some time, and I presume that for the present
you have turned banker.   I am in a bad state, and like
lightning the thought comes to me that you might help
me.   The edition of my three operas has been undertaken by myself; the capital I have borrowed in various
quarters; I have now received notice to repay all the
money, and I cannot hold out another week, for every
attempt to sell my copyrights, even for the bare
outlay, has in these difficult times proved unsuccessful.
From several other causes the matter begins to look
very alarming to me, and I ask myself secretly what is
to become of me.   The sum in question is 5,000 thalers;
after deducting the proceeds that have already come in
and without claim to royalties, this is the money that
has been invested in the publication of my operas.   Can
you get me such a sum ?   Have you got it yourself, or
has some one else who would pay it for the love of you ?
Would it not be interesting if you were to become the
owner of the copyright of my operas ?   My friend
Meser would continue the business on your account as
honestly as he has done on mine ; and a lawyer could
easily put the thing in order.   And do you know what
would be the result ?   I should once more be a *human
being*, a man for whom existence would be possible, an
artist who would never again in his life ask for a shilling,
and would only do his work bravely and gladly.   Dear
Liszt, with this money you will buy me out of slavery!

Do you think I am worth that sum as a serf ?   Let that be known soon to

Your most devoted
RICHARD WAGNER.

DRESDEN, *June 23rd*, 1848.

6.

BEST OF FRIENDS,

Here am I fighting for death or life, and do not know what the end will be. I have written to my lawyer to tell him of my last hope : that by your energetic interference my affairs may possibly be arranged. Your name will go far in the transaction, but your person still farther ; let me have the latter for a day, but *very soon*. According to news which has reached me here, I shall next Wednesday or Thursday have to undertake a journey which will keep me away from Dresden for a fortnight. Performances of my operas I cannot, for that and other reasons, offer you. Could you make up your mind to come here very quickly even without the expectation of one of my operas ? If I offer you no performances, you shall, on the other hand (that is my most ardent wish), possess all my operas as your hereditary property. Do come ! Your personality will do much good, more than my personality will be able to do all my life; for I cannot help myself.

Best greetings, excellent friend !

Wholly yours,
RICHARD WAGNER.

DRESDEN, *July 1st*, 1848.

7.

MOST ESTEEMED FRIEND,

Last night I wrote to Herr von Villen and asked him to talk over and arrange with your lawyer and Herr Meser the affair of the scores, and then to let me have a positive and precise answer. I cannot possibly come to Dresden for the present. May God grant that the state of your affairs turn out to be such as to enable me to offer you my small and much-enfeebled services, being, as I am,

Your sincere and devoted admirer and friend,

F. LISZT.

WEYMAR, *July 4th*, 1848.

8.

BEST OF FRIENDS,

Cordial greetings, and best thanks for the many and manifold troubles you have taken on my behalf.

I had promised Princess Wittgenstein news as to the performance of my *Tannhäuser*; but I cannot for the present give you any other than that the opera will *not* be performed either Sunday or Monday, as I had promised, owing chiefly to the indisposition of Tichat-schek. Even if he were well, it could not take place, as we have first of all to satisfy a "star," Formes. Probably *Tannhäuser* will not be possible till about a week later.

In any case I hope soon to see you again, and am glad accordingly. May I ask you to remember me to the Princess ?

I am wholly yours,

RICHARD WAGNER.

DRESDEN, *September 6th*, 1848.

9.

MOST ESTEEMED FRIEND,

Although I dare scarcely hope that you can act upon it, I hasten to let you know that *Tannhäuser* is announced for performance here on Sunday next, September 24th.

On Friday, 22nd, there will be a jubilee concert of our orchestra in celebration of its existence for three hundred years, and on that occasion a piece of my latest opera, *Lohengrin*, will, amongst other things, be heard. According to a previous arrangement, I consider it my duty to let you know this, and should certainly be very glad to welcome you, and perhaps Princess Wittgenstein (to whom please give my best compliments), on these occasions, although I must fear that my news may come at an inconvenient moment.

Yours with all my heart,

RICHARD WAGNER.

DRESDEN, *September 19th,* 1848.

10.

MOST ESTEEMED FRIEND,

Cordial greetings, and best thanks for the kind remembrance in which you hold me. For a long time I have felt it my duty to write to you. Lord knows why I have never done so. May it not be too late even to-day.

Will you really in this evil time undergo the nuisance of tackling my *Tannhäuser*? Have you not yet lost your courage in this arduous labour, which only in the luckiest case can be grateful? "In the luckiest case," I say, for only if the actors, especially of the principal parts, are equal to their most difficult task, if the unaccustomed nature of that task does not frighten them and cripple their good intentions, only then the lucky case can happen of the performance being comprehensible and effective. If one circumstance gives me hope of success, it is that *you* have undertaken the task. You can do many, many things; of that I am persuaded.

I am very glad you are settled in Weimar, and I hope that not only Weimar, but you, will profit by it. At least, we shall remain near each other.

I live in a very humbled condition and without much hope. I depend on the goodwill of certain people. Every thought of enjoying life I have abandoned, but— let me tell you this for your comfort—I am alive in spite of it all, and do not mean to let any one kill me so easily.

Remember me kindly to Herr von Zigesar, who has written to me very courteously. The points mentioned in his letter have, I hope, been settled verbally by Herr Genast, especially that about the honorarium, which I am willing to give up altogether. Please remember me also to Herr Genast, and let me soon have some news of you.

I remain in cordial devotion yours,

RICHARD WAGNER.

DRESDEN, *January* 14*th*, 1849.

II.

(TO HERR VON ZIGESAR.)

HIGHLY ESTEEMED SIR,

Accept my most hearty thanks for your kind letter, which has given me much joy. I confess that

I scarcely thought this the time to gain sympathy for my works, less on account of the present political commotion, than because of the absence of all real earnestness, which has long ago disappeared from the public interest in the theatre, giving way to the most shallow desire for entertainment. You yourself are anxious about the reception of my opera at the hands of the Weimar public, but as at the same time you evince your sympathy for that work so cordially, you will, I may hope, agree with me when I openly charge your excellent predecessors with the responsibility for your being obliged to suspect the public of an ill-regulated and shallow taste. For as we educate a child, so he grows up, and a theatrical audience is equally subject to the effects of training. But I am unjust in accusing Weimar of a fault which during the last generation has invaded all the theatres in the world, the more so as I lay myself open to the suspicion of doing so in the self-conceited interest of a work which perhaps for different reasons, derivable from intrinsic faults, may be exposed to the displeasure of the public. However that may be, your care for my work is in the circumstances all the more gratifying and meritorious, and I offer you my most cordial thanks. The pleasure of a visit to you at Weimar I am compelled, for reasons connected with my local affairs, to leave to another time. That the performance of my opera would not answer my expectations is the least thing I fear; for from firm conviction I have the most favourable opinion of what diligence and good-will can do, while I know, on the other hand, how little without these two the amplest resources can achieve for true art. As I can be certain of these chief requirements at your theatre, I feel justified in offering to you, all others concerned, and especially my friend Liszt, my best thanks in advance; and no excessive anxiety shall trouble me. I sincerely wish that the exalted lady whose birthday is to be celebrated will think the success of your labour worthy of acknowledgment.

With much esteem, I have the honour to remain

Yours most sincerely,

RICHARD WAGNER.

DRESDEN, *February 8th*, 1849.

12.

MUCH-ESTEEMED FRIEND,

Herr von Zigesar has lately written to you to say with how much zeal and with what ever-increasing admiration and sympathy we are studying your *Tannhäuser*. If you could make it possible to come over for the last rehearsal on the 15th and attend the performance on the 16th, we should all be truly delighted. Let me know the day before, because of engaging a room, etc.

Cordial thanks for sending me the *Faust* overture.

Hoping to see you soon,

Your sincerely devoted

F. LISZT.

February 9th, 1849.

13.

DEAR FRIEND LISZT,

From all I hear you have recently added to the unequalled successes of your former life and artistic

activity a new one, which probably is not inferior to
the foremost of its predecessors, and in many respects
perhaps surpasses them all. Do you suppose I cannot
judge of this from a distance ? Hear if I can.

No theatre in the world has so far thought it
advisable to perform my opera *Tannhäuser* four
years after its production ; it was left to *you* to settle
down for a time from your world-wide travels at a small
court theatre, and at once to set to work so that your
much-tried friend might at last get on a little. You
did not talk or fuss ; you yourself undertook the unaccustomed task of teaching my work to the people.
Be sure that no one knows as well as I what it
means to bring such a work to light in existing circumstances. Who the deuce does not conduct operatic
rehearsals nowadays ? You were intent not only upon
giving the opera, but upon making it understood and
received with applause. That meant to throw yourself
into the work body and soul, to sacrifice body and soul,
to press and exert every fibre of the body, every
faculty of the soul, towards the one aim of not only
producing your friend's work, but of producing it
splendidly and to his advantage. You had to be sure
that it would succeed, for only with a view to success
had you begun the work ; and therein lies the force
of your character and of your ability—*you have succeeded.* If I have judged your beautiful action rightly,
if I have understood you, I hope you will understand
me too when, in words as brief and precise as was your
action, I say to you,

I THANK *you, dear friend !*

You, however, wished not only to benefit my work,

but to benefit me as well; you know that my position is
that of a somewhat hemmed-in, forsaken, solitary man·
You desired to make *friends* for me, and had a sufficiently
good opinion of my work to think that the spreading
of it abroad would gain friends for me.   Dear friend,
by that very means you have at this moment lifted me
up as by a charm.   It is not to complain, but merely
to convince you of the force of that impression, when
I tell you that just now, in the very week when you
gave my *Tannhäuser* at Weimar, our manager insulted
me in so gross a manner that for several days I was
discussing with myself whether I should bear any longer
to be exposed to such infamous treatment for the bite of
bread that my service here gives me to eat, and whether
I should not rather throw up art and earn my
bread as a labourer, to be at least free from the des-
potism of malignant ignorance.   Thank God!   The news
from Weimar and Tichatschek's greetings and accounts
have again strengthened me.   I once more have
courage to suffer.

This also I owe to you !

D.V.—I shall soon see you again, dear, worthy,
helpful friend.   Last week it was impossible to ask my
tormentor for a short leave of absence; otherwise I
should have liked to come, if only to spend a few
cheerful and animated hours with you and to tell you
the delight I feel in you.   In the meantime be satisfied
with this.   It comes from my fullest heart, and tears
are in my eyes.

From Herren von Zigesar, Biedenfeld, and Genast
I simultaneously received letters of joyfullest and
friendliest import; I answer them all at once by

making you my interpreter, and through you greet those gentlemen with all my heart. Hold me dear as before. I give to you in return what is in me, and what therefore I call my own.

God bless you, *dear* Liszt.

Your

RICHARD WAGNER.

DRESDEN, *February 20th,* 1849.

14.

DEAREST FRIEND,

So much do I owe to your bold and high genius, to the fiery and magnificent pages of your *Tannhäuser,* that I feel quite awkward in accepting the gratitude you are good enough to express with regard to the two performances I had the honour and happiness to conduct. However that may be, your letter has given me the liveliest pleasure of friendship. I thank you with all my heart for the thanks you proffer me. Once for all, number me in future amongst your most zealous and devoted admirers; far or near, count on me and dispose of me.

Herren Zigesar, Genast, and Biedenfeld have described to you in detail the impression which your masterpiece has made on our public. In the *Deutsche Allgemeine Zeitung* you will find a few lines I have sent to Brockhaus by his demand. Biedenfeld has put the little article into shape. I shall send you by post the article that appeared in our *Gemeindeblatt,* where is also printed the prologue of Schober, who had the sense to turn *Tannhäuser* to good account.

Talking of people with good sense, do you know what I mean to do ? No more nor less than to appropriate for the piano, after my fashion, the overture of *Tannhäuser* and the whole scene "O du mein holder Abendstern" of the third act. As to the former, I believe that it will meet with few executants capable of mastering its technical difficulties, but the scene of the "Abendstern" should be within easy reach of second-class pianists.

If you will propose to Meser to have it engraved, or if you will allow me to dispose of it for the benefit of H. or Sch., I should like to have it published soon. Perhaps, if you have no objection, I should dispose of it in favour of an album for which my assistance has been asked for the last two months—the album published by the "Ladies' Society for the German Fleet." In vain I told them that I suffered from a drought of both manuscripts and ideas; they would not leave me alone; and I have just received another letter from a nice lady, who gives it me nicely.

Write to me as to the destination you prefer for your "Abendstern;" and when we meet, I shall have the impertinence to play you with my two hands your overture, such as I have prepared it for my particular use.

Remember me very affectionately to Tichatschek ; he has been an admirable artist and a charming comrade and friend. It will be a true pleasure to me to see him here again in the month of May, according to his promise. If you could on the same occasion dispose of a few days, we should be only too happy to see you.

In the meantime, dearest friend, believe me from my heart and soul your devoted admirer and friend,

FR. LISZT.

February 26th, 1849.

P.S.—A very beautiful and accomplished hand wishes to add a few lines to this letter; if you have found it tedious to read me, you could have no better compensation.

15.

Allow me, dear sir, to add another voice to the chorus of admiration which sings "Gloria" to the author of the double poem of *Tannhäuser*. If others have more right than I to speak to you of the sublime artistic expression which you have given to such deep emotions, I yet venture to tell you how souls lost in the crowd who chant to themselves your *Sängerkrieg* are penetrated by your harmonies, which contain all the fine and delicate shades of idea, sentiment, and passion.

We had hoped to see you for a moment at Weimar, and I clung to that hope all the more as I wanted to express to you my thanks for the kindness you showed me during my stay at Dresden. Let me add to these the other thanks which I owe you for the wonderful moments during which I listened to your melodies, expressive of the fascinating charms of the sirens who dwell on the banks of our imagination, and of those piercing cries wrung from us by the extinction of the perfumes of their enchanted home,—for those thoughts which elevate us in their humility, that despair which throws us "without fear against swords, when the soul is pierced by a very different sword of grief," those elegies which one whispers only to the evening star, those prayers which bear away the soul on their wings.

Grant, sir, that the thoughts which so much passion and beauty awake in hearts knowing what strange secrets lie hidden in passion, and adoring splendour and beauty, may reach you and tell you how deep is the admiration which this master work will excite at all times and everywhere in those who have once visited these resplendent and dolorous regions of the soul.

Believe, above all, in the admiration which has been given to you here, and which we should be so happy to express to you personally. I am amongst those most desirous of seeing you, sir, and of repeating from mouth to mouth the expression of the admiring and devoted sentiments of which I ask you to be a thousand times assured.

CAROLYNE WITTGENSTEIN.

February 25th, 1849.

16.

DEAREST FRIEND,

A thousand thanks for your letter! We are going on nicely together. If the world belonged to us, I believe we should do something to give pleasure to the people living therein. I hope we two at least shall agree with each other; let those who will not go with us remain behind,—and thus be our alliance sealed!

What shall I do with the beautiful letter I received together with your own? Have I really so pleased your esteemed friend with my feeble work that she thought it worth while to give me such great and unexpected joy in return? She indeed has fully effected her purpose, but I can scarcely credit that my work alone should have produced a similar impression upon the *spirituelle* Princess; and I am probably right in surmising that here also my friend Liszt has wooed for me with his wondrous fire. However that may be, I feel too silly to-day to thank your esteemed friend otherwise than through your medium, through your mouth, and therefore I pray you with all my power to express my gratitude to her as fervently, as joyfully, as you are able. Will you grant me this favour?

Before I knew anything about your intention, several years ago, when I was writing the overture, I wondered whether I should ever hear it played by you. I should never have mentioned it to you, for in such matters one must not be too forward, but now that I hear you are employed in making this piece your own, after your own fashion, I must tell you that I feel as if a wonderful dream were realised. Is it possible? Why not? *All* is possible to you. About the "Abendstern," dear friend, do exactly as you like. I have spoken to Meser about it, and he will write to you at once to place himself at your disposal; but if you prefer another way of publication, do exactly as you like. In any case I feel highly flattered by your proposal.

To-day I read the account of my opera in the *Deutsche Allgemeine Zeitung* of which you speak; by its tenor Herr von Biedenfeld has once more obliged me very, very much; express to him my best thanks, dearest friend! I must also beg to convey my great and deeply felt gratitude to the artists who have deserved well of me by their successful zeal. To how many and how deeply have I reason to be grateful! I am looking forward to May, when I shall be with you in any case; I will then speak from my full heart as loudly as my breast will let me. Till May, then!

God bless you, dearest, best, of friends! Best remembrances to Zigesar and Genast. I throw myself at the feet of the Princess.

For ever your most grateful

RICHARD WAGNER.

DRESDEN, *March 1st*, 1849.

17.

(TO HERR O. L. B. WOLFF.)

DEAREST FRIEND,

It was impossible for me to write to you from Rorschach (where I arrived only yesterday) and to return your passport. Half an hour after the arrival of the steamer the express coach started for Zurich; and I felt bound to take advantage of it, as I had made up my mind to cut this journey as short as possible by avoiding unnecessary delay. Unfortunately I got on but slowly. From Coburg I could not start for Lichtenfels till early on Saturday, but fortunately I got through everywhere without notice, at Lindau only, where I arrived at midnight, they asked for my passport at the gate. The next morning I received it back without difficulty, but unfortunately it had on it a *visé* for Switzerland, adorned with which I am compelled to return it to Dr. Widmann. I hope that his political experience will understand this addition to his passport.

Luckily then I am in Switzerland. To your counsel and your active aid, dear friends, I owe my safety. The four days' journey in a frightful heat had, however, brought my blood to such a state of excitement, that I found it impossible to go on without risking a stroke of apoplexy. Moreover, I hope to employ my stay at Zurich in obtaining a passport for France. One of my early friends has been residing here for a long time ; to-day I expect him back from a pleasure trip, and I hope he will do what is necessary to save me the long détour by Geneva.

To my wife I write at length, and my request to you to communicate this news to my friends is therefore for the present limited to our Liszt. Greet my preserver and sovereign liege many thousand times, and assure him of my firm resolution to do all that is in my power to please him. The journey has freshened and roused my artistic courage, and I have quite made up my mind as to what I have to accomplish in Paris. I do not think much of fate, but I feel that my late adventures have thrown me into a path where I must do the most important and significant things which my nature can produce. Even four weeks ago I had no idea of that which now I recognize to be my highest task ; my deep-rooted friendship for Liszt supplies me with strength from within and without to perform that task ; it is to be our *common* work. More of this soon !

Liszt will shortly receive a parcel of scores, etc., from my wife; let him open it. The score of *Lohengrin* I want him to try at some leisure ; it is my last and ripest work. As yet I have not shown it to any artist, and therefore have not been able to learn from any one what impression it produces. How curious I am to hear Liszt about it ! As soon as he has finished looking through it, I want him to forward it at once to Paris, along with the other scores and books of words. Perhaps some acquaintance going to Paris will take them. The copy of the score of the *Flying Dutchman* is meant for the Weimar theatre; this and the book of words let Liszt therefore take from the parcel and keep back.

That wonderful man must also look after my poor wife. I am particularly anxious to get her out of Saxony, and especially out of that d——d Dresden. Therefore I have hit upon the idea of finding for her and her family a modest but cheerful refuge somewhere in the Weimar territory, perhaps on one of the grand-ducal estates, where, with the remainder of what is saved of our goods and chattels, she might prepare a new home for herself, and perhaps for me also—in the future. May my friend succeed in this!

Thanks, cordial thanks, to you for the great kindness you have shown to me! My memorials of it are so numerous that I cannot put my hand in my pocket without being reminded of the thoughtfulness and sympathy of friend Wolff. May my future be your reward!

Cordial greetings to Dr. Widmann, as whose double I have acted for four days; I return him to himself in his integrity, which I hope will not a little conduce to his perfect well-being. Best thanks to him!

And thanks, thanks also, to your dear wife and mother! The blessings of one saved are with them. Farewell, dear friend!

You will soon hear more from your

RICHARD WAGNER.

ZURICH, *May 29th*, 1849.

18.

My Dear Friend,

To you[1] I must turn if my heart is once more to open itself, and I am in need of such heart-comfortings ; that I cannot deny. Like a spoiled child of my homeland, I exclaim, " Were I only home again in a little house by the wood and might leave the devil to look after his great world, which at the best I should not even care to conquer, because its possession would be even more loathsome than is its mere aspect ! "

Your friendship—if you could understand what it is to me ! My only longing is to live with my wife always near you. Not Paris nor London—you alone would be able to hammer out what good there may be in me, for you fire me to the best efforts.

From Zurich you had news of me through Wolff. Switzerland did me good, and there I found an old friend of my youth, to whom I could talk much about you. It was Alexander Müller, whom you too know, a worthy and amiable man and artist. At Zurich also I read your article on *Tannhäuser* in the *Journal des Débats*. What have you done in it ? You wished to describe my opera to the people, and instead of that you have yourself produced a true work of art. Just as you conducted the opera, so have you written about it : new, all new, and from your inner self. When I put the article down, my first thoughts were these : " This wonderful man can do or undertake nothing without producing his own self from his inner fulness.

[1] In this and all the subsequent letters the familiar " Du " (" Thou ") instead of the formal " Sie " (" You ") is adopted.—Tr.

he can never be merely reproductive; no other action than the purely productive is possible to him; all in him tends to absolute, pure production, and yet he has never yet concentrated his whole power of will on the production of a great work. Is he, with all his individuality, too little of an egoist? Is he too full of love, and does he resemble Jesus on the Cross, Who helps every one but Himself?"

Ah, dear friend, my thoughts of you and my love of you are still too enthusiastic; I can only exclaim and rejoice when I think of you. Soon I hope to grow stronger, so that my selfish enthusiasm may allow me to give utterance to my anxiety for you. May Heaven grant me the power to do full justice to the love I have for you; as yet I live too much on your love for me, and mine vents itself in useless exclamations. I hope soon to gather the necessary strength from the intercourse with those who love you as I do; and truly *you have friends!*

I arrived in Paris soon after the publication of your article. We know better than any one that this was an accident, of which you had not in the least thought when you wrote and despatched the article. But this accident has at once given a distinct colour to my position in Paris, and—our friend M. considers that colour as black as possible. Dear Liszt, you ought to clear your mind as to this man. But why do I talk? Should not you have found out long ago that natures like that of M. are strictly opposed to yours and mine? Should not you have found out long ago that the only tie possible between you and M. was effected by magnanimity on your side and by prudence on his? Where the two threads of this woof met, there deception was possible for a time, but I believe that you gave way to that magnanimous deception with amiable intent. M. is thoroughly little, and unfortunately I do not meet a man who has the slightest doubt about it.

Honestly speaking, I am unable to engage in a drama of intrigue *à la Verre d'Eau*; if this were the only way open to me, I should pack my bundle to-morrow and settle down in a German village; work I will as much as I can, but to sell my ware in *this market* is impossible to me. Artistic affairs here are in so vile a condition, so rotten, so fit for decay, that only a bold scytheman is required who understands the right cut. Dearest friend, apart from all political speculation, I am compelled to say openly that in the soil of the anti-Revolution no art can grow, neither perhaps could it for the present in the soil of the Revolution, unless care were taken—in time. To speak briefly, to-morrow I shall begin a searching article on the theatre of the future for some important political journal. I promise you to leave politics on one side as much as possible, and therefore shall not compromise you or any one else; but as far as art and the theatre are concerned you must, with a good grace, allow me to be as red as possible, for a very determined colour is the only one of use to us. This, I think, is my most prudent course to adopt, and he who advises it for prudential reasons as the most effective one is none other than your representative Belloni. He tells me that here I want money as much as M. or really more than M., or else I must make myself feared. Well, money I have not, but a tremendous desire to practise a little artistic terrorism.

Give me your blessing, or, better still, give me your assistance. Come here and lead the great hunt; we will shoot, and the hares shall fall right and left.

I do not expect to reach the goal here so very soon, but must prepare myself. A libretto of Scribe or Dumas I cannot set to music. If I ever do reach the right goal in this Parisian hunt, I shall not compass it in the common way; I must in that case create something new, and that I can achieve only by doing it all myself. I am on the look-out for a young French poet sufficiently congenial to give himself up to my idea. My subject I shall arrange myself, and he must then write his French verses as spontaneously as possible; to anything else I could not agree.

During these slow preparations I shall have to occupy my leisure with London; I am ready to go there as soon as possible to do all in my power for the performance of my works. As to this I expect your friendly command.

I thank you from all my heart for Belloni; he is an able, honest, and very active man; every day he calls for me to show me the proper way to Parisian glory.

This is the cheerful part of my news; otherwise this horrible Paris presses on me with a hundredweight. Often I bleat like a calf for its stable and for the udder of its life-giving mother. How lonely I am amongst these people! My poor wife! I have had no news as yet, and I feel deathly soft and flabby at every remembrance. Let me soon have good news of my wife! With all my courage, I am often the most miserable coward. In spite of your generous offers, I frequently consider with a deadly terror the shrinking

of my cash after my doubly prolonged journey to Paris.
I feel again as I did when I came here ten years ago,
and when thievish longings would often get hold of me on
watching the dawn of the hot days that were to shine
on my empty stomach. Ah, how this vulgarest of cares
degrades man!

But one piece of news will rouse everything in me
again, especially if the little Weimar has remained
faithful to me. One single piece of good news, and
I float once more on the top of the ocean waves.

My dear, glorious friend, take me such as this
abominable Paris has excited me to-day. I do not
thank you; I call you blessed. Greet the dear Princess,
greet the small knot of my friends, and tell them that
you hope I shall do well. Soon you will hear more of
me. Be happy and remember me.

Yours,

RICHARD WAGNER.

PARIS, *June 5th*, 1849.

(Have you received the scores, and shall I see some
of them here by-and-bye?)

I have been with your mother, and she has given me
uncommon pleasure; *she* is a healthy woman! I shall
call on her again. She sends you best greetings.

19.

DEAREST FRIEND,

It is nearly four weeks since I left my wife, and
I have not yet had the least news of her. My grief
and depression are great. I must gain another home
and hearth; otherwise all is over with me. My heart
is greater than my sense.

With Belloni I have been in close consultation, and we have formed the following opinion and the resolution derived therefrom :—

In Paris I can do no good at present; my business is to write an opera for Paris; for anything else I am unfit. This object cannot be attained by storm; in the most favourable case I shall achieve the poem in half a year, and the performance in a year and a half. In Paris without a home, or—which is the same—peace of heart, I can do no work; I must find a new place where I am at home and can make up my mind to remain at home. For such a place I have selected Zurich. I have written to my wife to come there with her youngest sister, with the remnants of our household goods, so as once more to be united to me. I have a friend there, Alexander Müller, who will assist me in furnishing as cheap a home as is to be had. As soon as I can, I shall go there from this place. When I have my wife again, I shall forthwith and gladly set to work. The sketch of a subject for Paris I shall send from there to Belloni, who will arrange about a French version by Gustave Vaez. In October he may have finished his work, and then I shall for a short time leave my wife for Paris, and shall try every possible means to obtain a commission for the setting of the said subject. I may perhaps on the same occasion perform some of my music, and after that shall return to Zurich to set about the composition. Meanwhile I shall employ my time in setting to music my latest German drama, *The Death of Siegfried*. Within half a year I shall send you the opera completed.

I *must* commence some genuine work, or else perish,

but in order to work I want quiet and a home. With my wife and in pleasant Zurich I shall find both. I have one thing in view, and one thing I shall always do with joy and pleasure—*work*, *i.e.*, write operas. For anything else I am unfit; play a part or occupy a position I cannot, and I should deceive those whom I promised to undertake any other task.

You friends must get me some small yearly allowance, just sufficient to secure for me and my wife a quiet existence in Zurich, as for the present I am not allowed to be near you in Germany. I talked to you in Weimar of a salary of three hundred thalers which I should wish to ask of the Grand Duchess for my operas, alterations of the same, and the like. If perhaps the Duke of Coburg and possibly even the Princess of Prussia were to add something, I would willingly surrender my whole artistic activity to these three protectors as a kind of equivalent, and they would have the satisfaction of having kept me free and ready for my art. I cannot ask for myself nor find the proper form for the necessary agreement, but *you* can, and *you* and your intercession will succeed. Possible revenues from the opera I shall write for Paris I might then entirely devote to the payment of the debts I left in Dresden.

Dear Liszt, have I spoken plainly enough?

With the confidence of one *entirely* helpless, I further ask, Make it possible to let me have some money soon, so that I may leave here, go to Zurich, and exist there till I receive the desired salary. You are the best judge as to what I want for this. Whether my wife when, in accordance with my ardent prayer, she thinks of starting for Zurich, will be able to raise the necessary funds, I unfortunately cannot tell. Would you kindly ask her soon whether she wants anything? Write to her care of Eduard Avenarius, Marienstrasse, Leipzig.

Goodness, how I always try not to weep! My poor wife!

The best I can bring forth, I will bring forth,— all, all! But to battle about in this great world is impossible for me. Let me once more be at home somewhere!

I was unable to write more to-day; do not be angry on that account. But I know your kindness, and trust in it implicitly.

Take a thousand greetings from your

RICHARD WAGNER.

REUIL, *June 18th*, 1849.

(The scores my wife could bring to me at Zurich, could she not?)

(I had hoped to get some money from Berlin through Tichatschek; unfortunately nothing has arrived, and I cannot in any way relieve you, although I do not know where you are to get the money.)

20.

DEAR FRIEND,

Excuse me for applying to you again so soon. At last I received a letter from my wife, and many pangs of conscience were again roused by it. More than all, it lies heavy on my heart to-day that I have asked you to intercede with several royal personages for a salary for me. I had forgotten—to say nothing of my immediate past—that my sufficiently public participation in the Dresden rising has placed me towards those royal personages in a position which must make them think of me as one opposed to them on principle, and this perhaps will make it appear strange that now, when the collapse of that rising has reduced me to poverty, I turn for help to them of all others. My position is all the more painful because I can take no steps to free myself from the suspicion of such sentiments without incurring the worse suspicion of meanness and cowardice. You personally I may assure that the feeling manifested by my undisguised sympathy with the Dresden rising was very far from the ridiculously fanatical notion that every prince is an object of active hatred. If I concurred in this strange fanaticism, I should naturally have had scruples in approaching the Grand Duchess at Weimar with *perfect* openness. Before you, I trust, I need not defend myself; you know the bitter source of my discontent, which sprang from the condition of my beloved art, which I nourished with passion, and which finally I transferred to every other field, the connection of which with the ground of my deep dissatisfaction I had to acknowledge. From this feeling came the violent longing which finds its expression in the words, " There must be a change ; thus it cannot remain." That now, taught by the experience of my participation in that rising, I could never again mix myself up with a political catastrophe, I need not say ; every reasonable person must know it. What rejoices me, and what I may safely affirm, is that in all my aims I have once more become entirely an artist. But this I cannot possibly tell the princes at the moment when I am about to claim their assistance. What would they think of me!

A general and public declaration also would bring me
nothing but disgrace. It would have to appear as an
apology, and an apology in the only correct sense time
and my life alone can tender, not a public declaration,
which in the present threatening circumstances and in
my helplessness must needs appear cowardly and low.

I am sure you will agree with my view of the matter,
and I surmise that already you have found yourself in a
very awkward position towards the Grand Duchess on
my account. My wife, who still thinks it necessary to
live on amongst the dregs of Dresden vulgarity, tells
me a thousand unpleasant things which in the eyes of
miserable creatures make me appear much more compromised by the revolution than I really am. This
feeling towards me is probably spread far and wide,
and therefore may have affected the Weimar court. I
can well imagine that you think it at present inadvisable to raise your voice for me at a court which, with a
natural prejudice, at first sight recognizes in me only
the political revolutionary, and forgets the artistic revolutionary whom at bottom it has learnt to love.

How far you will think it good to comply with my
application of yesterday in such circumstances you will
best decide for yourself. Is it possible that our princes
nowadays should be magnanimous enough to exercise
a beautiful, old privilege, unmoved by the currents of
the time and without weighing conditions ? Think this
over ; perhaps you have more confidence than I.

My wife suffers, and is embittered ; for her I hope
everything from time. I asked you yesterday to inquire
of her as to the pecuniary aid she may need ; I ask you
to-day not to do so—not now. If you will do me a

kindness, send me a little money, so that I can get away,—anywhere, perhaps after all to Zurich, to my old friend Müller. I should like to be at rest, so as to write the *scenario* for Paris ; I don't feel up to much just now. What should I do in London ? I am good for nothing, except perhaps writing operas, and that I cannot do in London.

Best greetings to any one who will accept them from me ; there will not be many. Farewell, dear, much-troubled friend. Could I but make you returns !

Your most faithful

RICHARD WAGNER.

REUIL, *June* 19*th*, 1849.

21.

DEAR FRIEND,

With the contents of your letter No. 2 I agree more than with No. 1. For the present it would not be very diplomatic to knock at battered doors. Later on, when you stand revealed as a *made* fellow, even as you are a *created* one, protectors will easily be found ; and if I can serve you then as a connecting and convenient instrument, I shall be quite at your disposal with my whole heart and with a certain slight *savoir-faire*. But a period of transition you cannot avoid, and Paris is for everything and before everything a necessity to you. Try to make it possible that your *Rienzi* (with a few modifications intended for the Paris public) is performed in the course of next winter. Pay a little court to Roger and Madame Viardot. Roger is an amiably intelligent man, who will probably fall in love with the part. I think, however, that in any case you will have to spare him a little more than Tichatschek, and will have to ease his task by some abbreviations. Also do not neglect Janin, who, I feel sure, will give you a helping hand, and whose influence in the press can secure the early performance of the opera.

In a word, very dear and very great friend, make yourself possible in possible conditions, and success will assuredly not fail you. Vaez and A. Royer will be of great assistance to you both for the translation and rearrangement of *Rienzi* and for the design of your new work. Associate and concur with them strictly for the realisation of that plan from which you must not swerve :—

1. To give *Rienzi* during the winter of 1850 at the Paris Opera, whence it will take its flight to all the theatres of Germany, and perhaps of Italy. For Europe wants an opera which for our new revolutionary epoch will be what *La Muette de Portici* was for the July revolution, and *Rienzi* is conceived and written for those conditions. If you succeed in introducing into it a slight element of relief, were it only by means of stage machinery or of the ballet, success is certain.

2. To write a new work for the winter of '51 in collaboration with Vaez and A. Royer, who know all the mysteries of success. In the interval you cannot do better than take a good position in the musical press. Forgive me for this suggestion, and manage so that you are not of necessity placed in a hostile position towards things and people likely to bar your road to success and fame. A truce to political commonplaces, socialistic stuff, and personal hatreds ! On the other hand, good

courage, strong patience, and flaming fire, which latter it will not be difficult for you to provide, with the volcanoes you have in your brain ! Your idea of retiring to Zurich for some time in order to work more at ease seems good, and I have charged Belloni to remit to you three hundred francs for travelling expenses. I hope that Madame Wagner will be able to join you, and before the autumn I shall let you have a small sum which will keep you afloat.

Kindly let me know whether I shall send your works to Madame Wagner, and at what address.

The admirable score of *Lohengrin* has interested me profoundly ; nevertheless I fear at the performance the *superideal* colour which you have maintained throughout. Perhaps you will think me an awful Philistine, dear friend, but I cannot help it, and my sincere friendship for you may authorise me to tell you. . . .[1]

22.

Dear Friend,

Thanks to your intercession, I have been able to fly to the friendly place from which I write to you to-day. I should trouble you unnecessarily were I to tell you all that latterly has passed through my heart ; perhaps you will guess it. Belloni has taken care of me with the greatest kindness and consideration ; there are, however, things in which no friend in the world can be of assistance. One thing more by way of explanation : during my journey through Switzerland and on my arrival in

---

[1] The letter breaks off here in the original edition.—Tr.

Paris, I met with some Saxon refugees in a position which induced me to assist them in your name. I shall not be tempted again.

I hope to find some rest and collectedness for the completion of my intended Paris work in the intimate intercourse with a dear friend who is also a friend of yours—Alexander Müller. About *Rienzi* and the plans which you have commended to us regarding that opera, Belloni will give you details in so far as the purely practical part of the matter is concerned. He thinks it impossible, especially at first, to place it at the Grand Opéra. I, as an artist and man, have not the heart for the reconstruction of that to my taste superannuated work, which, in consequence of its immoderate dimensions, I have had to remodel more than once. I have no longer the heart for it, and desire from all my soul soon to do something *new* instead. Besides, the erection of an operatic theatre in Paris is imminent where only foreign works are to be produced; that would be the place for *Rienzi*, especially if some one else would occupy himself with it. I want you to decide about this as soon as you have heard our reasons. I have settled everything with Gustave Vaez as regards the external part of our common enterprise. The work, which I shall now take in hand at once, will, I hope, soon open to him and to you my inner view of the matter. Heaven grant that in this also we may understand each other or at least come to an understanding. Only from the *one* deep conviction which is the essence of my mental being can I draw inspiration and courage for my art, for only through this conviction can I love it; if this conviction were to separate me from my friends, I should bid farewell to art—and probably turn clodhopper.

By all accounts I am in fine repute with you! The other day, I hear, I was accused, together with another person, of having set fire to the old Dresden opera house. All right. My dear wife lives in the midst of this slough of civic excellence and magnanimity. One thing grieves me deeply; it wounds me to the very bone : I mean the reproach frequently made to me that I have been ungrateful to the King of Saxony. I am wholly made of sentiment, and could never understand, in the face of such a reproach, why I felt no pangs of conscience at this supposed ingratitude. I have at last asked myself whether the King of Saxony has committed a punishable wrong by conferring upon me undeserved favours, in which case I should certainly have owed him gratitude for his infringement of justice. Fortunately my consciousness acquits him of any such guilt. The payment of 1,500 thalers for my conducting, at his intendant's command, a certain number of bad operas every year, was indeed excessive ; but this was to me no reason for gratitude, but rather for dissatisfaction with my appointment. That he paid me nothing for the best I could do does not oblige me to *gratitude* ; that when he had an opportunity of helping me thoroughly he could not or dared not help me, but calmly discussed my dismissal with his intendant, quieted me as to the dependence of my position on any act of grace. Finally, I am conscious that, even if there had been cause for any particular gratitude towards the King of Saxony, I have not knowingly done anything ungrateful towards him ; proof of this I should be able to furnish.

Pardon, dear friend, this unpleasant deviation; unfortunately I am not yet again in that stage of creating which shuts out anything but the present and the future from my cognisance. My spirit still writhes too violently under the impression of a past which, alas! continues wholly to occupy my present. I am still bent on justification, and that I wish to address to *no one* but you.

As soon as I have anything ready I shall send it to you. For the present I must urgently ask you to forward me here at once the scores and other literary tools which my wife has sent to you. I want to get into some kind of swing again so that the bell may ring. Be good enough to give the parcel to a carrier to be forwarded here by express conveyance (care of Alexander Müller, Zurich).

Müller greets you most cordially. He will write to you soon to inform you of the success of Herr Eck, the instrument-maker, whose company is doing very well.

Dear Liszt, do not cease to be my friend; have patience with me, and take me as I am. A thousand compliments to the Princess, and thank her in my name for the kind memory she has preserved of me; she may find it difficult to remain my friend.

Be healthy and happy, and let me soon hear some of your works, even as I promise you on my part. Farewell, and take my cordial thanks for your constancy and friendship.

Your

Richard Wagner.

Zurich, *July 9th*, 1849.

23.

My Dear Liszt,

Are you in a good temper? Probably not, as you are just opening a letter from your plaguing spirit. And yet it is all the world to me that you should be in a good temper just to-day, at this moment! Fancy yourself at the most beautiful moment of your life, and thence look upon me cheerfully and benevolently, for I have to proffer an ardent prayer. I receive to-day a letter from my wife, unfortunately much delayed in the post. It touches me more than anything in the world; she wants to come to me, and stay with me, and suffer with me once more all the ills of life. Of a return to Germany, as you know well yourself, I must not for the present think; therefore our reunion must take place abroad. I had already told her that the hoped-for assistance from Weimar would come to nothing; this she will easily understand and bear. But in order to carry out her idea to come to me, she and I lack no less than all. To get away from Dresden in the most difficult circumstances she wants money; quite lately she told me she had to pay sixty-two thalers without knowing where to get it. She will now have to pack and send to me the few things we have saved; she must leave something for the immediate wants of her parents, whom formerly I kept entirely. She then has to travel to Zurich with her sister, and I must at least be able to offer her the bare necessaries of life for the beginning. At this moment I can offer her nothing in the world. I live at present only on the remainder of the money which I received from you through Belloni before my departure from Paris. But, dear friend, I take

care not to be a burden to you alone, and this care is
partly the reason why I have not yet thoroughly set to
work, although the anxiety about my wife is chiefly to
blame. I have again tried hard to get paying work
and assistance, so that I might ease your burden, and in
the worst case need only ask you to assist me again
for my journey to Paris in the autumn. But now in this
moment of the most painful joy at the imminent return
of my wife—now I know of no one but you to whom to
apply with the firm hope of seeing my wishes speedily
accomplished. You therefore I implore by all that is
dear to you to raise and collect as much as you
possibly can, and to send it, not to me, but to my wife,
so that she may have enough to get away and to join
me with the assurance of being able to live with me
free from care for some time at least. Dearest friend,
you care for my welfare, my soul, my art. Once more
restore me to my art ! I do not cling to a home, but I
cling to this poor, good, faithful woman, to whom as
yet I have caused almost nothing but grief, who is of
a careful, serious disposition, without enthusiasm, and
who feels herself chained for ever to such a reckless
devil as myself. Restore her to me ; by doing so you
will give me all you can wish for me, and, believe me,
for that I shall be *grateful to you, yea grateful !*

You will see how quickly I shall turn out things.
My preparations for Paris, the pamphlet, and even two
sketches for subjects will be ready and on their way
next month. Where I cannot agree with you I shall
win you over to me ; that I promise, so that we may
always go hand in hand and never separate. I will
obey you, but give me my poor *wife* ; arrange it so that

she may come cheerfully, with some confidence, soon and quickly. Alas! this, in the language of our dear nineteenth century, means, Send her as much money as you can possibly get. Yes, such is my nature; I can beg, I could steal, to cheer up my wife, were it only for a little while. Dear, good Liszt, see what you can do! Help me, help me, dear Liszt. Farewell, and— help me!

Your grateful

RICHARD WAGNER.

Write straight to my *wife*: Minna Wagner, Friedrich-strasse No. 20, Dresden.

24.

DEAR FRIEND,

In answer to your letter, I have remitted one hundred thalers to your wife at Dresden. This sum has been handed to me by an admirer of *Tannhäuser*, whom you do not know, and who has specially asked me not to name him to you.

With Y. B., who paid me a visit yesterday, I talked over your position at length. I hope his family will take an active interest in your affairs.

All the scores (excepting the overture to *Faust*) I sent to Zurich last week. The separation from your *Lohengrin* was difficult to me. The more I enter into its conception and masterly execution, the higher rises my enthusiasm for this extraordinary work. Forgive my wretched pusillanimity if I still have some doubt as to the wholly satisfactory result of the performance.

Permit me one question: Do you not think it advisable to add to *Tannhäuser* a dedication (*post scriptum*) to the Lord of Wartburg, H.R.H. Carl Alexander, Hereditary Grand Duke of Saxe-Weymar-Eisenach ?

If you agree to this, have a very simple plate to that effect engraved, and send me in advance, together with your next letter, a few lines to the Hereditary Grand Duke, which I shall hand to him at once. For the present you must expect no special donation in return, but the sympathy of the prince for your masterpiece fully justifies this attention.

Friendly greetings to Alexander Müller, to whom I am still very grateful for his friendly reception at Zurich. If you should see J. E., assure him of my sincere interest in his further welfare. He is an honest, able, excellent man.

Hold me in kind remembrance, even as I am cordially devoted to you.

F. LISZT.

WEYMAR, *July 29th*, 1849.

P.S.—Be careful in your articles in the newspapers to omit all political allusions to Germany, and leave royal princes alone. In case there should be an opportunity of paying Weymar a modest compliment *en passant,* give free vent to your reminiscences with the necessary kid gloves.

25.

DEAR LISZT,

I herewith send you my last finished work ; it is a new version of the original article which I

sent to Paris last week to have it translated for
the *feuilleton* of the *National*. Whether you will be
pleased with it I do not know, but I feel certain
that your nature is at one with me. I hope you
will find in it nothing of the political commonplaces,
socialistic balderdash, or personal animosities, against
which you warned me ; but that, in the deepest depth
of things, I see what I see, is entirely owing to the
circumstance that my own artistic nature and the
sufferings it has to go through have opened my
eyes in such a manner that death alone can close
them again. I look forward either to an entirely
useless existence, or to an activity which responds
to my inmost being, even if I have to exercise it
afar from all external splendour. In the former case
I should have to think of abbreviating that existence.

Please address and send the manuscript, together
with the enclosed letter, to the publisher Otto
Wigand in Leipzig. Perhaps I shall succeed in
drawing from my inferior literary faculty some small
support for my existence. Since my last letter, which
I posted at the same time with my stormy petition
to you, I have had no news from my wife, and am
slightly tortured accordingly.

From a letter written by Baron Schober to Eck at
Zurich, I see with great pleasure that your prospects
are cheerful, and that you are resolved to settle in
Weimar. I presume that the excellent Princess is
also happy and well. Heaven be thanked ! Whether
you ought to show her my manuscript I am not quite
certain ; in it I am so much of a *Greek* that I have not
been able quite to convert myself to Christianity. But

what nonsense I talk! As if you were not the right
people! Pardon me.

Farewell, dear, unique friend! Remember me in
kindness.

Your

RICHARD WAGNER.

ZURICH, *August 4th*, 1849.

Have you been good enough to see about the
forwarding to me of my scores and writings? I
am anxious at not having seen anything of them.

26.

DEAREST FRIEND,

A thousand thanks for your letter, and for
kindly taking care of my wife. The unknown donor
is wrong in wishing to be hidden from me. Thank
him in my name.

The day before yesterday I sent you a long article;
probably you have read it. I am glad that I can
agree to your wish to dedicate *Tannhäuser* to the
Grand Duke without the slightest abnegation of my
principles, for I hope you will see that I care for
something else than the stupid political questions of
the day.

It would be best if you could have the dedication
page and the special copy done through Meser, in
which case you might also, if necessary, promise to
bear the trifling expense, for of that copyright not
a single note is mine. I hope you like the verses.
Will you put the letter to the Grand Duke in an addressed envelope?

Oh, my friends, if you would only give me the

wages of a middling mechanic, you would have pleasure in my undisturbed work, which should all be yours.

Thanks for sending the scores. *Lohengrin* will be especially useful to me, for I hope to pawn the score here for some hundreds of florins, so as to have money for myself and my wife for the next few months.

Your doubts as to a satisfactory effect of the performance of the opera have frequently occurred to me. I think, however, that if the performance is quite according to my colour, the work—including even the end—will be all right. One must *dare*.

Müller and Eck were delighted by your greetings, and return them with enthusiasm.

Dear, good Liszt, I also thank you most cordially for all the care you take of me. Consider that I can give you nothing better in return than the best I can accomplish. Give me perfect peace, and you shall be satisfied. I hope my wife will be here soon; then you shall soon have good news of me.

Farewell, and continue to be my friend.

Your

RICHARD WAGNER.

ZURICH, *August 7th,* 1849.

27.

MY DEAR FRIEND,

After a silence of several months, I cannot address you without first of all thanking you once more with all my heart for the friendly assistance which enabled me to have my poor wife back again.

By this assistance my wife made it possible to preserve and bring with her some favourite trifles of our former household and, before all, my grand piano. We are settled here as well as possible; and after a long interruption, full of pain and unrest, I am once more able to think of the execution of my great artistic plans for the future.

After this final reunion with my much-tried wife, nothing could have given me greater pleasure than to learn about the produce of your artistic activity. The pieces written by you for the centenary of Goethe's birth I have now seen in the pianoforte score, and have occupied myself with them attentively. With all my heart I bid you welcome, and am glad—especially also in sympathy with your friend—that you behave so valiantly in this field of honour, selected by you with glorious consistency. What I felt most vividly, after my acquaintance with these compositions, was the desire to know that you were writing an opera or finishing one already begun. The aphoristic nature of such tasks as those set you by this Goethe celebration must involuntarily be transferred to the artistic production, which therefore cannot attain to perfect warmth. Creative power in music appears to me like a bell, which the larger it is is the less able to give forth its full tone, unless an adequate power has set it in motion. This power is internal, and where it does not exist internally it does not exist at all. The purely internal, however, cannot operate unless it is stimulated by something external, related to it and yet different. Creative power in music surely requires this stimulus no less than does any other great artistic power; a great incitement alone can make it effective. As I have every reason to deem your power great, I desire for it the corresponding great incitement; for nothing here can be arbitrarily substituted or added: genuine strength can only create from necessity. Wherever in the series of your pieces Goethe himself incites your strength, the bell resounds with its natural full tone, and the clapper beats in it as the heart does in the body. If you had been able to ring the whole *Faust*-bell (I know this was impossible), if the detached pieces had had reference to a great whole, then that great whole would have thrown on the single pieces a reflex which is exactly the certain *something* that may be gained from the great whole, but not from the single piece. In single, aphoristic things we never attain repose; only in a great whole is great power self-contained, strong, and therefore, in spite of all excitement, reposeful. Unrest in what we do is a proof that our activity is not perfectly self-contained, that not our whole power, but only a detached particle of that power, is in action. This unrest I have found in your compositions, even as you must have found it too often in mine without better cause. With this unrest I was, however, better pleased than if comfortable self-contentment had been their prominent feature. I compare it to the claw by which I recognise the lion; but now I call out to you, Show us the complete lion: in other words, write or finish soon an opera.

Dear friend, look upon me with an earnest but kind glance! All the ills that have happened to me were the natural and necessary consequences of the discord of my own being. The power which is mine is quite unyielding and indivisible. By its nature it takes violent revenge when I try to turn or divide it by external force. To be wholly what I can be, and therefore, no doubt, should be, is only possible for me if I renounce all those external things which I could gain by dint of the aforesaid external force. That force would always make me fritter away my genuine power, would always conjure up the same evils. In all I do and think I am only artist, nothing but artist. If I am to throw myself into our modern publicity, I cannot conquer it as an artist, and God preserve me from dealing with it as a politician. Poor and without means for bare life, without goods or heritage, as I am, I should be compelled to think only of acquisition; but I have learnt nothing but my art, and that I cannot possibly use for the purpose of acquiring nowadays; I cannot seek publicity, and my artistic salvation could be brought about one day only by publicity seeking me. The publicity for which alone I can work is a small nucleus of individuals who constitute my whole publicity at present. To these individuals, therefore, I must turn, and put the question to them whether they love me and my art-work sufficiently to make it possible for me, as far as in them lies, to be *myself*, and to develop my activity without disturbance. These individuals are not many, and they live far from each other, but the character of their sympathy is an energetic one. Dear friend, the question with me is bare life. You have opened Paris to me, and I most certainly do not refuse it; but what I have to choose and to design for that place cannot be chosen and designed in a moment; I must there be some one else and yet necessarily remain the same.

All my numerous sketches are adapted only to treatment by myself, and in the German language. Subjects which I should have been prepared to execute for Paris (such as *Jesus of Nazareth*) turn out to be impossible for manifold reasons when I come to consider closely the practical bearings of the thing, and I must therefore have time and leisure to wait for inspiration, which I can expect only from some remote region of my nature. On the other hand, the poem of my *Siegfried* lies before me. After not having composed a note for two years, my whole artistic man is impelled towards writing the music for it. What I could possibly hope for from a Paris success would not even be able to keep me alive ; for, without being thoroughly dishonest, I should have to hand it over to my creditors.

The question, then, is, How and whence shall I get enough to live ? Is my finished work *Lohengrin* worth nothing ? Is the opera which I am longing to complete worth nothing ? It is true that to the present generation and to publicity as it is these must appear as a useless luxury. But how about the few who love these works ? Should not they be allowed to offer to the poor suffering creator—not a remuneration, but the bare possibility of continuing to create ?

To the tradesmen I cannot apply, nor to the existing nobility—not to human princes, but to princely men. To work my best, my inmost salvation, I am not in a position to rely on merit, but on grace. If we few in this villainous trading age are not gracious towards each other, how can we live in the name and for the honour of art ?

Dear friend, you, I believe, are the only one on

whom I can implicitly rely. Do not be frightened! I have tried to relieve you of the burden of this exclusive reliance; I have turned elsewhere, but in vain. From H. B., about whom you wrote to me, I have heard nothing, and am glad from my heart that I have not. Dear Liszt, let us leave the *tradesmen* alone once for all. They are human and even love art, but only as far as *business* will allow.

Tell me; advise me! Hitherto my wife and I have kept ourselves alive by the help of a friend here. By the end of this month of October our last florins will be gone, and a wide, beautiful world lies before me, in which I have nothing to eat, nothing to warm myself with. Think of what you can do for me, dear, princely man! Let some one buy my *Lohengrin*, skin and bones; let some one commission my *Siegfried*. I will do it cheaply! Leaving our old plan of a confederation of princes out of the question, can you not find some other individuals who would join together to help me, if *you* were to ask them in the proper manner? Shall I put in the newspaper " I have nothing to live on ; let him who loves me give me something"? I cannot do it because of my wife; she would die of shame. Oh the trouble it is to find a place in the world for a man like me! If nothing else will answer, you might perhaps give a concert "for an artist in distress." Consider everything, dear Liszt, and before all manage to send me soon some—some money. I want firewood, and a warm overcoat, because my wife has not brought my old one on account of its shabbiness. Consider!

From Belloni I soon expect an invitation to Paris, so as to get my *Tannhäuser* overture performed at the

Conservatoire, to begin with. Well, dear friend, give one of your much-occupied days to the serious and sympathetic consideration of what you might do for me. Your loving nature, free from all prejudice and only occupied with the artist in me, will suggest to you a great work of love which will be my salvation. Believe me, I speak sincerely and openly; believe me that in you lies my only hope.

Farewell. Receive, together with mine, the most ardent wishes of my good wife. Remember me, as one cordially devoted to her, to Princess Wittgenstein, and thank her in my name if she should think of me now and then.

Farewell, you good man, and let me soon hear from you.

Wholly yours,

RICHARD WAGNER.

ZURICH, *October 14th*, 1849.
(Am Zeltwege, in den hinteren Escherhäusern, 182.)

28.

DEAR FRIEND,

For more than a month I have been detained here by the serious illness of the young Princess M. W My return to Weymar is in consequence forcibly postponed for at least another month, and before returning there it is impossible for me to think of serving you with any efficiency. You propose to me to find you a purchaser for *Lohengrin* and *Siegfried*. This will certainly not be an easy matter, for these operas, being essentially—I might say exclusively—German, can at most be represented in five or six German towns. You know, moreover, that since the Dresden affair *official*

Germany is not favourable to your name. Dresden, Berlin, and Vienna are well-nigh impossible fields for your works for some time to come. If, as is not unlikely, I go to Berlin for a few days this winter, I shall try to interest the King in your genius and your future; perhaps I shall succeed in gaining his sympathy for you and in managing through that means your return by way of Berlin, which would certainly be your best chance. But I need not tell you how delicate such a step is, and how difficult to lead to a good end. As to the "confederation of princes" which you mention again in your letter, I must unfortunately repeat to you that I believe in its realisation about as much as in mythology.

Nevertheless I shall not omit to sound the disposition of H.H. the Duke of Coburg during the visit I shall probably have the honour of paying him at the beginning of January. By his superior intelligence and personal love of music, access to him will be made easier. But as to the other thirty-eight sovereigns of Germany (excepting Weymar, Gotha, and Berlin), I confess that I do not know how I shall manage to instil into them so subtle an idea as would be the positive encouragement and the active protection of an artist of your stamp.

As to the dedication of *Tannhäuser*, the Hereditary Grand Duke, while graciously receiving your intention, has sent me word that it would be more convenient to defer the publication for a few months, so that I have not been in a hurry to make the necessary arrangements for the engraving of the dedication plate.

Try, my dear friend, to get on as best you can till Christmas. My purse is completely dry at this moment;

and you are aware, no doubt, that the fortune of
the Princess has been for a year without an admini-
strator, and may be completely confiscated any day.
Towards the end of the year I reckon upon money
coming in, and shall then certainly not fail to let you have
some, as far as my very limited means will go ; you
know what heavy charges are weighing upon me. Before
thinking of myself I must provide for the comfortable
existence of my mother and my dear children in Paris,
and I can also not avoid paying Belloni a modest salary
for the services he renders me, although he has always
shown himself most nobly disinterested on my behalf.
My concert career, as you know, has been closed for
more than two years past, and I cannot resume it
imprudently without serious damage to my present
position and still more to my future.

However, on my way through Hamburg I have
yielded to numerous solicitations to conduct in April
a grand "Musical Festival," the greater part of the
receipts of which will be devoted to the "Pension Fund
of Musicians," which I founded about seven years ago.

Your *Tannhäuser* overture will of course figure in
the programme, and perhaps also, if we have sufficient time and means, the finale of the first or second
act,—unless you have some other pieces to propose.
Kindly write on this subject to your niece, who is
engaged for the whole winter at Hamburg, and ask her
to come to our assistance on this occasion. For it is
my firm intention (not *avowed* or *divulged*, you understand, for there would be much inconvenience and no
advantage in confiding it to friends or the public) to
set aside part of the receipts for you.

Could not you, on your part, arrange some concerts at Zurich, the proceeds of which would enable you to get through the winter tolerably ? Why should you not undertake this ? Your personal dignity, it seems to me, would not in the least suffer by it.

Yet another thing, another string to your bow. Should you think it inconvenient to publish a book of vocal compositions,—lieder or ballads, melodies or lyrical effusions, anything ? For a work of this class signed with your name I can easily find a publisher and insist upon a decent honorarium, and there is surely nothing derogatory in continuing in a path which Mozart, Beethoven, Schubert, and Rossini have not disdained. I quite understand what you say of my compositions in the " Goethe Album," and only regret you did not hear my *Tasso* overture, which, I flatter myself, would not have displeased you. In consequence of the good opinion which you kindly express of my talent as a composer, I am going to ask you a favour if the idea meets with your approval. While recently glancing through the volume of Lord Byron which has scarcely ever quitted me on my travels, I came again upon the mystery *Heaven and Earth*, and on reading it once more felt persuaded that one might turn it to good account by preserving the difference of character between the two women Anah and Aholibamah and by keeping of course the Deluge as a *purely instrumental* piece for the dénouement. If in your free moments you could think of cutting out of this an oratorio of moderate length, as in Byron, I should be truly obliged to you.

Read over the Mystery, and tell me whether you like

my plan. In the course of the summer my *Sardanapalus* (in Italian) will be completely finished, and I shall be delighted to undertake another work at once.

If you reply before the end of November, address Bückeburg, for I shall not return to Weymar, for the rest of the winter, till the beginning of December.

Remember me very kindly to Madame Wagner, and in all circumstances rely upon my devoted friendship and admiration.

F. LISZT.

BÜCKEBURG, *October 28th,* 1849.

29.

MY DEAR FRIEND LISZT,

God knows, the more I look into my future, the more I feel what I possess in you. Such as I am and such as you are, I come to understand better and better what a rare degree of friendship and kindness you must have towards me to show me the most active sympathy of all my friends, in spite of many sides of my nature which cannot possibly be agreeable to you. You resemble in this the true poet who, with perfect impartiality, takes every phenomenon of life as it is according to its essence. As regards your anxiety about me, I can assure you that if you had sent me some assistance in answer to my last request, I should not have been more touched than I was in feeling with you your sorrow at having to confess that for the time being you could not send me anything. I helped myself as well as I could by applying to my friends here. If I had not a wife, and a wife who has already gone with me through such hard times, I should be much less anxious about

the future; but for her sake I frequently sink into
deep dejection. But that dejection does not help me
on; and, thanks to my healthy nature, I always nerve
myself to renewed courage. Having lately expressed
my whole view of art in a work entitled "The Art-
work of the Future," I am now free from all theoretic
hankerings, and have got so far as to care about nothing
but doing art-work. I should have liked best to complete
my *Siegfried*, but this wish I could realise only in
exceptionally favourable circumstances, namely if I
could look forward to a year free from material care.
This is not the case, and the care for my future
makes it my duty altogether to think more seriously
of my appointed tasks than has hitherto been possible
amidst the most conflicting impressions. Listen, dear
friend: the reason why for a long time I could not
warm to the idea of writing an opera for Paris was a
certain artistic dislike of the French language which
is peculiar to me. You will not understand this, being
at home in all Europe, while I came into the world
in a specifically Teutonic manner. But this dislike I
have conquered in favour of an important artistic
undertaking. The next question was the poem and
a subject, and here I must confess that it would be
absolutely impossible for me simply to write music
to another man's poems, not because I consider this
beneath me, but because I know, and know by experience, that my music would be bad and meaningless.
What operatic subjects I had in my head would not
have done for Paris, and this was the cause of my
hesitation in the whole affair which you had initiated so
well. Since then I have clearly discovered what task I

have in reality to perform in Paris, so as to remain true
to myself and yet keep Paris always in my mind's eye.
As to this, dear friend, we shall perhaps understand
each other perfectly, and you will agree with me when
I determine not to become a Frenchman (in which I
should never succeed, and which the French do not want
from a German), but to remain as I am and in my own
character to speak to the French comprehensibly. Well,
in this sense the subject for a poem has quite recently
occurred to me, which I shall immediately work out and
communicate to Gustave Vaez; it is highly original and
suitable to all conditions. More I will tell you as soon
as I have finished the *scenario*. Belloni has asked me
for the scores of my overtures to *Tannhäuser* and
Rienzi, the first for a concert at the Conservatoire;
I believe it is to be performed next January, and at that
time I shall go to Paris myself to conduct the overture,
to settle everything with Gustave Vaez, and to co-operate
with him in obtaining a commission for an opera. One
thing more : I cannot allow my *Lohengrin* to lie by
and decay. Latterly I have accustomed myself to the
notion of giving it to the world at first in a foreign
language, and I now take up your own former idea of
having it translated into English, so as to make its production in London possible. I am not afraid that this
opera would not be understood by the English, and for
a slight alteration I should be quite prepared. As yet,
however, I do not know a single person in London.
With the publisher Beal I made acquaintance *par
distance* when he printed the overture to *Rienzi*, but
apart from this I have no connection with London.
Could you manage, dear friend, to write to London and

to introduce my undertaking, and could you also let me know to whom to apply further ?   From Paris I should then go to London, in order to settle the matter if possible.

You perceive that I am only intent on carrying out the scheme originally suggested by you.   Do not be angry with me for taking it in hand so late.   At first it was your plan exclusively, and I had to make it mine ; my awkwardness in this you must kindly attribute to my extraordinary position and mental trouble.

But now it is important, dear Liszt, to provide me with means for this definite object.   That you alone cannot support me I realised long ago ; and knowing as I do your position, it is altogether with a heavy heart that I ask you for further sacrifices.   I have therefore applied to a friend at Dresden (himself poor), and have asked him to see if he could get me some money from my other friends, so as to help me, in conjunction with you, over my immediate and greatest difficulties.   His news so far does not lead me to expect any great success from his efforts, and in any case it will not amount to much.   You were kind enough to promise me some assistance from your own means towards the end of the year.   Do not be angry if I assure you that I shall be compelled to count upon your kind fulfilment of this promise.

I trust in no one else, and do not indulge in any further illusions.   Of a concert in Zurich I have thought myself.   The local concert society have asked me to study with their orchestra, which is feeble, a sym-phony by Beethoven and one of my compositions, in return for which they would arrange a benefit concert for me. The necessary increase of the strings, which I had to demand as a point of honour, has delayed the matter up till now, and it will be probably the beginning of January before the subscription concert takes place which is to be, so to speak, the *captatio benevolentiæ* for my benefit concert. It is therefore not unlikely that I shall not be able to wait for the favourable moment, as I expect to be summoned to Paris by Belloni towards the beginning of next year. Any assistance from that quarter is therefore very problematic. Your thought of me in wishing to set aside part of the receipts of an intended concert at Hamburg has touched me deeply. You are a good man ; and every day, alas ! I feel more sure that I have no friend like you. In any case my niece shall interest herself in the concert; that small errand I willingly undertake.

All I want is to provide my poor wife during my absence with the money necessary for her subsistence, which will not amount to much, also to enable me to pay for my journeys and my stay in Paris and London. Belloni must get me a small, cheap room, and I promise to be as careful as possible in every way. I trust you and the above-mentioned friends will be able to provide me with the necessary means. Let us hope that success will reward your beautiful and rare sympathy.

Farewell, dear and valued friend ! Remember me and my wife cordially to Princess Wittgenstein, and be assured at all times of my enthusiastic recognition of your rare and beautiful nature.

Always your deeply obliged friend,

RICHARD WAGNER

ZURICH, *December 5th,* 1849.

The subject from Byron I shall certainly consider. As yet I do not know it, nor have had time to make myself acquainted with it, for which you must pardon me. I should be too glad to be of any service to you, and am thankful to you for showing me the way to do it. Let me only finish my opera sketch for Paris first.

My address is "Am Zeltweg, in den hinteren Escherhäusern," No. 182.

30.

DEAR FRIEND,

I have just returned to Weymar, and hasten to send you a bill on Rothschild for five hundred francs. According to what you tell me, I hope it will be of service to you in Paris, where, I am convinced, you will find the best field for your activity and your genius.

I quite agree with your decision "to remain thoroughly faithful to yourself and yet always to have Paris before your eyes in the conception and execution of your designs." I anticipate soon the most excellent and satisfactory results. You are quite right in not wishing to become a Frenchman; apart from the fact that you would scarcely succeed, your task is a different and even a contrary one, viz., to Germanize the French in your sense of the word, or rather to inspire them and fill them with enthusiasm for more general, more comprehensive, more elevated, dramatic art-work.

I should be delighted to learn what operatic subject you have selected, and my earnest desire is that you will use all your time in hastening the representation. In actual circumstances it is almost impossible for you to think of a speedy return to Germany, where, moreover, you would find nothing but disagreeable things, envy, and enmity. Paris and perhaps London are absolutely necessary for your present and future career. Whatever the annoyances and sufferings may be which you will have to go through during the period of transition in which you are unhappily placed, take courage and have full confidence in the star of your genius. The day after your first performance in Paris you will be "as one new-born and content like a Greek god."

Regarding London, it will be somewhat difficult to place your *Lohengrin* there. It depends very much upon the chance of a good opportunity, which I hope will turn up. I shortly expect M. Ernst on his return from London, and he will give me some details as to the actual situation and the *personnel* of the London theatres. Italian opera not being suitable to you in any form, you will have to attach yourself to one of the ephemeral enterprises of the English stage, ensuring, of course, every possible precaution and guarantee. I shall one of these days write direct to Mr. Chorley, an excellent friend of mine, who will give me the necessary information and help you during your stay in London. Before the spring I shall perhaps be able to give you some favourable news. You on your part must strike every iron while it is hot, and before all "stick to our Paris plans." For the *fête* of the Grand Duchess I shall conduct *Iphigenia in Aulis*, which Herr von Zigesar has got for me from Dresden, and this in spite of the opposition, from want of intelligence or evil intention, which I shall have to encounter. Herr von Lüttichau has declined all responsibility for the loan of your score, and I have boldly undertaken to be answerable to you for it.

At the end of the week we shall repeat *Tannhäuser*, which, by some miracle of taste, the Weymar public and many people from the surrounding towns have demanded ever since the beginning of the theatrical season, and which has been postponed only on account of my absence.

Let me hear from you soon, dear friend, and continue to dispose of me as of your sincerely devoted friend,

F. LISZT.

WEYMAR, *January 14th*, 1850.

P.S.—Kindly give my best remembrances and compliments to Madame Wagner.

31.

MY DEAR LISZT,

You will know by this time how I have fared in Paris. The performance of my overture came to nothing, and all your trouble about it has been in vain. Poor man!

In my life some decisive events have happened ; the last shackles have fallen that tied me to a world in which I must have perished soon, not only mentally, but physically. Through the eternal compulsion imposed upon me by my immediate surroundings, I have lost my health, and my nerves are shattered. In the immediate future I must live only for my recovery ; my existence is provided for ; you shall hear from me from time to time.

Dear friend, I have just been looking through the

score of my *Lohengrin*. I very seldom read my own works. An immense desire has sprung up in me to have this work performed. I address this wish to your heart :—

Perform my *Lohengrin* ! *You are the only one* to whom I could address this prayer ; to none but you I should entrust the creation of this opera ; to you I give it with perfect and joyous confidence. Perform it where you like, even if only in Weimar ; I feel certain you will procure every possible and necessary means, and they will refuse you nothing. Perform *Lohengrin*, and let its existence be *your* work. There is a correct score of the opera at Dresden. Herr von Lüttichau has bought it of me for the price of the copying (thirty-six thalers). As he is not going to perform it—against which I should protest, considering the musical direction in that city—it is possible that he will let you have the copy on repayment of the thirty-six thalers, or else he will in any case have it copied out for you. This letter may be your authority for receiving it.

If you comply with my wish, I shall send you soon a complete libretto, with exact indications of my view as to the *mise-en-scène*, etc.

Do what you can and what you like. You shall soon hear from me again.

Belloni tells me that you have promised him to get me an additional five hundred francs for the score of *Iphigenia*. If you succeed in this, remit the money for me to Belloni ; I shall in my thoughts dispose of it.

Farewell, dear friend and brother. Remember me to my few friends. If the Grand Duchess and the

Hereditary Grand Duke will accept a greeting, greet them most cordially from me.

Farewell, and think well of

Your faithful and grateful

RICHARD WAGNER.

PARIS, *April 21st*, 1850.

32.

DEAREST LISZT,

I herewith send you the promised directions for the performance of *Lohengrin*. Pardon me if they come too late. I heard only recently with what amiable and speedy readiness you have complied with my wish for the performance of this opera. When we meet again, I shall have many things to tell you. Of my immediate past I only say that my intended journey to Greece has come to nothing; there were too many impediments, which I found it impossible to overcome. Better than anything else I should have liked to get out of the world altogether. Of this more later on.

As I understand that you are going to perform *Lohengrin* as early as August 28th, I must not delay my instructions any longer, leaving other matters for a later communication.

First of all, I have in the enclosed treated of scenery and decorations. My drawings made for that purpose will give you great delight ; I count them amongst the most successful creations of my genius. Where my *technique* forsook me, you must be satisfied with the good intention, which will be clear to you from the literary explanation attached to it. The trees especially presented me with insuperable difficulties, and if every painter has to perspire over perspective as I have done, his art is by no means an easy calling. As to the rest, I have in my notes always referred to the full score, in which I have indicated—much more fully and clearly than in the libretto—the scenic action in conjunction with the music. The stage-manager will have to go exactly by the score, or at least an arrangement of it.

As to the orchestra, I have also put down some remarks for you.

But now I have first of all a great wish to address to you :

Give the opera as it is ; cut nothing !

One single cut I will indicate to you myself, and I even insist upon the omission of the passage, viz., the second part of Lohengrin's tale in the final scene of the third act. After the words of Lohengrin—

"Sein Ritter ich bin Lohengrin ge "=[nannt fifty-six
    bars must be omitted]

"Wo ihr mit Gott mich landen" ["saht" therefore,—
    "nannt" instead of "saht"].

I have frequently sung it to myself, and have come to the conclusion that this second part of the tale must produce a depressing effect. The passage is therefore to be omitted in the libretto as well.

As to the rest, I must request you urgently, Let me for once do as I like. I have been intent upon establishing so unfailing, so plastic, a connection between the music and the poem and action, that I feel quite certain as to the result. Rely upon me, and do not attribute it to my being in love with my own work. If you should feel compelled to make cuts on account of excessive difficulty,

I should ask you to consider whether it would not be better to leave the performance alone on account of insufficiency of means. I assume, however, that all possible means will be readily placed at your disposal, and also that you will succeed in conquering every difficulty if you are fully determined to do so. If you make up your mind that it must be, then I am sure that it will be, or else that you would rather give up the whole thing. As to this, I think, we agree.

Concerning the chief thing, the cast of vocalists, I rely upon you with perfect confidence. You will not undertake impossible things. Our friend Götze, to whom I am in any case much indebted for his Tannhäuser, will find more difficulties in Lohengrin, because he lacks in external appearance and voice that resplendent quality which, where nature has vouchsafed it, must make the part easy. Let him supply that resplendence as far as possible by means of art. To look at him ought to make one's eyes smart. A newly revised libretto intended for the printer I send at the same time with this. It will arrive by the ordinary mail. As to this libretto, I have the following wish to express : Sell it, or if you can get nothing for it, give it to a publisher who will undertake to bring it out beautifully, at least as well as the libretto of *Tannhäuser;* the Weimar theatre then gets as many copies from the publisher as it wants for sale in the house, allowing a certain commission. This is exactly what we did with *Tannhäuser.* As I should like you to dispose of the pianoforte score, made by Uhlig in Dresden, to a music-publisher, the best way would be to offer the libretto to the same man whom you have in your eye

for the pianoforte arrangement. That libretto, if sold
at a moderate price, is, however, by no means a bad
business. Of *Tannhäuser* we sold over two thousand
copies. One thing more : tell me, dear Liszt, how could
we make it possible that I could attend the first performance in Weimar *incognito?* This is a desperate question, especially as at this moment it is no longer, as it
recently was, a matter of indifference to me whether
I am to dwell in a royal Saxon prison or not. Listen :
I hold the Grand Duchess in high regard ; would not
this lady, to whom I attribute real nobility, at your
suggestion be inclined for the stroke of genius of
duping the police of united Germany, and of getting
me a safe conduct under an assumed name from
Switzerland to Weimar and back again to Zurich ?
I promise faithfully to preserve my *incognito* in the
most stoical manner, to lie *perdu* in Weimar for a little
time, and to go straight back, guaranteeing all the time
the strictest secrecy from abroad also. Or would this
be more easily achievable through the Duke of Coburg ?
Of him I hear many things that delight me. Anyhow
look into this ; you would give a poor devil like me
real joy, and perhaps a new stimulus and much-needed
encouragement.

If it is possible, or even if it is impossible, I ask
further, Would you like to pay me a short visit in
Zurich soon ? You are devilish quick at such things.
If I could see you again now, I should go half mad
through joy, therefore *wholly mad*, as people have
surely taken me for half mad a long time since. I
would sing *Lohengrin* to you from A to Z ; that would
be a real pleasure !

Enough for to-day. I shall soon write again. Whether I have got any money from Weimar for *Iphigenia* I cannot tell yet; there has latterly been much confusion around me. I am about to crush some most absurd rumours which have been spread abroad concerning me by returning to Zurich. Address to me there " Enge, Sterngasse, Hirzel's Haus, Zurich."

Farewell, old, dear, only friend! I know you love me. Believe that I respond from my fullest heart.

Ever thine,

RICHARD WAGNER.

THUN, *July 2nd*, 1850.

33.

DEAR LISZT,

Would you be kind enough to answer the following simple question briefly by "Yes" or "No"? Did the management of the Weimar theatre intend to pay me five hundred francs for my version of *Iphigenia*, as Belloni told me after his return to Weimar? Further, have these five hundred francs been sent anywhere for me, and to whom and where should I in that case have to apply? or if they have not been sent, may I still count on them? Lastly, if the latter should be the case, will you ask Herr von Zigesar to send three hundred francs of the sum to Belloni in Paris, in settlement of a tailor's bill falling due July 15th, and remit the balance of two hundred francs to me at Zurich as soon as possible?

My question has become more complicated than I

thought, as complicated, indeed, as is the demand on Herr von Zigesar to pay me five hundred francs for a mere arrangement. That you have managed to insist upon this demand I must in any case look upon as one of your miracles.

Dearest friend, you have, I hope, received my long letter from Thun. Shall I soon hear from you, or could you really manage to pay me a flying visit?

Best greetings from your most faithful

RICHARD WAGNER.

ZURICH, *July 10th*, 1850.
(Bei Frau Hirzel, Sterngasse, Enge.)

34.

DEAREST FRIEND,

Believe me, you have not for a moment ceased to be very near to my heart. The serious, enthusiastic admiration I have for your genius would not be satisfied with sleepy habits and barren sentiments. All that I can possibly do, either in the interest of your reputation and glory or in that of your person, you may feel perfectly certain will in no circumstances remain undone. Only a friend like you is not always quite easy and convenient to serve, for those who understand you must wish, before all, to serve you in an intelligent and dignified manner. I hope that so far I have not been wanting in these two essential conditions, and I do not mean to depart from them for the future. You may therefore have full confidence in me, and listen to me, and believe me as one who is frankly and without restriction devoted to you.

But let us speak definitely of your affairs, which, for some time at least, I have made seriously my own.

1. I found it impossible to get the five hundred francs for *Iphigenia* from the management. Nevertheless, you shall not be disappointed, for at the same time with this letter I forward to Belloni in Paris three hundred francs from my private purse, which he will hold at your disposal, and pay at your order either to your tailor or to any other person you may indicate. Apart from this, I have good hope that Herr von Zigesar, from whom I enclose a few lines, will be able to send you in a few days one hundred thalers, independently of the honorarium for *Lohengrin*, which will be about thirty louis d'or.

2. Your *Lohengrin* will be given under exceptional conditions, which are most favourable to its success. The management for this occasion spends about 2,000 thalers, a thing that has not been done in Weymar within the memory of man. The press will not be forgotten, and suitable and seriously conceived articles will appear successively in several papers. All the *personnel* will be put on its mettle. The number of violins will be slightly increased (from sixteen to eighteen), and a bass clarinet has been purchased. Nothing essential will be wanting in the musical material or design. I undertake all the rehearsals with pianoforte, chorus, strings, and orchestra. Genast will follow your indications for the *mise-en-scène* with zeal and energy. *It is understood that we shall not cut a note, not an iota*, of your work, and that we shall give it in its *absolute beauty*, as far as is in our power.

The special date of August 28th, on which *Lohengrin* will be performed, cannot be but favourable to it. To speak truth, I should not be allowed to put so extra-ordinary a work on the stage in the ordinary course of the theatrical season. Herr von Zigesar has fully realised that *Lohengrin* must be an *event*. For that reason they have curtailed the theatrical holidays by one-half, and have asked my friend Dingelstedt to write a prologue *ad hoc*, which he will bring us himself towards the middle of August, the first perform-ance being fixed for August 28th, the anniversary of Goethe's birth, and three days after the inauguration of the Herder monument, which will take place on the 25th. In connection with that Herder monument we shall have a great concourse of people here; and besides that, for the 28th the delegates of the Goethe foundation are convoked to settle the definite pro-gramme of that foundation at Weymar.

After two consecutive performances of *Lohengrin* the theatre will close again for another month, and *Lohengrin* will not be resumed till some time in the course of the winter.

3. With regard to the sale of the score, the matter is not quite so simple, and I need not enumerate and explain to you the commercial difficulties. Neverthe-less, if you charge me with this matter, I shall try to bring it to a good end; but a little time will be necessary. If, as I have no doubt, the success of *Lohengrin* is once firmly established at Weymar, you will perhaps find means to influence the B.'s so that they may have it done at Leipsic. In that case Tichatschek would be required for the principal

part, and your most devoted capellmeister would, if you should think it necessary, take care of the rest on certain conditions.

If the work succeeds at Leipzig, a publisher will easily be found; but I must not conceal from you that the success of *Lohengrin* seems to me somewhat doubtful, unless the necessary preliminary precautions with regard to study, rehearsals, and the press are taken. In leaving it to its fate—although, no doubt, it deserves a propitious fate—I have serious apprehensions from the ill-will which attaches to you personally and from the envy and stupidity which still combat your genius. Consider therefore carefully what plan you had better adopt in this matter. In the meantime I thank you cordially for the indications and hints which you give me about the score. I shall obey them with respect and friendship. Kindly write two words to Herr Uhlig in Dresden so as to prevent him from making difficulties about sending me the pianoforte score, which will be very useful to me.

I come to a point which pains me much, but which it is my duty not to conceal from you. Your return to Germany and visit to Weymar for the performance of *Lohengrin* is an *absolute impossibility*. When we meet again, I can give you verbally the details, which it would be too long and useless to write. Once more, it is necessary that you should be served with intelligence and dignity, and you would not be served in that manner by hazarding steps which must infallibly lead to an unfavourable result. What I think of most, and what, with God's help, may bring about "a turn in your situation," is the success of *Lohengrin;* and if that is once well established, I shall propose to their Highnesses to authorize me to write to you or to let Herr von Zigesar write to you commissioning you to finish your *Siegfried* as soon as possible, and sending you for that purpose a suitable honorarium in advance, so that you may be able to work for some six months at the completion of that opera free from material care.

Speak to no one of this plan, which I hope to carry out in due time.

Till then keep your head and your health in good condition, and count entirely upon your sincerely devoted and affectionate friend,

F. Liszt.

Herr von Zigesar will write to you direct about the sale of the libretto of *Lohengrin.* The best thing would be if Brockhaus would undertake the edition, and Z. has written to him on the subject. You, on your part, might write to him to the same effect, which would be a good beginning of the plan which I shall submit to your ultimate decision. Yet another and quite different question : Should you be inclined to undertake in connection with *Alceste, Orphée, Armide,* and *Iphigenia en Tauride,* by Gluck, a similar task to that which you have already performed for *Iphigenie en Aulide,* and what sum would you expect by way of honorarium ? Write to me on this subject when you have time ; there is no hurry about it, but perhaps I might be able to suggest the idea of such a commission to the proper person.

35.

My Dear Liszt,

I must say, *You are a friend.* Let me say no more to you, for although I always recognized in friendship between men the noblest and highest human relation, it was you who embodied this idea in its fullest reality by letting me no longer imagine, but feel and grasp, what a friend is.

I do not thank you, for you alone have the power to thank yourself by your joy in being what you are. It is noble to have a friend, but still nobler to be a friend.

Having found you, I can put up with my banishment from Germany, and I must look upon it almost as fortunate, for I could not have possibly been of such use to myself in Germany as you can be. But then I wanted you of all others. I cannot *write* your praise, but when we meet I will *tell it* you. Kindly and considerately as you treat me, you may feel sure that I as fully understand and appreciate the manner of your care of me. I know that you must act as you act, and not otherwise ; and for the *manner* of your taking care of me I am especially thankful. One thing gives me anxiety : you forget yourself over me, and I cannot replace what you lose of yourself in this. Consider this well.

Your letter has in many respects made a great impression on me. I have convictions which perhaps you will never share, but which you will not think it necessary to combat when I tell you that they in no manner interfere with my artistic activity. I have felt the pulse of our modern art, and know that it must die, but this does not make me melancholy, but rather joyful, because I know that not *art*, but only *our* art, standing as it does outside of real existence, must perish, while the true, imperishable, ever-new art has still to be born. The monumental character of our art will disappear ; the clinging and sticking to the past, the selfish care for continuity and possible immortality, we shall cast off; the Past will be Past, the Future will be Future, to us, and we shall live and create only in the To-day, in the full Present. Remember that I used to call you happy in your particular art, because you were an immediate artist, actually present, and appealing to the senses at every moment. That you could do so only by means of an instrument was not your fault, but that of the inevitable conditions of our time, which reduces the individual man wholly to himself, and in which association, enabling the single artist to expend his power in the common and immediately present work of art, is an impossible thing. It was not my purpose to flatter you. I only expressed half consciously my knowledge that the *representative* alone is the true artist. Our creations as poets and composers are in reality volition, not power; representation only is power—art.[1] Believe me, I should be ten times happier if I were a *dramatic representative* instead of a dramatic poet and composer. With this conviction which I have gained, I am naturally not desirous to create works for which I should have to resign a life in the present in order to give them some flattering, fictitious immortality. What cannot be made true

[1] In the German original there is here a play upon the word *können* and its derivative, *kunst*, which cannot be translated.

to-day will remain untrue in the future. The vain desire of creating beyond the present for the future I abandon, but if I am to create for the present, that present must appear to me in a less disgusting form than it actually does. I renounce fame, and more especially the ridiculous spectre of posthumous fame, because I love my fellow-men too much to condemn them, for the sake of my vanity, to the poverty in which alone the posthumous fame of dead people finds its nourishment.

As things are, I am incited to artistic creativeness, not by ambition, but by the desire to hold communion with my friends and the wish to give them joy; where I know this desire and this wish to be satisfied I am happy and perfectly content. If you in little Weimar give my *Lohengrin* with zeal and love, joy and success, and were it only for the two performances of which you write, I shall be happy in the thought that my purpose has been perfectly accomplished, that my anxiety about this work is wholly at an end, and that now I may begin another effort at offering something new in a similar manner. Judge then, can you blame my conviction which rids me of all egoism, of all the small passions of ambition? Surely not. Ah, that I might be able to communicate to all of you some of the blissful strength of my convictions!

Hear now what effect your letter has had upon me.

Last May I sent the poem of my *Siegfried* to a bookseller to be published, such as it is. In a short preface I explained that the completion and the performance of my work were beyond hope, and that I therefore communicated my *intention* to my friends. In fact, I shall

not compose my *Siegfried* on the mere chance for the
reasons I have just told you. Now, you offer to me
the artistic association which might bring *Siegfried* to
light. I demand representatives of heroes such as
our stage has not yet seen; where are they to come
from ? Not from the air, but from the earth, for I
believe you are in a good way to make them grow from
the earth by dint of your inspiring care. Although our
theatrical muddle is hopelessly confused, the best soil
for all art is still to be found in our foolish actors and
singers; their nature, if they have kept their hearts at
all, is incorruptible; by means of enthusiasm you can
make anything of them. Well then, as soon as you have
produced *Lohengrin* to your own satisfaction I shall
also produce my *Siegfried*, but only for *you* and for
Weimar. Two days ago I should not have believed
that I should come to this resolution ; I owe it to *you*.

My dear Liszt, from what I have told you you will see
that, according to my view of the thing, your amiable
anxiety for the further promulgation of my *Lohengrin*
has my sympathy almost alone on account of its
material advantages—for I must live—but not with a
view to my fame. I might have the desire to communicate myself to a larger circle, but is he likely to be
listened to who intrudes ? I cannot and will not in-
trude. You surely have done enough to attract the
attention of people towards me; shall I too buttonhole
them and ask them for a hearing ? Dear friend, these
people are flabby and cowardly ; they have no heart.
Leave them alone ! If I am to succeed, it must be
through people who care about the matter. Where
I must offer myself I lose all my power. How can

I care about a "Leipsic representation"? It would have to be a *good* representation, and how is that to be achieved unless some one like you undertook the thing? Do not forget that Weimar also would not exist for me if you did not happen to exist in Weimar. Good Lord! All depends upon *one* man in our days; the rest must be dragged along anyhow; nothing will go of itself. Even money considerations could not determine me to arrange performances which would of necessity be bad. Lord knows, although I have no money, I do not trouble about it excessively, for I have a notion that somehow I shall not starve. Just when I have nothing at all something always turns up, as, for instance, your last news, and then I feel suddenly calm and free of care. You see, dear friend, as long as you remain true to me I do not despair. As to your excellent proposal with regard to the treatment of Gluck's operas, which has given me great pleasure, I shall soon write more definitely.

Although I have many more things to tell you, I think it better to conclude on this page. You say so many things to me that I become quite confused when I have to think of a detailed answer. I know that I am safe with you as a child in its mother's bosom. What more is required beyond gratitude and love? Farewell, and let me press you to my heart.

Your friend, happy through you,

RICHARD WAGNER.

Herr von Zigesar will have a letter very soon; for the present I send him my best thanks for his valuable letter and his touching sympathy with my work.

One more thing : a certain conductor, Abt, from this place will be at Weimar on August 28th to hear *Lohengrin*. Kindly reserve a seat for him.

My best remembrances to Genast and my brave singers. I rejoice when I think of these good people. A whole family, Ritter by name, will come from Dresden to Switzerland next year, to settle near me ; they also will be at Weimar. I am writing to Uhlig.

36.

DEAR FRIEND,

I have been asked to forward to you the enclosed bill for one hundred thalers. Do not thank me, and do not thank Herr von Zigesar either, who has signed the bill. You will perhaps remember that about a year ago I sent you the same amount; this time it comes again from the same source, which, for official reasons, desires to remain hidden.

We float in the full ether of your *Lohengrin*. I flatter myself that we shall succeed in giving it according to your intentions. We rehearse every day for two or three hours, and the solo parts as well as the strings are in tolerable order. To-morrow and afterwards I shall separately rehearse the wind, which will be complete, in accordance with the demands of your score. We have ordered a bass clarinet, which will be excellently played by Herr Wahlbrül. Our violoncellos will be strengthened by the arrival from Paris of Cossmann, who will join our orchestra on August 15th. This is an excellent acquisition, which will, I hope, be followed by some others of the same sort, etc., etc. In short, all that it is humanly possible to do in Weimar in the year of grace 1850, you may be sure, will be done for your *Lohengrin*, which, in spite of much stupid talk, some false anxiety, and some too real impediments, will, you may take my promise, be very decently performed on the 28th inst., after which I have invited myself to supper at Zigesar's, who is fire and flame for *Lohengrin*. When he sends you your honorarium of from twenty-five to thirty louis d'or, towards the end of the month, kindly write to him a *fairly long and friendly* letter, for he fully shares my sympathy and admiration for your genius, and is the only person who can assist me in giving external significance to those sentiments. At his last stay in Berlin he spoke of *Tannhäuser* to the King and the Prince of Prussia, so as to let them know in Berlin how the matter stands. Two or three days later please write also a few lines to Genast, who has behaved extremely well in all the transactions preceding *Lohengrin*, and who will zealously execute your indications as to the *mise-en-scène*.

If you will do me a service, dear friend, send me, if possible by return of post, some metronomical indications for the introduction and several other important pieces, the duet between Lohengrin and Elsa in the third act amongst others. I believe I am not mistaken as to your wishes and intentions, but should still prefer to have conviction *in figures* as to this matter.

There will be no cut, no curtailment, in your score, and I shall do my best to have no lack of $<$ *fp*. *fp*. $>$, and especially of ... —, which is the most difficult thing for the string instruments.

Farewell, dear friend! I think your work is sublime, and am your sincerely devoted   F. LISZT.

37.

My Dearest Friend,

Many thanks for your letter received yesterday ;
also convey my cordial thanks to the donor. Dear
friend, we all know who it is. Why this official secrecy ?
I must confess that formerly I thought it more desirable
to have an honorarium for my version of *Iphigenia in
Aulis* than a present, but on second consideration I
find that such an honorarium would have been little more
than a present. Who knows better than myself that
in our dear world of the Mine and Thine, of work and
payment, I am a pure luxury ? He who gives anything
to me receives something quite superfluous and unnecessary in return. What do you think, who have taken
such infinite pains to dispose of my works ? Much as
I think of my *Lohengrin*, which you are bringing to
light, I think as much and almost more of you and
your terrible exertions. I know what these exertions
are. When I saw you conduct a rehearsal of *Tannhäuser*, I knew at once what you were to me. What
curious creatures we are ! We can be happy only by
the complete annihilation of our whole being ; to be
happy means with us to lose consciousness of ourselves.
Stupid as it may sound, I call to you, Reserve yourself
—as much as you can.

The arrival of a letter from you is always a feast to
me, and all my friends are invited to it. If possible, let
me have a few lines now and then as to the success of
the rehearsals. I control myself violently, and let no
one see it, but to you I must confess my sorrow is great
not to hear my work under your direction. But I have
to bear so many things, and shall bear this also. I think

of myself as if I were dead. Whenever I have news of you, I am filled with new desire to commence some large artistic work ; for literary work I have no longer any great inclination. Upon the whole, I preach to deaf ears ; only he whom artistic experience has taught to find the right thing can understand what I mean ; so it is better that every one should arrive by the aid of experience and do for himself what he can do. But I still feel enthusiasm for the work of art itself ; the music of my *Siegfried* vibrates through all my nerves ; it all depends upon a favourable mood, and that you, dear friend, will procure for me.

To Zigesar I shall write according to your wish. I have every reason to feel friendly towards him, and do so in very deed. To Genast I shall write to-morrow.

Another young friend of mine goes specially from Zurich to Weimar for the two performances of my opera ; I shall give him a few lines of introduction to you. For the present I only ask you to get him a good seat for the two performances ; please do not forget it. For a Herr Abt, from here, I asked the same favour last time.

You forgot in your last letter to reply as to the book of words. I wrote to you that I should like to see a proof ; it would be too late now, and therefore useless, to repeat that wish ; therefore I ask you to see that the proof is read as carefully as possible. Perhaps Professor Wolff, whom I greet cordially a thousand times, would be kind enough to correct a proof. This reminds me that I have corrected a mistake in the manuscript of the libretto, but not in the score. In the last words of Lohengrin's leave-taking of Elsa it should be, instead of—

> "*mein* zürnt der Gral wenn ich noch bleib,"
> "*mir* zürnt," etc., etc.

You ask me also for a few metronomical indications of the tempo. I consider this quite unnecessary, because I rely in all things on your artistic sympathy so thoroughly as to know that you need only be in a good humour with my work to find out the right thing everywhere ; for the right thing consists in this only : that the effect corresponds with the intention. But, as you wish it, I send you the following, in confirmation, no doubt, of your own views :—

INSTRUMENTAL INTRODUCTION.

(The triplets *molto moderato*.)

ACT I., SCENE 2, ELSA'S SONG (page 35).

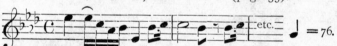

Later on—*e.g.*, in the finale—this theme of course grows quicker.

(At the arrival of Lohengrin (A major) perhaps a little *più moderato*.)

The slow movement in E flat 3—4 (*ensemble*) in the finale of the first act you will, I presume, not take too slow, but with solemn emotion. The last bar of the orchestral *ritornel* must be played a good deal *ritardando*, so as to make the tempo of this postlude even more majestic where the trumpets enter, by which means also the violins will be enabled to bring out the lively *staccato* figures strongly and clearly.

ACT II., SCENE I.

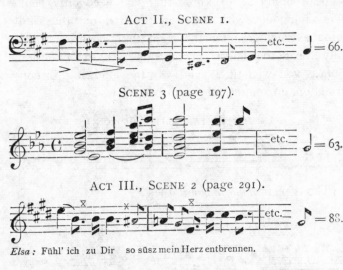

SCENE 3 (page 197).

ACT III., SCENE 2 (page 291).

Elsa: Fühl' ich zu Dir so süsz mein Herz entbrennen.

Grand and perfect repose is here the chief thing. In singing the passage, I found that I paused a little on the second and fourth part of the bar, but of course in such a manner as to be scarcely perceptible in a rhythmical sense, only as a matter of expression.

Lohengrin: Ath-mest Du nicht mit mir die süss - en.

Page 39.

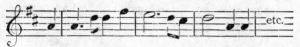

Dein Lie-ben muss mir hoch ent - gel - - ten.

(Here the tempo becomes a little slower.)

But enough, perhaps too much already. With all
these indications, I appear mean before you. You will
do it all right, perhaps better than I should. Only see
that we soon meet again; I long to be with you. Or
do you find me too effusive? No! Farewell, my dear,
good Liszt. Write to me soon.

Yours,

RICHARD WAGNER.

ZURICH, *August* 16*th*, 1850.
(Abendstern-Enge, Zurich.)

38.

At this moment, dearest friend, after having closed
the letter already, I begin to feel a doubt whether you
have received my last letter, which I sent you about
eighteen days ago. I am uncertain because you make no
mention of its contents, which were—

1. A letter from me to Zigesar.

2. One bar of music (full score), which was to be added
at the end of Lohengrin's tale in Act III. (the cut which
I want in this scene—omission of the second part of
Lohengrin's tale—you also do not mention; I assume
that you agree).

3. My asking you to send me a proof of the libretto
(now too late).

If you have not received this letter, kindly let me

know at once, because in that case I should like to send you the aforementioned additional bar, which might still arrive in time for the general rehearsal.

R. W.

39.

Dear Liszt,

The bearer of this greeting is my young friend Karl Ritter, whose visit I announced to you in my last letter. His family has migrated from Russia, where they formerly lived, to Dresden ; and their intention is later on to settle in Switzerland near me. Karl has preceded them in any case, and will stay for the summer with me. He is thoroughly cultured and full of talent, and his musical gift especially is considerable. He was unable to resist the desire to hear my *Lohengrin*, the score of which he knows thoroughly, under your direction ; and therefore he has journeyed to Weimar, to return to me after the second representation. I need scarcely ask you to be kind to him, for I know that it is your nature to be amiable. Please take him with you to the general rehearsal and see that he gets a good place at the performances, which his family from Dresden also will attend. I thank you in advance for this kindness.

I shall spend the day and evening of the 28th with my wife alone on the Righi. This little trip to the Alps, which has been made possible by your kindly care, will, I hope, benefit my bodily and mental condition, especially in these days, when I am naturally moved by many feelings. Farewell, dear friend. Write soon, and be always sure of my most devoted love.

Your

Richard Wagner.

Zurich, *August 22nd*, 1850.

40.

DEAREST FRIEND,

Your *Lohengrin* is a sublime work from one end to the other. The tears rose from my heart in more than one place. The whole opera being one indivisible wonder, I cannot stop to point out any particular passage, combination, or effect. A pious ecclesiastic once underlined word for word the whole "Imitatio Christi;" in the same way I might underline your *Lohengrin* note for note. In that case, however, I should like to begin at the end; that is, at the duet between Elsa and Lohengrin in the third act, which to my thinking is the acme of the beautiful and true in art.

Our first representation was, comparatively speaking, satisfactory. Herr von B., who will see you soon, will bring you very accurate news. The second performance cannot take place before ten or twelve days. The court and the few intelligent persons in Weymar are full of sympathy and admiration for your work; and as to the public at large, they will think themselves in honour bound to admire and applaud what they cannot understand. As soon as I have a little rest I shall begin the article which will probably appear in the *Débats*; in the meantime Raff, about whom B. will speak to you, will write two notices in the journal of Brockhaus and in the *Leipzig Illustrirte Zeitung*. Uhlig will look after Brendel's paper, etc.

If you have a moment, do not forget to write to Genast, who has very warmly interested himself in the success of *Lohengrin*. You may be quite assured of the fate of the masterpiece in Weymar, which is, no doubt, a little surprised at being able to produce such things. Before the end of the winter *Lohengrin* will certainly become a "draw."

When shall we have *Siegfried*? Write to me soon, and always count on your devoted friend and servant,

F. LISZT.

WEYMAR, *September 2nd.*

41.

DEAR FRIEND,

I can no longer delay writing to you, although I should have preferred to wait for another letter from you, so as to answer any possible questions of yours. As far as I can at present form an opinion of the character of the *Lohengrin* performance at Weimar from the accounts that have reached me, there is one thing that stands forth in the surest and most indubitable manner, viz., your unprecedented efforts and sacrifices in favour of my work, your touching love for me, and your marvellous faculty of making the impossible possible. I can see after the event quite clearly what a gigantic task you have undertaken and performed. How can I ever reward you? I should scarcely have anything to communicate to you beyond these exclamations of gratitude if I had not discovered in Herr von Zigesar's letter (received the day before yesterday, together with the honorarium) a certain disappointment—the disappointment involuntarily expressed by one who does not see his warmest zeal for a beloved cause crowned by the desired success, and who therefore assumes a certain pensive and doubtful attitude. Zigesar is doubtful whether the success of my opera is certain; he professes the warmest desire to work for that certainty with all his might, but appears to hesitate as to the best means for the purpose.

Knowing that your zeal in the same cause is more active and energetic than that of any one else, I must turn to you alone in considering the means which may bring about our common desire.

So much is certain : that the performance has caused fatigue by the length of its duration. I confess I was horrorstruck when I heard that the opera had lasted until close upon eleven at night. When I had finished the opera, I timed it exactly, and according to my calculation the first act would last not much over an hour, the second an hour and a quarter, the third again a little more than an hour, so that, counting the *entr'actes*, I calculated the duration of the opera from six o'clock to a quarter to ten at the latest. I should have been doubtful whether you had taken the tempi according to my calculation if musical friends, well acquainted with the opera, had not assured me particularly that you had taken the tempi throughout as they knew them from me, and now and then rather a little quicker than slower. I must therefore assume that the dragging took place where you, as conductor, lost your immediate power, viz., in the recitatives. I have been assured that the recitatives were not attacked by the singers as I had performed them to my friends at the piano. Allow me to explain myself a little more particularly, and forgive my mistake of not having done so before.

Owing to the deplorable fact that at our German theatres scarcely anything but operas translated from a foreign language is given, our dramatic singers have been most thoroughly demoralised. The translations of French and Italian operas are generally made by blunderers, or at least scarcely ever by people who would be able to effect between the music and the translation a similar concordance to that which existed in the original version, as, for example, I tried to do in the most important parts of Gluck's *Iphigenia*. The result has been in the course of time that the singers got into the way of neglecting altogether the connection between word and tone, of pronouncing an unimportant syllable to an accentuated note of the melody, and of putting the important word to a weak part of the bar. In this way they gradually became accustomed to the most absolute nonsense, to such an extent that it was frequently quite indifferent whether they pronounced at all or not. It is most amusing to hear German critics boast that only Germans understand dramatic music, while experience teaches that every bad Italian singer in the worst Italian opera declaims more naturally and expressively than the best Germans can do. The recitative has fared worst; in it singers have become accustomed to see only a certain conventional sequence of tonal phrases, which they can pull about and draw out according to their sweet will. When in opera the recitative commences, it means to them, " The Lord be praised, here is an end to that cursed tempo, which off and on compels us to a kind of rational rendering; we can now float about in all directions, dwell on any note we like until the prompter has supplied us with the next phrase; the conductor has now no power over us, and we can take revenge for his pretensions by commanding him to give us the beat when it suits us," etc. Although perhaps not all singers are conscious of this privilege of their genius, they, as a rule, involuntarily adopt this free-and-easy method, which confirms them in a certain natural laziness and flabbiness. A composer writing for German singers has therefore to take every care in opposing an artistic necessity to this lazy thoughtlessness. Nowhere in the score of my *Lohengrin* have I written above a vocal phrase the word " recitative ; " the singers ought not to know that there are any recitatives in it; on the other hand, I have been intent upon weighing and indicating the verbal emphasis of speech so surely and so distinctly that the singers *need only sing the notes, exactly according to their value in the given tempo,* in order to get purely by that means the declamatory expression. I therefore request the singers particularly to sing all declamatory passages in my operas at first in strict tempo, as they are written. By pronouncing them throughout vividly and distinctly *much* is gained. If, proceeding from this basis with reasonable liberty and accelerating rather than holding back, they manage to obliterate the painful effect of the tempo altogether, and produce an emotional and poetic mode of speech, then *all* is gained.

Dingelstedt's sympathetic and clever notice of the performance of my *Lohengrin* has impressed me very much. He owns that previously he had known nothing by me, and chiefly attributes to this circumstance a certain puzzled feeling which the first performance of *Lohengrin* has produced in him. That puzzled feeling he transfers to the character of the work itself, speaking of numberless intentions crossing each other, with which he supplies me, but never guessing, as far as I can see, the only intention which guided me—I mean the simple and bare intention of the *drama*. He speaks of the impression which flutes, violins, kettle-drums, and trumpets made on him, but nowhere of the dramatic representatives in whose stead, as he puts it, those instruments spoke. From this I conclude that at the performance the *purely musical execution* preponderated, that the orchestra — as connoisseurs have also told me—was excellent, and that friend Liszt, together with all that immediately depended on him, was the real hero of the performance. If we consider honestly and unselfishly the essence of music, we must own that it is in large measure a means to an end, that end being in rational opera the *drama*, which is most emphatically placed in the hands of the *representatives on the stage*. That these representatives disappeared for Dingelstedt, that in their stead he only heard the utterance of orchestral instruments, grieves me, for I see that, as regards fire and expression, the singers remained behind the support of the orchestra. I own that a singer supported by the orchestra in such a manner as is here the case must be of the very highest and best quality, and I fully believe that such singers could not easily be found in Weimar, and in Germany generally. But what is really the essential and prin-cipal thing here ? Is it voice only ? Surely not. It is *life and fire,* and in addition to that earnest endeavour and a strong and powerful will. In Dresden I made the experience with our best singers that, although they had the most laudable intentions and the greatest love for their tasks, they were unable to master a certain flabby laziness, which in our actual artistic muddle appears to be the characteristic trait of all our operatic

heroes. I there caused all the remarks in the score of
Tannhäuser to be inserted in the parts of the singers
with the utmost accuracy—I mean the remarks which
had reference to the meaning of the situation and the
dramatic action. At the performance I perceived with
dismay that all these had remained unnoticed, and I had
to see—imagine my horror!—for example, that my
Tannhäuser in the contest of the singers shouted the
hymn of Venus—

> "Wer dich mit Gluth in seine Arme geschlossen,
>   Was Liebe ist, weiss der, nur der allein!"

at Elizabeth, the chastest of virgins, before a whole
assembly of people. The only possible result could be
that the public was, to say the least, confounded, and
did not know what to make of it. Indeed, I heard at
Dresden that the public became acquainted with the
dramatic meaning of the opera only by reading the book
in extenso; in other words, they understood the performance by disregarding the visible performance and
making additions from their own imagination. Are
your singers at Weimar more advanced than our famous
people of Dresden? I think not. Probably they also
will, in the first instance, be satisfied with getting over
the difficulty of hitting the notes and committing their
parts to memory, and on the stage they will at best
take notice only of what the stage-manager tells them
in the most general way. Genast, however, was always
one of those artists who do not rely upon the stage-
manager for the comprehension of their parts; he who
has heard him and seen him knows so much. Being
now a stage-manager himself, he probably thinks it

unnecessary to play for the singers the schoolmaster, whom he, as a singer, never wanted. In this, however, he is mistaken; the present generation has run wild from its birth. I also can understand too well that, in his friendly zeal for my work, he remained entirely on the proper standpoint of the stage-manager, who arranges things in a general way, and justly leaves it to the individual actors to find out for themselves what concerns them only. In spite of this, I ask him now to interfere even there, where the power and the natural activity of the stage-manager ceases; let him be the trustee of infant actors. At the rehearsal of my *Tannhäuser* in Weimar I had occasion to point out the neglect of some scenic indications on the part of individual singers. Elizabeth, for example, during the postlude of the duet with Tannhäuser in the second act, has to justify the re-entry of the tender theme in the clarinet in slower tempo by looking—as is indicated in the score —after Tannhäuser in the court of the castle and by beckoning to him. By neglecting this and merely standing in front, waiting for the conclusion of the music, she naturally produces an unbearable feeling of tedium. Every bar of dramatic music is justified only by the fact that it explains something in the action or in the character of the actor. That reminiscence of the clarinet theme is not there for its own sake as a purely musical effect, which Elizabeth might have to accompany by her action, but the beckoned greeting of Elizabeth is the chief thing I had in my eye, and that reminiscence I selected in order to accompany suitably this action of Elizabeth. The relations of music and action must therefore be deplorably perverted where, as in this

instance, the *principal thing*—*i.e.*, the dramatic motive—
is left out, while the *lesser thing*—*i.e.*, the accompani-
ment of that motive—alone remains. Of the performance of *Lohengrin* one fact has been related to me which,
although it may appear of little consequence, must
serve me to show how important, nay decisive, for a
proper understanding such individual cases may be.

When I conceived and wrote the second act, it had
not escaped me how important it would be for the
proper mood of the spectator to show that Elsa's
contentment at the last words of Lohengrin is not really
complete and genuine; the public should feel that
Elsa violently forces herself to conquer her doubt, and
we should in reality fear that, having once indulged
in brooding over Lohengrin, she will finally succumb
and ask the prohibited question. In the production of
this general feeling of fear lies the only necessity for
a third act in which that fear is realised; without it the
opera should end here, for the chief problem would
not only have been mooted, but satisfactorily solved.
In order to produce this feeling very distinctly and
tangibly, I invented the following dramatic point : Elsa
is led by Lohengrin up the steps on the minster; on
the topmost step she looks downwards with timid appre-
hension; her eye involuntarily seeks Frederick, of whom
she is still thinking ; at that moment her glance falls
on Ortrud, who stands below, and raises her hand in
a threatening manner. At this moment I introduce
in the orchestra in F minor ff. the warning of Lohengrin,
the significance of which has by this time been distinctly
impressed upon us, and which, accompanied by Ortrud's
impressive gesture, here indicates with absolute certainty,

"Whatever happens, you will disobey the command in spite of all." Elsa then turns away in terror, and only when the king, after this interruption, once more proceeds towards the entrance of the minster with the bridal pair, does the curtain drop. What a pity then that that dramatic point was not made on the stage, and that the curtain dropped before the entry of the reminiscence in F minor! This not unimportant mistake was, no doubt, caused by the probably accidental neglect of a remark in the full score which, according to my previous wish, should, like similar other remarks, have been extracted for the benefit of the actors. I must fear that several other things have also remained unnoticed and unexecuted, and nothing confirms me so much in this fear as the account of Dingelstedt, who, in spite of his unmistakable goodwill, has evidently not taken in my opera because of the music.

Dearest Liszt, was I right when in the preface of my "Kunstwerk der Zukunft" I wrote that not the individual, but the community alone, could create genuine works of art? You have done the *impossible*, but, believe me, *all* must nowadays do the impossible in order to achieve what is really possible. What delights me more than all is to hear that you have not lost courage, and are going to try everything in order to support the opera, in spite of a certain disappointment around you, and even to put it on its legs. To assist you in this most laudable zeal I give you the following advice : Let Genast, whom I cordially thank for his friendship, before the resumption of *Lohengrin*, call the whole *personnel* to a *reading rehearsal*; let the singers *read* their parts in connection, distinctly and expressively, from the printed libretto, in which there are unfortunately many misprints. Let Genast take the score, and from the remarks therein inserted explain to the singers the meaning of the situations and their connection with the music bar by bar. The devil must be in it if the matter could not then be put right, provided the intentions of the actors are good. Once more, let Genast go beyond his position as stage-manager, which, no doubt, he fills as well as any one, and let him become the *guardian of the infants and the neglected.*

By these words I by no means wish to express a definite doubt as to your singers in general or their achievements in this particular case. The fact that in a purely musical sense they took such care of their parts that you ventured with them upon the performance of this enormously difficult, because unfamiliar music is an excellent testimony in their favour. In the above I asked them for something which perhaps they have never been asked for before. I hope Genast will find it worth his while to explain this most specially to them, and that he will succeed in making them do justice to my demand. In that case he may boast of having been the chief participant in a revolution which will lift our theatrical routine out of its grooves.

The representative of Lohengrin alone appears, according to all accounts, really incapable. Would it not be possible to make in this instance a change of persons? To my mind everybody ought to be glad when Lohengrin enters, instead of which it appears that people were more pleased when he left the stage. At this moment I receive your letter, assuring me of your joy and friendship. What good spirits you are in!

I will close this long letter, which must have bored you very much, by comprising all the single points I have mentioned to you in a final and weighty bundle of prayers.

1. Arrange by the intervention of Genast that before the second performance the singers have another rehearsal according to the above indications. Let no scenic remark remain unnoticed.

2. Insist firmly and sharply that the singers perform in decisive and lively tempo what they take to be recitatives in my opera. By this means the duration of the opera will, according to my experience, be shortened by nearly an hour.

3. Further, I desire that, with the exception of the second part of Lohengrin's tale, which I determined from the beginning to cut, my opera should be given *as it is*, without any omissions.

If cuts are made, the chain of comprehension will be torn asunder, and my style, which the public are only just beginning to take in, so far from being made more accessible, will be further removed from the public and the actors. To capitulate to the enemy is not to conquer; the enemy himself must surrender; and that enemy is the laziness and flabbiness of our actors, who must be forcibly driven to feel and think. If I do not gain the victory, and have to capitulate in spite of my powerful ally, I shall go into no further battles. If my *Lohengrin* can be preserved only by tearing its well-calculated and artistic context to pieces, in other words if it has to be cut owing to the laziness of the actors, *I shall abandon opera altogether.* Weimar in that case will have no more interest for me, and *I shall have written my last opera.* With you, dear Liszt, who have so bravely accepted my battle, it lies to gain a complete victory for me. I do not know what more I could say; to you I have said enough. To Genast, for whom also this letter is intended, I shall write separately as soon as I know that my demand has not offended him. To Zigesar I write to-morrow.

In the meantime I post this letter in order not to incur the reproach of delay.

Farewell, then, dearest, splendid friend. You are as good as refreshing summer rain. Farewell. Be thanked, and greet my friends.

Always your most obliged
RICHARD WAGNER.

ZURICH, *September 8th,* 1850.

One thing more: as you have no organ and no harmonium (*physharmonika*), I want you to let the short organ-passage at the end of the second act be played *by wind instruments behind the scenes.*

Lohengrin should sing the words " Heil dir, Elsa! nun lass vor Gott uns gehen!" with *tender* emotion.

42.

(TO HERR VON ZIGESAR.)

MOST ESTIMABLE HERR INTENDANT,

On my return from a little trip to the Alps, I find the copies of the libretto of *Lohengrin* which you have kindly sent to me, and have every reason to rejoice heartily at the remarkable care with which you have had it done. This is another ocular proof of the sympathy with which you have gone to work in everything concerning my last opera, and I must not omit to express my warmest thanks to you. Your last letter, in which you kindly enclosed the honorarium for my *Lohengrin*, tells me of the success of all your extraordinary exertions for the performance of the opera, and I see with regret from your friendly communication that satisfaction, in the measure desired by you, has not been the result, and that a permanent success appears doubtful to you. As with this statement you combine no objection to the work itself, but, on the contrary, assure me that to the best of your intention and power you will try to secure that desired success for my opera, I feel bound to add to the expression of my gratitude for your kind feeling my opinion as to how our mutual wishes might be realised.

Most esteemed Herr Intendant, with full knowledge of the matter at stake, you have undertaken by its performance at your theatre to give life to a dramatic work the essence of which is that it is in all its parts a continuous whole, and not something incongruous, made up of many different parts. The author of this work does not wish to shine by the effect of single musical pieces; music to him is altogether no more than the most exalted and most comprehensive mode of expression of what he desired to express—the drama. Even where music became a mere ornament I remained conscious of having acted in accordance with a certain artistic necessity, and each necessary effect was brought about only by the fact that, like the link of a well-forged chain, it derived its significance from the preceding links. If this chain were torn asunder by the removal of the whole, or a half, or a quarter of a link, the whole context would be torn along with it, and my intention would be destroyed. You admitted to me yourself that in certain cases about which at first you had doubts you had been finally convinced of the necessity of this concatenation, but the impression made upon you by the performance has again renewed this doubt, to the extent, at least, that you think it advisable, in consideration of the public, to consent to certain omissions in my opera. Permit me to think a little better of the public. An audience which assembles in a fair mood is satisfied as soon as it distinctly understands what is going forward, and it is a great mistake to think that a theatrical audience must have a special knowledge of music in order to receive the right impression of a musical drama. To this entirely erroneous opinion we have been brought by the fact that in opera music has wrongly been made the aim, while the drama was merely a means for the display of the music. Music, on the contrary, should do no more than contribute its full share towards making the drama clearly and quickly comprehensible at every moment. While listening to a good—that is, rational—opera, people should, so to speak, not think of the music at all, but only feel it in an unconscious manner, while their fullest sympathy should be wholly occupied by the action represented. Every audience which has an uncorrupted sense and a human heart is therefore welcome to me as long as I may be certain that the dramatic action is made more immediately comprehensible and moving by the music, instead of being hidden by it. In this respect the performance of my *Lohengrin* at Weimar does not as yet seem to have been adequate, in so far as the purely musical part was much more perfect than the dramatic, properly so called, and the fault I attribute solely to the general state of our opera, which from the outset has the most confusing and damaging influence on all our singers. If during the performance of my *Lohengrin* the music *only* was noticed, yea almost only the orchestra, you may be sure that the actors remained far behind their task. Yesterday I wrote at length to my incomparable friend Liszt about this, and explained to him my views as to how the matter might be managed so as to place the performance in the right light. If in future the so-called recitatives are sung as I have asked Liszt to insist upon their being sung, the halting and freezing impression of whole, long passages will disappear, and the duration of the performance will be considerably shortened. If cuts were resorted to, you would gain comparatively little time, and would sacrifice to our modern theatrical routine every possibility of thorough reform. I can imagine, for instance, that the speeches of the king and the herald may have made a fatiguing impression, but if this was the case because the singers sang them in a lackadaisical, lazy, and slovenly manner, without real utterance, is then the interest of art benefited by curtailing or omitting these speeches ? Surely not. Art and artists will be equally benefited only if those singers are *earnestly* requested to pronounce those speeches with energy, fire, and determined expression. Where no effect is made no impression can be produced, and where no impression is produced people are bored ; but is it right, in order to shorten that boredom, to remove what with a proper expression would produce

the necessary effect? In that case it would be better
to drop the whole work, which, for want of proper
expression, would be in danger of failing to produce
the necessary effect. For if we yield in small and
single things, if we make concessions to laziness and
incompetence, we may be sure that we shall soon be
obliged to do the same throughout; in other words,
that we must give up every attempt at making a work
like the present succeed. It appears to me preferable
to find out with the utmost care where the real cause
of the existing evil lies, and then to attack the enemy
in his own camp with perseverance and power. You
will see from this, most esteemed Herr Intendant, how
important it is for me not to gain toleration for my
Lohengrin by accommodating it to existing evils, but to
secure for it a decisive success by making it *conquer*
existing evils. Otherwise I confess openly that the
future chances of this opera would have no value for me;
in that case I should only regret the amount of exertion,
trouble, and sympathy which you have kindly wasted on
this work. Fame I do not seek, gain I had to renounce
long ago, and if now I have at last to experience
that even my most energetic friends and patrons think
themselves obliged to make concessions for my benefit
where a real victory can alone be of value, I shall lose
every wish and every power to be further active in my
art. If you can keep my *Lohengrin* going only by
truncating its healthy organism, and not by operating
to the best of your power on the diseased organism
of our truncated operatic body, then I shall be cordially
glad if you are rewarded for your pains according to
circumstances, but I must ask you not to be angry

with me if I look upon such a success with indifference. What to you is a matter of benevolence towards me is for me, unfortunately, a vital question of my whole mental existence in art, to which my being clings with bleeding fibres.

May Heaven grant that you, highly esteemed sir and patron, will take the contents and expression of these lines in good part, and that you will not for a moment doubt that always and in all circumstances I shall look upon you as one of the most sympathetic phenomena that have entered my existence. In all respects I owe you love and unbounded gratitude. If I should never be able to show this to you, as from my whole heart I desire, I ask you fervently to attribute it, not to the wish of my inmost soul, but to the position which I, as an artist with a passionate heart, must, according to my firm conviction, take towards the state of deep depravity of our public art-life.

With the highest esteem and veneration, I remain yours obediently,

RICHARD WAGNER.

ZURICH, *September 9th*, 1850.

43.

DEAREST LISZT,

I must to-day write you a few additional lines with reference to my recent long letter.

Karl Ritter arrived here last night from his journey; and from his account I see that in my surmises as to certain points in the performance of *Lohengrin*, founded chiefly on some striking remarks in Dingelstedt's notes, I have not hit the right thing. Ritter tells me that,

contrary to what I thought, you have kept up the
tempo of the recitatives according to my indications,
and that therefore the dreaded caprice of the singers,
as far, at least, as the tempo was concerned, had no
licence. For *this* also I must thank you, but am a
little perplexed as to the advice I recently gave you.
By keeping up the tempi of the recitatives I had
chiefly intended to shorten the duration of the performance, but I see now that you had already done the
right thing, and therefore remain astounded at my
own error as to the length of the opera, which is certainly detrimental. My opinion is that if, as I much
desire, the higher context is not to be destroyed by
cuts, the public must be *deceived* as to the duration of
the performance by your making the singers pronounce
the recitatives as vividly and as speakingly as possible ;
it is quite possible for them to sing them in the proper
tempo without giving interest to them by warmth and
truth of declamation. Moreover, the performance will,
of its own accord, become more compact as time goes
on. I have made this experience at the performances
of my operas which I conducted myself, the first performances always lasting a little longer than the subsequent ones, although nothing had been cut in these.
This will probably be the case with the performance
of *Lohengrin* in Weimar, which only now that I have
been able to ask about many difficult details I can appreciate in its *excellence* and *perfection* as regards the
musical portion.

I now come to the principal thing. You cannot believe
how delighted I was to hear some particulars of your
music to *Prometheus*. Our friend Uhlig, to whom

I attribute excellent judgment, sends me word that he values this single overture more than the whole of Mendelssohn. My desire to make its acquaintance is raised to the highest pitch. Dearest friend, will you be kind enough to let me have a copy soon, if I ask you particularly? You would please me immensely, and I already contemplate the possibility of having it played to me at a concert here in Zurich. Now and then I shall take an interest in the local musical performances, and I promise you that your work will not be heard otherwise than in the most adequate conditions that can be obtained. Could I also have your overture to *Tasso*? When I look upon your whole life and contemplate the energetic turn which you have given to it of late years, when I further anticipate your achievements, you may easily imagine how happy I shall be to give my sincerest and most joyous sympathy to your works. You extraordinary and amiable man, send me soon what I ask you.

Enough for to-day.

I am always and wholly yours,

RICHARD WAGNER.

ZURICH, *September 11th*, 1850.

44.

DEAREST FRIEND,

The second performance of your masterpiece has answered my expectations, and the third and fourth will bring home to every one the opinion I expressed as soon as we began rehearsing *Lohengrin*, namely, that this work will confer on a public making itself worthy

of understanding and enjoying it more honour than that
public could confer upon the work by any amount of
applause.

"Perish all theatrical mud!" I exclaimed when we
tried for the first time the first scenes of *Lohengrin*.
"Perish all critical mud and the routine of artists and
the public!" I have added a hundred times during the
last six weeks. At last, and very much *at last*, I have
the satisfaction to be able to assure you very positively
that your work will be better executed and better heard
and understood from performance to performance.
This last point is, in my opinion, the most important
of all, for it is not only the singers and the orchestras
that must be brought up to the mark to serve as
instruments in the *dramatic revolution*, which you so
eloquently describe in your letter to Zigesar, but also,
and before all, the *public*, which must be elevated to
a level where it becomes capable of associating itself
by sympathy and intelligent comprehension with
conceptions of a higher order than that of the lazy
amusements with which it feeds its imagination and
sensibility at our theatres every day. This must be
done, if need be, by violence, for, as the Gospel tells us,
the kingdom of heaven suffers violence, and only those
who use violence will take it.

I fully understand the motive which has made you
speak with diplomatic reserve of the *audiences* of *Lohengrin* in your letter to Zigesar, and I approve of it. At the
same time, it is certain that, in order to realise completely
the *drama* which you conceive, and of which you give us
such magnificent examples in *Tannhäuser* and *Lohengrin*,
it is absolutely necessary to make a breach in the old

routine of criticism, the long ears and short sight of "Philistia," as well as the stupid arrogance of that self-sufficient fraction of the public which believes itself the destined judge of works of art by dint of birthright.

The enemy to whom, as you, my great art-hero, rightly put it, one should not capitulate—that enemy is not only in the throats of the singers, but also very essentially in the lazy and at the same time tyrannical habits of the hearers. On these as well as on the others one must make an impression if necessary by a good beating. This you understand better than I could tell you.

In accordance with your desire, we have at the second performance of *Lohengrin* not omitted a single syllable, for after your letter it would, in my opinion, have been a crime to venture upon the slightest cut. As I took occasion to tell those of my friends who were here on August 28th, the performance of your works, as long as you entrust me with their absolute direction, is with me a question of principle and of honour. In these two things one must never make a concession ; and, as far as I am personally concerned, you may rest perfectly assured that I shall not fail in anything which you have a right to expect from me. In spite of this, both Herr von Zigesar and Genast feel bound, in the interest of your work, to address you some observations, which I, for my part, have declined to submit to you, although I think them somewhat justified by the limits of our theatre and of our public, which are as yet far behind my wishes and even my hopes. If you think it advisable to agree to some cuts, kindly let me know your resolution as to this subject. Whether you accept those proposed by Genast, or whether you determine upon others, or whether, which is probable, you prefer to keep your work such as we have given it twice, I promise you on my honour that your wish shall be strictly carried out, with all the respect and all the submission which you have a right to demand by reason of your genius and of your achievements.

Whatever determination you come to in this regard, be certain that in all circumstances you will find in me zeal equal to my admiration and my devotion.

Wholly yours,

F. LISZT.

September 16th, 1850.

P.S.—Remember me kindly to Herr Ritter. I am very thankful to him for not having spoken too ill of our first performance of *Lohengrin* ; the second has been much more satisfactory, and the third and fourth will no doubt be still more so. Herr Beck, who takes the principal part, endeavours in the most laudable manner not to be below the task allotted to him. What is more, he begins to feel enthusiasm for his part and for the composer. If one considers fairly the enormous difficulty of mounting such a work at Weymar, I can tell you sincerely that there is no reason for dissatisfaction with the result which has so far been attained, and which beyond a doubt will go on improving with every representation.

I do not know whether the sublimity of the work blinds me to the imperfection of the execution, but I fancy that if you could be present at one of our next representations you would not be too hard upon us.

45.

DEAREST FRIEND,

In a week or so I shall send you a *very long* article of mine about *Lohengrin*. If personal reasons of your own do not prevent it, it will appear in Paris in the course of October. You are sufficiently acquainted with the habits of the Paris press to know how reluctantly it admits the entire and absolute eulogium of a work by a foreign composer, especially while he is still living. In spite of this, I shall try to overcome this great obstacle, for I make it a point of honour to publish my opinion of your work ; and if you were fairly satisfied with my article, you might perhaps give me a pleasure which would not cost you more than a day or two of tedium. This would be to make a translation, revised, corrected, augmented, and authenticated, which, by the help of your and my friends, could be inserted in two or three numbers of the *Augsburg Allgemeine Zeitung* or the journal of Brockhaus, signed with my name.

If you should prefer to have it printed separately as a little pamphlet by Weber, of Leipzig, I should not object ; and if you would say a word to Weber, I feel convinced that he would willingly undertake it. But before all you must be acquainted with my article, and tell me very frankly whether or not you would like to have it published in Germany. In France I will manage it a little sooner or a little later, but in case of a German publication I should make it an absolute condition that you undertook the trouble of translating it and of having it copied under your eyes, so that I should not be charged with the blunders of the translator, etc., etc.

You will see that the style is carefully French, and it would therefore be very important not to destroy the *nuances* of sentiment and thought in their passage to another language.

Always and wholly yours,

F. LISZT.

WEYMAR, *September 25th*, 1850.

46.

DEAREST FRIEND,

I have little to tell you unless I write to you about all the things which we two need scarcely discuss any more. After your last letter, which has given me great and genuine joy, such as few things could, we are almost so absolutely near each other on the most important questions that we may truly say, we are one. I only long for the pleasure of your company, for the delight of being united with you for a season, so that we may mutually no longer say, but *do* to each other what we cannot express in writing. In fact, *to do something* is always better and leads to the goal much quicker than the cleverest discussion. Cannot you get free for a little time and have a look round Switzerland? or cannot you at least send me your scores, for which I recently asked you? You ignore my request in your letter; why is that?

I have again many things to think about—alas! to think about only. I have once more arrived at a point where retreat is impossible; I *must* think out my thoughts before becoming once more a naïve and confident artist, although I shall be that again, and look forward with pleasure to reaping the richest benefit.

You lay stress in your letter upon the fact that the enemy whom we have to fight is not only in the throats of our singers, but in the lazy Philistinism of our public and in the donkeydom of our critics. Dearest friend, I agree with you so fully that I did not even mention it to you. What I object to are the perverse demands which are made on the public. I will not allow that the public is charged with *want of artistic intelligence*, and that the salvation of art is expected from the process of grafting artistic intelligence on the public from above; ever since the existence of connoisseurs art has gone to the devil. By drilling artistic intelligence into it we only make the public perfectly stupid. What I said was this: that I wanted nothing of the public beyond *a healthy sense and a human heart*. This does not sound much, but it is so much that the whole world would have to be turned upside down to bring it about. The noble-minded, the refined, those who have the courage of their feelings, believe themselves at the top of the tree; they are mistaken! In our actual order of things the *Philistine*, the vulgar, common, flabby, and at the same time cruel *man of routine*, reigns supreme. He, and no one else, is the prop of existing things, and against him we all fight in vain, however noble our courage may be; for unfortunately all things are in this slavery of leathern custom, and only fright and trouble of all kinds can turn the Philistine into a man *by thoroughly upsetting him*. Pending an entirely new order of things, we must, dearest friend, be satisfied with ourselves and with those who, like ourselves, know but one enemy

—the Philistine. Let us show each other what we can do, and let us feel highly rewarded if we can give joy to each other. " *A healthy sense and a human heart !*"—we ask nothing more, and yet all, if we realise the bottomless corruption of that sense, the wicked cowardliness of the heart of the so-called public. Confess, a deluge would be necessary to correct this little fault. To remedy these ills I fear our most ardent endeavour will do nothing that is efficacious. All we can do—while we exist, and with the best will in the world cannot exist at any other time but the *present*—is to think of preserving our dignity and freedom as artists and as men. Let us show to one another in *ourselves* that there is worth in man.

In the same sense I was intent, in connection with my *Lohengrin*, upon considering only the thing in itself; that is, its adequate embodiment on the part of the actors. Of the public I thought only in so far as I contemplated the one possibility of leading the half-unconscious, healthy sense of that public towards the real kernel of the thing—the drama—by means of the dramatic perfection of the performance. That otherwise this kernel is overlooked by the most æsthetic and most intelligent hearers I have unfortunately again been shown by the clearest evidence, and I confess that in this respect Dingelstedt's account of my opera is present to my mind, causing me deep grief. You, best of friends, have taken such infinite care of me in *every respect* that I can only sincerely regret that your efforts are sometimes responded to in so perverse a manner. In Dingel-

stedt's account I recognize two things : his friendly
disposition towards me, with which he has been inspired
by you, and his most absolute incapability, with all his
æstheticism, of conceiving the slightest notion of what
had to be conceived. The total confusion engendered
in him by listening to my opera he transfers with bold
self-reliance to my intentions and to the work itself.
He, who apparently can see in opera nothing but
kettledrums, trombones, and double-basses, naturally
in my opera did not see the wood for the trees ; but,
being a clever and glib-penned littérateur, he produces
a witty and many-coloured set of variorum notes which
he could not have done better if it had been his intention to make fun of me, and this stuff he sends to the
newspaper with the *largest circulation* in the German
language. If I cared in the least to be in a certain
sense recognized, I should have to perceive that Dingelstedt has thoroughly injured me.   I read in some papers
notices of my opera, evidently founded upon that of
Dingelstedt, somewhat to this effect : " Wagner has
written another opera, in which he seems to have surpassed the coarse noise of his *Rienzi*," etc.   I am grieved
that this happened in *the same Allgemeine Zeitung*
where five years ago Dr. Hermann Franck discoursed on
my *Tannhäuser* in an intelligent, calm, and lucid manner.
If it should interest you, please read this article.
It is printed in the *A.A.Z.*, No. 311, November 7th,
1845. You can imagine how I must feel when I
compare the two articles.

If you have not given up the hope of being useful
to me in wider circles, I should make bold to ask
you whether you could manage to have another and

more appropriate notice of my *Lohengrin* inserted in the *A.A.Z.* It has, as I said before, the *largest circulation.*

How glad, on the other hand, was I to see your indications and hints worked up into an intelligent sketch by a Frenchman who is so much further removed from me. This has been done by Nerval, in the *feuilleton* of the *Presse.* Many mistakes occur, but that does not matter. The man has formed for himself from your utterances a picture of me which at least indicates clearly and distinctly my intention. The most terrible of all things is a German æsthetic littérateur.

But to return once more to you. I should like almost for your sake to gain a widespread reputation. You blow up a hundred mines, and wherever I look I come upon you and your more than friendly care for me ; it is touching, and almost without example. Remember me very kindly to Herr Raff, and thank him most cordially in my name. Some of my friends thought it would have been better if he had spoken of my " faults as a man " rather than of my " faults as a *subject* ; " but that, surely, does not matter, and every one must have understood it in that sense. A better intention to serve me I can look for in none except you.

To Genast I wrote a few days ago. This nasty bargaining about twopence-halfpenny in the matter of cuts is repulsive to me ; but Genast remains a fine, brave fellow.

Behold, my paper is at an end, and I have done nothing but gabble. I have many and more im-

portant things to write to you about. Lord, forgive
me! I am not in a mood for it to-day. I shall soon
write again. My best greetings to Zigesar. Truly
this warm, true heart does me much good. Farewell
for to-day, noblest and best of men.

Your

RICHARD WAGNER.

ZURICH, ABENDSTERN, ENGE,
October 2nd, 1850.

47.

DEAR LISZT,

You make me blush! without a blush I can
scarcely read what you are going to tell the world of
me; and now you want me to interpret it. Only if
you earnestly desire it will I grant your prayer, a
prayer which flatters me too much to call it a "prayer."
Would that I could be of use to you! My last letter must
have appeared dissonant to you. I do not know what
moved me to speak bitterly of newspaper notices. One
reason, however, I may tell you: many things have
determined me at last to speak in a literary way *once
more*. I am occupied with a work the title of which is
to be "The Essence of Opera." In it I mean to speak
clearly and definitely about opera as a type of art, and
to indicate as plainly as possible what should be done
to it in order to develop the hidden germs to full bloom.
I should have liked to dedicate this book to you, because
in it I announce the salvation and justification of the
musician quâ musician. I should do this if I did not
think it better not to drag you into this address to
the musical world. In that manner I shall preserve

greater liberty to you. The book therefore shall be a surprise to you. As in this book I intend to explain my view of the essence of the musical drama, I can find nothing more annoying than to see the most contradictory opinions of me spread amongst the public by witty littérateurs. The world must take me for a muddle-headed and false priest if I preach the drama in words while it is said of my works that musical confusion and noise reign in them. But enough of this.

Your letter to B.'s mother was another noble thing of yours. Best thanks.

I once more go to battle with my deadly enemy the winter. I must think a great deal of the preservation of my health, and before the spring I cannot work at *Siegfried* with a will, but in the summer it shall be ready. Let me soon hear something of your works.

One word more in confidence : at the end of this month I shall have spent all my money ; Zigesar has sent me less than you made me hope. Towards the new year I again hope for some assistance from Frau R. in D., but that also is uncertain. Can you— but how shall I express it ? If you have to do something beneath your or my dignity, you cannot ; that I know. The rest will be all right. God bless you. I think the devil will not get hold of me just yet.

Farewell, best of men. Send me your scores. Farewell, and remain kind to me.

Your

RICHARD WAGNER.

ZURICH, *October 8th*, 1850.

48.

HIGHLY ESTEEMED MADAM,

Your kind letter has, as you may imagine, made a great impression. I see, to my genuine joy, that I may count you amongst the small number of the friends who by the weight of their sympathy richly compensate me for the absence of popular acclamation. That you have remained faithful to me is more important to me than perhaps you know yourself. Accept my cordial thanks for the friendship you have preserved for me.

You ask me about my *Wiland*. I have more designs than I have the power to execute. Therefore I want a helper, yea more than a helper, an artistic bosom friend, who works in the same spirit, and, I hope, better than I could work myself. I request you to persuade Liszt to undertake the musical execution of *Wiland* in my stead. The poem in its present condition, such as herewith I send it to you, is the result of sorrowful and deeply emotional enthusiasm, which has stirred me up to imaginings on which as an artist I may, I think, congratulate myself. But it takes me back to a time to which I do not want to be taken back. I cannot finish the poem *now*, either in words or music. If later on I could gain sufficient repose for the purpose, I should be afraid of having cooled towards it. In consequence I have lately become accustomed to the thought of giving up the poem altogether.

But if this *Wiland*, when Liszt makes its first acquaintance, should inspire him as I was once inspired by it, I ask him to consider it as his property. The design is quite complete; all that remains to be done is simple versification, which every fairly skilful writer of verse might execute: Liszt will easily find one. In the more important places, I have written the verses myself. To do more is at present impossible to me; even the copying out gave me much trouble.

I hope, dear madam, you will not think my poem unworthy of your warm recommendation to the friend whom, as you tell me to my great joy, you will soon make happy by calling your own.

With sincere thanks for your kindness, and with cordial esteem, I remain, dear madam,

Your obedient servant,

RICHARD WAGNER.

ZURICH, *October 8th,* 1850.

49.

DEAREST FRIEND,

I really do not know how to thank you; for the only equivalent I could offer you would evidently be to send you a masterpiece in exchange; and this kind of return is difficult to make even with the best intention in the world. Allow me to look upon your manuscript of *Wiland* as a sacred trust, which I shall hold at your disposal till the time you reclaim it. My very numerous engagements will prevent me from occupying myself with it for a year or eighteen months; and if after that time you still think that I am capable of undertaking the composition, we can easily arrange the matter either verbally or by letter. To-day I send you by post a fair copy of my article on *Lohengrin*. As this is the only one I possess, I must ask you kindly to return it to me at Eilsen (Bückeburg), where I shall spend the months of November and December. I foresee the difficulties I shall have to encounter in publishing through the Paris press an article so extensive and so sincerely in praise of a German opera by a German composer, in whose success no one has an interest, rather the reverse. Nevertheless I do not absolutely despair of having it inserted some day in some review, and consequently want the manuscript.

If in the meantime you think my article worthy of publication in Germany, I repeat the request already made that you undertake to translate it freely, and improve it by completing it.

In the quotations it would naturally be better to reproduce exactly the *verses* of your poem, and perhaps one might make the comprehension of your work easier by adding two plates of music type showing the five or six principal themes,

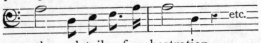

and two or three details of orchestration.

However, as regards both the translation and the publication, I attach value to them only in so far as you approve; for this article has been written solely with the intention of serving, as far as in me lay, the great and beautiful cause of art with the French public, such as it is in 1850. If you think that I have not succeeded, I ask you not to hesitate for a moment in telling me so frankly. In this, any more than in other things, you will not find in me any stupid *amour-propre*, but only the very modest and sincere desire to suit my words and actions to my sentiments.

I have just received a letter from Seghers, director of the *Union Musicale*, Paris, who tells me that your *Tannhäuser* overture will be performed at the first concert of the Society (November 24th). You may rely upon his zeal and intelligence in preparing a good performance.

By the way, have you heard of an intended performance of *Lohengrin* at Dresden? I do not know how far this Dresden performance would benefit you in actual circumstances, while you are forcibly prevented from looking after the rehearsals, etc.

Uhlig has probably told you that Tichatschek will study the part of Lohengrin with him. Soon after my return Herr von Zigesar intends to give the fourth performance, and for the fifth we shall have Tichatschek.

I am really much obliged to you for taking interest in my overtures, and must ask you to forgive me for not having thanked you before; but the fact is, the greater part of my time is occupied with other things than me and my works.

Unfortunately I possess only a single copy of *Prometheus* and *Tasso*, and of that I cannot dispose, as it belongs to the theatre. If, as I am in hopes, next summer I can at last make a trip to the Rhine, we must meet somewhere, possibly at Basle, and then I shall unpack my *sac de nuit*, full of obscure scores.

In the meantime I am very happy to learn that you have not lost hold of your *Siegfried*, which is sure to be *una gran bella cosa*, as the Italians say. I thank you for it in advance.

The day after to-morrow I start for Eilsen, where

please address me until further notice. Do not fail to return the manuscript of my *Lohengrin* article, of which, *if necessary*, you might have a copy made at Zurich. I shall want it between the 5th and 10th of November.

Once more be thanked cordially for your *Wiland*, and rest assured that, *with* or *without* the welded wings of genius, I always remain

Your truly devoted friend,

F. LISZT.

WEYMAR, *October 18th*, 1850.

50.

MY DEAREST FRIEND,

Do not be angry with me because I am so late in answering your last letter. I had to see to the return of the manuscript, entrusted to me, and this I was unable to do sooner. Your letter of October 22nd, together with the manuscript, did not reach me here till November 8th, *viâ* Berlin. As you wanted your manuscript back by November 10th, I must assume that some delay had taken place which you had not foreseen. I return herewith the French original, and in a few days I shall send the translation, which by then will have received its proper form.

Dear friend, your article has impressed me in a grand, elevating, stirring manner. That I have succeeded in thus acting upon you by my artistic work, that you are inclined to devote no small part of your extraordinary gift to opening, not only an external, but an internal, path to my movement—this fills me with the deepest and most joyous emotion. I feel as if in us two men had

met who had proceeded from the two most distant
points in order to penetrate to the core of art, and who
now, in the joy of their discovery, fraternally clasped
hands. This joy alone enables me to accept your admiring exclamations without bashfulness ; for I feel that
when you praise my gifts and my achievements you
express thereby only your joy at having met me at the
core of art. Be thanked for the pleasure you have thus
given me.

I shall say something more about the translation when
I send it to you, which, as I mentioned before, will be
in a few days.

I have also read your *feuilleton* in the *Journal des
Débats*. Your restless energy in serving me I can only
compare with the spirit in which you do it. Indeed,
dear, good Liszt, I owe it to you that soon I shall be
able once more to be entirely an artist. I look upon
this final resumption of my artistic plans to which I
now shall turn as one of the most decisive moments in
my life. Between the musical execution of my
Lohengrin and that of my *Siegfried* there lies for
me a stormy, but, I feel convinced, a fruitful, world. I
had to abandon the entire life lying behind me, to bring
into full consciousness everything dawning in it, to
conquer any rising reflection by its own means—that is,
by the most thorough entering into its subject—in order
to throw myself once more with clear and cheerful consciousness into the beautiful unconsciousness of artistic
creation. The winter I shall spend in completing this
abandonment. I want to enter a new world unburdened,
free, and happy, bringing nothing with me but a glad
artistic conscience. My work on "The Essence of

Opera," the last fruit of my contemplation, takes larger
dimensions than I at first expected. If I show that music,
the woman, becomes co-parent with the poet, the man, I
must take care that this splendid woman is not given
over to the first comer who desires her, but only to the
man who longs for woman with true, irresistible love.
The necessity of this union with the full power of
music desired by the poet himself I was unable to prove
by abstract æsthetic definitions alone, which generally
are not understood and remain without effect. I had
to derive that necessity with tangible distinctness from
the state of modern dramatic poetry, and I hope I shall
fully succeed. When I have finished this book, I intend,
provided I can find a publisher, to bring out my three
romantic opera-poems, with a preface introducing them
and explaining their genesis. After that, to clear off
all remains, I should collect the best of my Paris
writings of ten years ago (including my Beethoven
novelette) in a perhaps not unamusing volume; in it
those who take an interest in me might study the
beginning of my movement. In this manner I should
get to the spring pleasantly and in an easy frame of
mind, and should then work at my *Siegfried* without
interruption and complete it. Give your blessing
to this.

I recently had a letter from a friend in Paris who
witnessed several rehearsals of the *Tannhäuser* overture under Seghers's direction. He has completely
satisfied me that the performance is carefully prepared,
and that the understanding of the public will be aided
as much as possible by a programme taken from your
article upon my opera. In spite of this, I am very

doubtful whether in the most favourable case I shall derive any benefit from it.

My request to you to accept my poem of *Wiland*, you apparently have not quite understood. It is a sincere wish and request. Your present and imminent occupations might delay the fulfilment of my wish, which, however, would become impossible only if my sketch did not inspire you with the desire to complete it. In that case please be frank with me. If you intend, however late, to finish *Wiland*, I will undertake its proper versification.

For the present, dearest friend, I must take leave of you ; I do so with cordial wishes for your well-being. Commend me to the Princess in the best way you can, so that she also may keep me in friendly remembrance.

Farewell, and be greeted from the full heart of

Your grateful friend,

RICHARD WAGNER.

ZURICH, *November 25th*, 1850.

51.

DEAREST FRIEND,

Quite against my custom, I have just spent about ten days in bed fighting with a violent fever. As it is a very long time since I heard from you, I begin to be somewhat anxious as to the fate of my *Lohengrin* article, which, before leaving Weymar, I gave to Raff, asking him to send it to you as soon as he had read it. In case you have received it, write me a few lines to reassure me with regard to it, and at the same time tell me frankly, and without compliments of any kind, whether the analysis has pleased or displeased you, whether you think it worth publishing, and what I had better do with it.

My whole correspondence has fallen into the most lamentable arrears through the sad condition I have lived in for more than a fortnight. I owe an answer especially to Herr Ritter, who has made me a most courteous offer, the value of which I quite appreciate. Be good enough, dear friend, to thank him in my name (before I can do so myself) for his friendly conduct, for which I shall prove myself grateful, as far as lies in my power, on all occasions.

How far have you got with *Siegfried*? Have you continued your volume about the opera, and when will it appear ?

Send me soon one of those long letters which you write so beautifully. It will serve excellently well to relieve of his grief and sorrow

Your affectionate and devoted friend,

F. LISZT.

EILSEN, *November 26th,* 1850.

Address Eilsen (Bückeburg) till December 30th. In the first week of the new year I shall be back in Weymar.

52.

MY DEAR LISZT,

At last I am able to send you the translation of your article. As you probably cannot understand why it has been delayed so long, and may perhaps even suspect that I was indifferent to your more than kind

intention, I must tell you first of all how it has
happened.

I was so moved by your work that I at once felt *one
thing* distinctly, viz., that in something so encouraging
and deeply touching I could not myself collaborate. I
felt as shy and bashful as possible when I thought
of writing with my own hand the praise which you
dictated to me in your extremely brilliant article. I
hesitated and wavered, and did not know how to begin.
Then my young friend Ritter came to my aid, and
asked me to let him do the translation. I consented, and
reserved to myself the right of revising it afterwards, so
as to set forth less my praise than the animation of your
original style. R. and B. translated it between them,
and I looked through it together with them. R. then
went to work again, and the result of these careful
endeavours I now lay before you, asking you to explain
to yourself from these indications why the whole thing
has been delayed so long. Of the actual version I can
assure you with a good conscience that, according to
my firm conviction, it is not unworthy of your original,
which it renders adequately in the sense that one does not
suspect a laborious translation, but might let it pass
without hesitation for the German original of a not
unaccomplished German author. I can advise you,
therefore, without scruple to give your signature to this
version, and leave it to you whether you will announce
it to be a translation. In all you have said about the
work and its author, the version contains nothing but
an absolutely faithful translation of the original, every
conceivable care having been taken to render its very
brilliant, novel, and thoroughly artistic language as

adequately as its individual flavour and fulness would allow. In places, however, where you indicate the subject matter and the material aspect of situations and scenes, the translator has made bold to use a little more liberty. He considered that in these respects the German original of the poem was nearer to him than to the author of the French description. The situations are therefore treated a little more exhaustively, and the German text has been immediately drawn upon, as was indeed your own wish. Perhaps the scenes have now and then been given a little too fully ; but as in print the verses will appear in smaller type, I hope that this also will upon the whole add to the comprehension of the dramatic situations. Therefore I live in good hope that you will not be dissatisfied with the work ; and if you still intend to give me an almost excessive proof of your love of my artistic being and to supply my friends with an important means of realising what they love in my art, I shall feel highly honoured and pleased by the publication of this version, which I think had best take the form of an independent pamphlet, especially because in that way the important musical supplement suggested by you would be possible.

If I were to tell you what I felt while reading this article repeatedly and most carefully, I should scarcely be able to find words. Let this suffice : *I feel more than fully rewarded for my efforts, my sacrifices, and my artistic struggles by recognizing the impression I have made upon you of all others. To be so fully understood was my only longing, and to have been understood is the most blissful satisfaction of that longing.*

Truly, dear friend, you have turned the little Weimar

into a very focus of my fame. When I read the numerous, comprehensive, and often very brilliant articles about *Lohengrin* which now come from Weimar, and compare them with the jealous enmity with which, for example, the Dresden critics used constantly to attack me, working with sad consistency for the systematic confusion of the public, I look upon Weimar as a blessed asylum where at last I can breathe freely and ease my troubled heart. Thank Lobe very cordially in my name; his judgment has surprised and delighted me. Also tell Biedenfeld and the author of the article in the *Frankfort Conversationsblatt* that I still hope to thank them by endeavouring with all my power to justify by new works their great opinion of me. Greet them kindly, also Raff, and Genast, and Zigesar, without forgetting the brave artists to whom I owe so much gratitude.

I am deep in my work on "Opera and Drama;" it is, as I told you, of the greatest importance to me, and I hope it will not be without importance to others. But it will be a great, stout volume. Ah, would it were spring, and that I might be once more a full-blooded, poetising musician! I am not very well off; *care, care,* nothing but *care,* is the funereal chant which I have to sing to every young day.

You also have been in a very pitiable plight. Your serious indisposition and the depressed mood it left behind were strange things to you, and have affected me very much. For my comfort I assume that your illness is quite gone; but was I not right, dear friend, when I warned you and expressed to you my anxiety for your health, because I knew what

unheard-of exertions you had made for my sake?
Please set my fear at rest soon and comfort me thereby.

Finally, I ask you to transmit my sincerest and most
cordial respects to your faithful, highly esteemed friend.
May you two extraordinary people be happy! Farewell, and accept my heartfelt thanks for your friendship,
which is now the richest source of my joy.

Your

R. W.

ZURICH, *December 24th,* 1850.

53.

DEAR FRIEND,

I have just received a letter from Brussels, sent
by desire of the management of the Royal. Theatre
there.   In consequence of the brilliant success—so they
write—which my opera *Lohengrin* has recently obtained,
and seeing that the subject of the opera belongs to
Belgian history, they contemplate translating the work
into good French, if that should be possible, and
producing it forthwith at the Royal Theatre.   They
therefore want at once a copy of the score and of the
libretto.

Dear friend, I place the whole matter at your feet.
If you wish that it should come to something, and if you
think that it may come to something, then acquire the
further merit of taking this thing in hand, which, in
your position as protector and generally speaking, you
are infinitely more capable of doing than I.   You are sure
to know Brussels.   If you will undertake this, I should
ask you before all to see about a score.   Lüttichau
claims his copy as his property, and Zigesar was

obliged to have another copy made. Seeing that Lüttichau, as I hear positively from Dresden, does not intend to give the opera at least just yet, one might hope that he would give back the score *for a time, if you were to ask him.* Of course *I* cannot apply to him.

To send my own original score so far away, I should not like at all; it is all the little property I have. To have a copy made here would exceed my limited means, and would also take too long, as they are pressing at Brussels. A libretto I shall send them direct from here.

See what you can and will do, dear friend. If it should succeed, and some good come of it, I should like to owe it entirely to *you*, as you have altogether assumed the paternal responsibility for this opera with the care attaching to it. I shall ask them at Brussels to apply to you, as you have full power to act in the matter. Farewell for to-day; a thousand blessings in return for your love

from your sincerely grateful

RICHARD WAGNER.

ZURICH, *December 27th*, 1850.

I have to reply to "M. Charles Hanssens jeune, che d'orchestre et directeur du Théâtre Royal à Bruxelles."

54.

DEAR FRIEND,

I have just received your letter addressed Weymar, and hasten to place my humble services gladly at your disposal as regards the score of *Lohengrin* and the correspondence with Herr von Lüttichau. Probably his Excellency will not be very willing to lend the work a second time; but I hope for a favourable result all the same.

In your place (forgive my friendly impertinence) I should certainly accept the Brussels offer, but with the one condition—*conditio sine quâ non*—that they let you revise the translation and attend the general rehearsals. The performance and the success will have quite a different chance if you go to Brussels, and I am afraid that in your absence your *Lohengrin* might be a little compromised. The actual state of the Brussels theatre I do not know; some years ago it was somewhat in a muddle and very little adapted to serious work. Some time will in any case be required for the translation and rehearsals, but I advise you to make the condition of your presence at once and firmly. The travelling expenses are so small that the management can easily bear them; and if you agree, I shall answer the gentlemen in that sense as soon as they write to me.

Herr von Zigesar wrote to me urgently some days ago not to delay my return to Weymar any longer. Unfortunately I shall be detained here for about another fortnight by the serious illness of Princess M. About January 20th *Tannhäuser* and *Lohengrin* will again be given, and towards the end of the season Tichatschek will probably be there and take the part.

By repeated desire, I have determined to publish my article on the Herder festival, together with the analysis of *Lohengrin*, in a separate form. If you want to add some further remarks on it, let it be soon, so that I may be able to make use of them.

I enclose a few lines to Ritter. Kindly excuse me to him, and allow me to restore to you the possession and absolute disposal of your property after my return to Weymar. Great as is the temptation to weld at your *Wiland*, I must abide by my resolution *never* to write a German opera.

I feel no vocation for it, and I lack the necessary *patience* to bother myself with German theatrical affairs. Altogether I think it more appropriate and easier to risk my first dramatic work on the Italian stage (which probably may happen in the spring of next year—1852 —in Paris or London), and to stick there if I should succeed.

Germany is your property, and you her glory. Complete your *Siegfried* soon. Of power and genius you have plenty; only do not lose patience. Perhaps we shall soon see you again in Germany; then you will reap what you have so nobly sown.

Your sincerely devoted

F. LISZT.

EILSEN, *January 3rd,* 1851.

Have you made much progress with your book on the opera? I am very curious to see this work.

55.

DEAREST FRIEND,

Have you all forgotten me? I have felt so lonely of late that I am often afraid. Should you be angry with me about anything? perhaps about the absurd misunderstanding with B.? He wrote to me that he had heard that I was annoyed at his great article on *Lohengrin*. I was quite confounded, and thought that some misapprehension of an expression in one of my letters might have led you and B. after you to a completely erroneous opinion about me. Therefore I requested him to ask you in my name to let him explain to you the passage in my letter, because I was anxious, not only for his sake, but for yours, to dispel so ugly an error. Has any unpleasantness resulted from it?

From Brussels I have heard nothing. Could you give me some news, or are you angry that I have troubled you with this affair? Anyhow I have no illusions as to Brussels.

My very stout book is ready. Its title is "Oper und Drama." I have not yet a publisher; and as I must take care to get a little money for it, I am a little anxious about the matter.

Next month I shall devote to the edition of my three romantic opera-poems. A longish introduction will explain the origin of these poems and their position towards music.

At the beginning of spring I hope to commence the composition of *Siegfried*, and to continue the work without interruption.

As to the rest, my pleasure in life is not great. All is quiet and lonely around me, and I frequently feel as if I were dead and forgotten.

But how are you? Have you quite recovered? I frequently dream of Weimar and of you—wild, confused things.

Let us say nothing more about *Wiland*; I am heartily sorry that—you are right.

Have you still courage? Are you in good spirits? Do you really still care to live amongst the majestic people of the Philistines who rule the world nowadays? Ah! as long as we possess *fancy* we can pull along somehow.

My poor dear little parrot is also dead! He was my *spiritus familiaris*, the good brownie of my house.

Farewell, and forgive me.

Always and wholly thine,
RICHARD WAGNER.

ENGE, ZURICH, *February* 18*th*, 1851.

56.

DEAR WAGNER,

By the date of these lines you will sufficiently see in what grief and sorrow I have been living for months. I was, it is true, in Weymar for three weeks, but immediately after the birthday of the Grand Duchess (February 16th) I returned here, where unfortunately I found the Princess still very ailing and in bed. On the 7th I have to be back in Weymar to conduct Raff's opera ; the work is too important for Raff's career for me to neglect it. But the thought of that journey, while my whole soul, my whole faith, and all my love must remain here at the sick-bed, is terrible to me. Let us talk of you.

I could never think of forgetting you, and, if possible, still less of being angry with you. Forgive me that I did not sooner thank you cordially for B. and R.'s German version of my *Lohengrin* article. Your letter especially has pleased and flattered me highly. That you are satisfied with my conception of that splendid masterpiece of heart and soul *Lohengrin* is my exceeding rich reward. Immediately after my return to Weymar I shall have it printed (perhaps the *Illustrirte Zeitung* will publish it in *one* number), and shall send you the proof, which I must ask you to correct and return straight to Weber *as quickly as possible.*

R. can carefully read the article in one day, and send it to Leipzig by return of post.

As to the French original, I shall probably publish it as a separate pamphlet, together with my article on the Herder festival, and without the alterations and omissions made by Janin in the *Journal des Débats* of October 22nd. The title will be " Fêtes de Herder et Goethe à Weymar, 25 et 28 Août, 1850."

From Brussels not a line ! Without repudiating altogether the musical soil of Belgium, barren though hitherto it has been, with the exception of some individual talents, I can only advise you again to protest absolutely against a performance of your works under any direction but your own. The first condition you should impose on the management of the theatre is that they call you to Brussels. In that sense I shall answer in case they apply to me.

About B. I could tell you many things in a half-and-half way, but you had better think them out for yourself. Let me speak French, and don't repeat it.

B. is a nobleman who has spent long years in becoming a literary good-for-nothing. If he had possessed or acquired the necessary talent, he would in that direction have made himself a position as a nobleman. As it is, he is an amphibious creature, living in bogs on one side and getting dry in his water on the other. He has

shown me the letter you wrote to him, but with this kind
of people little is gained by explanation. They are not
wanting in the *good* where the better would be required,
and it is generally more advisable to be cautious with
them than to complain, or correct their opinions.   I
think you might have been satisfied with thanking
him simply for his article about *Lohengrin,* however
awkward and badly argued certain passages may have
been. *Apropos* of this, have you read the articles on
Lohengrin in the *Frankfort Conversationsblatt*?   They
are certainly better meant and better written; and as you
have thanked B., you might, I think, appropriately write
a few lines to the author, who is a very decent man
and one of your sincere and enthusiastic proselytes.
Enclose the lines to him in the first letter you address
to me at Weymar, and I will forward them to him at
once.

Wiland is still imprisoned at Weymar, together with
my manuscripts and scores.   As soon as my valet
returns I shall send you *Wiland* at once, but I am not
going to call in a common, prosaic locksmith to set
him at liberty.

I am looking forward to your book.   Perhaps I may
try on this occasion to comprehend your ideas a little
better, which in your book " Kunst und Revolution "
I could not manage very well, and in that case I shall
cook a French sauce to it.

Brockhaus published a few days ago my pamphlet
on the Goethe foundation ("De la Fondation Goethe
à Weymar").   I shall send it you on the first opportunity.
Of my articles on Chopin in the *France Musicale,* which
I am likely to spin out through fifteen numbers, you have

probably not heard at Zurich. B. read the original at Weymar. Farewell, be happier than I, and write soon to

Your truly devoted friend,

F. LISZT.

EILSEN, *March* 1*st*, 1851.

57.

BEST OF FRIENDS,

Cordial thanks for your letter, which was a sure sign of your continued interest in me. Your domestic troubles have alarmed me very much; be assured of my genuine sympathy with any grief that may befall you. I hope this letter will find you in an easier state of mind with regard to the health of your very dear friend. If only my wish could contribute to this! But necessity compels me to gain some certainty as to my own position through your means. Listen, and do not be angry.

The communication of your plans in my favour last summer roused in me a hope as to which I must now know whether I am to look for its fulfilment or to abandon it altogether. You told me that in case of the desired success of my *Lohengrin* you intended to make use of the presumably friendly disposition of the Grand Duchess, with a view to inducing her to allow me the necessary means of subsistence during the composition of my *Siegfried*. Just at that time I had given up all thoughts of setting the opera to music, and had sent the poem of *Siegfried* to the printer in order to place it before the public in the form of an intention never carried out. Your communication changed my mind, as I acknowledged to you at the time in the most joyous and grateful manner. I cancelled the order for printing the poem, and prepared myself for the composition instead. For the commencement of the work I fixed upon the coming spring, partly in order, first, to get rid of my always depressed winter humour, and partly to give you time for carrying out your kind intention without hurry. For the winter I chose a literary work, for which I had plenty of material, and which I took in hand at once, hoping that I might make something by it. This work, a book of four hundred to five hundred pages, small octavo, entitled "Oper und Drama," has been ready these six weeks; but as yet none of the publishers to whom I wrote about it has replied, and my expectations at least of *gain* from this work are therefore very small. During the whole of six months, after spending the honorarium for the production of *Lohengrin* at Weimar, I have lived entirely by the assistance of Frau R. in D., because latterly I have not been able to earn anything beyond a small fee for conducting two of Beethoven's symphonies at the miserable concerts here. I know that my Dresden friend has for the present exhausted herself, because the family is not wealthy, but has only just a sufficient income, which, moreover, owing to some awkward complications with Russia, is at present placed in jeopardy. I am therefore compelled to try and make money at any price, and should have to abandon a task like the composition of *Siegfried*, which in a pecuniary sense is useless. If I were to have any inclination for a task undertaken for the sake of money, it would have to be so-called " æsthetic literature," and in order to get money for such literature I should have to spend *all* my time in writing for magazines at so much "per sheet." The thought is very humiliating.

If I am to undertake an important artistic task, my immediate future—say for the current year, at least—must be secured; otherwise I shall lack the necessary cheerfulness and collectedness. If I am to have peace of mind for devoting myself to artistic labour without interruption, I must, as I said before, be without anxiety for my immediate subsistence. Necessity, as the proverb says, breaks iron, and therefore I put this question to you once more simply, so as to be sure as to my position. I am aware that everything has turned out unfavourably for your plan of helping me. The Grand Duchess was ill, and could attend only the third perform-ance of *Lohengrin* ; soon afterwards you left Weimar, and therefore had no opportunity of preparing the Grand Duchess for your plan in a proper and dignified manner. All this I know, and therefore no blame attaches to you in the remotest degree. Only I must know *now* where I am. For that reason I pray you with all my heart to tell me plainly and definitely whether, as things are, I still may hope for something or not, so that I may make all my arrangements accordingly ; uncertainty is the worst of tortures. *One* request I further make without hesitation. If you are compelled by the state of affairs to tell me that your plan cannot now be realised, and that therefore I must not hope for any further assistance in favour of the composition of my *Siegfried*, then kindly see at least whether you cannot get me *at once* SOME *money*, were it only as much as my immediate difficulty requires, in order to gain me some time for settling to my altered plan. It is very sad that I have to trouble you with this ugly request.

But enough of this.

May Heaven grant that you will soon be relieved from your domestic troubles. I wish the Princess a quick and perfect recovery with all my heart.

Farewell, dear friend. Good luck and the best success to Herr Raff!

Farewell, and be happy.

Your sincerely devoted

RICHARD WAGNER.

ENGE BEI ZURICH, *March 9th*, 1851.

58.

DEAR FRIEND,

I passed the whole of March in such trouble and distress, that I could not write to you. Since April 4th I have been back here. *Lohengrin* was to be given on the 8th, but Beck's hoarseness compelled us to postpone the performance till next Saturday. In any case the opera will be given twice more during this season.

By to-day's post I send you my *Lohengrin* article, which in the first instance will appear in German in the *Illustrirte Zeitung*. Be kind enough to read the proof *quickly* and to return it direct to Weber, Leipzig. It will probably be published in the next number. About the French edition I shall arrange soon afterwards; it will be the same size and type as my pamphlet on the Goethe foundation, of which also I send you a copy to-day. Brockhaus will be the publisher.

Have you received the hundred thalers? Your last letter has made me very sad, but I do not relinquish all hope of leading the somewhat difficult diplomatic transaction concerning your *Siegfried* to a successful issue. Perhaps I shall succeed in settling the matter by the middle of May. Tell me in round figures what sum you require, and (quite *entre nous*, for I must ask you specially to let *nobody* know) write me a full letter which I can show to Z. You must excuse me for troubling you with such things, and I am grieved, deeply grieved, that the matter cannot be brought more simply to a good result; but, in my opinion, it will be necessary for you to explain by letter your position as well as the plan of the work and the artistic hopes which may justly be founded upon it. I need not tell you that I do not want this for *myself*. You know me, and are aware that you can have implicit confidence in me.

Müller's letter I sent yesterday, after thinking from day to day that I should return. He will doubtless soon write to you, and you will find him a trustworthy, prudent friend, who genuinely esteems you.

Can you tell me, under the seal of the most absolute secrecy, whether the famous article on the Jews in music ("Das Judenthum in der Musik") in Brendel's paper is by you?

The Princess has remained in Eilsen, still confined to her bed; and I do not expect her till the end of this month. You may imagine how deeply her long illness has grieved me.

Write soon, and do not forget to correct the proofs of the *Illustrirte Zeitung* at once.

Your

F. Liszt.

April 9th, 1851.

P.S.—*The "Lohengrin" article must be signed thus:* "From the French of F. Liszt." Request the printer's reader kindly not to omit this and to call the editor's special attention to it.

59.

DEAREST LISZT,

I did not write to you at once in order to write to you more at length and more calmly on a favourable day. Then came the number of the *Illustrirte Zeitung* of April 12th, and once more I read your printed article from beginning to end. It is difficult for me to describe the impression your work of friendship has made on me just at this time. I was once more cold and diffident, and looked with something like bitter irony on the thought of having to begin a new artistic labour. The artistic misery far and wide around me was so great, my mood so hopeless, that I felt inclined to laugh at myself when I thought, for example, of the composition of my *Siegfried*; and this mood I transferred to all my other works. Recently I glanced through my score of *Lohengrin*; it filled me absolutely with disgust, and my intermittent fits of laughter were not of a cheerful kind. Then you approached me once more, and moved, delighted, warmed, inspired me in such a manner that the bright tears welled forth, and that once more I knew no greater delight than that of being an artist and of creating works. I have no name for the effect you have produced upon me. Everywhere around me I see nothing but the most beautiful spring life, full of germs and blossoms, and together with it such voluptuous pain, such painfully intoxicating joy, such delight

in being a man, in having a beating heart—although it
feel nothing but sorrow—that I regret only to have to
write all this to you.

And how strangely everything happens with you!
Would I could describe my love for you! There is
no torture, but, on the other hand, no joy, which does
not vibrate in this love. One day jealousy, fear of what
is strange to me in your particular nature, grieve me;
I feel anxiety, trouble, yea doubt; and then again
something breaks forth in me like a fire in a wood,
and everything is devoured by this conflagration,
which nothing but a stream of the most blissful tears
can extinguish at last. You are a wonderful man, and
wonderful is our love. If we had not loved, we might
have terribly hated, one another. All that I wanted
to write to you with well-balanced composure must
now come out just as it happens to strike me at the
moment. My *Siegfried* I shall begin at the commencement of May, happen what will. Perish all
guarantee of my existence! I shall not starve. For my
book I have at last a publisher, Avenarius, in Leipzig;
he pays me one hundred thalers; it is very little, but
I don't think I can get any more. Now and then you
will put a groat by for me; and when my necessity
grows breast-high, you will help me with as much as
you may happen to have for a poor friend. Frau R.
in D. will also do her part off and on, and in the winter
I shall earn again a few louis d'or by conducting
symphonies, so that I shall not go to the devil after all if
only my wife will keep calm. So let us leave the Grand
Duchess alone; I can and will not ask her for anything
even in the most indirect manner. If she made me an

offer of her own free will, it would touch and delight me, all the more coming from a princess, but this possibility, even if it never should happen, I must not turn into an impossibility by *asking* her for a proof of her kindness. Away with all business transactions as to this question! Up till now the sympathy of that princely lady has made so beautiful an impression upon me, that I do not wish to spoil it. Are we agreed? I think so.

You ask me about the *Judenthum*. You must know that the article is by me. Why do you ask? Not from fear, but only to avoid that the Jews should drag this question into bare personality, I appear in a pseudonymous capacity. I felt a long-repressed hatred for this Jewry, and this hatred is as necessary to my nature as gall is to the blood. An opportunity arose when their damnable scribbling annoyed me most, and so I broke forth at last. It seems to have made a tremendous impression, and that pleases me, for I really wanted only to frighten them in this manner; that they will remain the masters is as certain as that not our princes, but the bankers and the Philistines, are nowadays our masters. Towards Meyerbeer my position is a peculiar one. I do not hate him, but he disgusts me beyond measure. This eternally amiable and pleasant man reminds me of the most turbid, not to say most vicious, period of my life, when he pretended to be my protector; that was a period of connections and back stairs when we are made fools of by our protectors, whom in our inmost heart we do not like. This is a relation of the most perfect dishonesty; neither party is sincere towards the other; one and the other assume the appearance of affection, and both make use of each other as long as their mutual interest requires it. For the intentional impotence of his politeness towards me I do not find fault with Meyerbeer; on the contrary, I am glad not to be his debtor as deeply as, for example, B. But it was quite time that I should free myself perfectly from this dishonest relation towards him. Externally there was not the least occasion for it, for even the experience that he was not sincere towards me would not have surprised me, neither did it give me a right to be angry, because at bottom I had to own that I had intentionally deceived myself about him. But from inner causes arose the necessity to relinquish all considerations of common prudence with regard to him. As an artist I cannot exist before myself and my friends, I cannot think or feel, without realising and confessing my absolute antagonism to Meyerbeer, and to this I am driven with genuine desperation when I meet with the erroneous opinion even amongst my friends that I have anything in common with Meyerbeer. Before none of my friends I can appear in clear and definite form, with all that I desire and feel, unless I separate myself entirely from the nebulous outline in which many see me. This is an act necessary for the perfect birth of my matured nature; and if God wills, I hope to be of service to many by performing this act so zealously.

What you will think of this—that—just imagine—I do not as yet know exactly. I know who you are and perfectly feel what you are, and yet it must appear to me as if in this point you could not as yet be entirely your own self. But enough of this. There are earthly things on which we may occasionally be of different opinion without ever parting from each other in divine things. If you don't approve of something here, shut your eyes to it.

Let me at last have some good news of you. In your most intimate relations you seem to me so sadly placed that I am quite melancholy about it. Is the illness of the Princess so serious that, apart from its long duration, it inspires you with real anxiety? I must almost fear this unless you reassure me about it. Do this *as soon as* you can, and tell the highly esteemed lady how cordially I sympathise with her sufferings.

Dear, dear Liszt, arrange that we soon may see each other. Perhaps the Princess would benefit by Swiss air; send her here and come with her.

I cannot go on to-day. I wanted to write to you about your Goethe foundation, but must wait for a calmer hour to meet your splendid idea with dignity.

Farewell, and be pressed to the heart of your

RICHARD WAGNER.

ENGE, ZURICH, *April 18th*, 1851.

I doubt whether the correction of the proof will still be necessary, but have sent it to Leipzig nevertheless.

60.

Then we are to have *Young Siegfried*! You are truly a most incredible fellow, to whom one must doff hat and bonnet three times. The satisfactory settlement of this matter rejoices me cordially; and, as you may imagine, I have perfect *faith* in your work. But let us *say nothing about it* until you send in *Young Siegfried* (July 1st, 1852), so as to avoid the useless preliminary talk of people. Here nobody knows about it, excepting Zigesar; and we are anxious to keep it from the public. *Lohengrin* at its last performance (the fifth) on Sunday was appreciated more than ever, and actors and orchestra also came nearer to the understanding and the interpretation of the work. The house was filled for the greater part, it is true, by Erfurters, Naumburgers, and other curious people from the neighbourhood, for, to speak candidly, our Weymar public, with the exception of about a dozen persons, are not yet sufficiently advanced to be in real sympathy with so extraordinary a work. That *Lohengrin* has reached its fifth performance in one season is a kind of miracle which must be attributed to the *Court.* The Hereditary Grand Duchess had especially asked for this performance on the occasion of her first visit to the theatre after her confinement. From Leipzig came David and Moscheles, from Halle Robert Franz, from Eisenach Kühnstedt. Professor Stahr, who has become a dear friend, and Fanny Lewald have been here about a fortnight.

Stahr is going to write about *Lohengrin* in the *National Zeitung* or *Kölnische Zeitung.* If after reading his article you feel inclined to write him a few lines, send them to Weymar (Hotel Zum Erbprinzen). Müller has written another *Lohengrin* article in the *Weimar Zeitung,* which he has probably sent to you. After the performance of *Lohengrin* I received your letter about the Goethe foundation, and I thank you cordially for it. I may mention, however, that perhaps no less than two years' time and trouble will be required to make the idea of the Goethe foundation a reality. I am prepared to devote that time to it, because I am

firmly convinced that without my activity the thing
here will simply come to nothing, as has already happened at Berlin.

Should you not be inclined to publish your letter in
its actual form of a letter to me in some newspaper
which is open to you ?   I will send it back to you in a
few days for that purpose, asking you, however, to return it to me at Weymar as soon as you have done with it.

The day after to-morrow I have to go to Eilsen for
the third time, but hope to be back here at Whitsuntide.
At the close of the theatrical season we shall have either
Tannhäuser or *Lohengrin* once more.   The direction of
the former work I think I may now leave to Götze.

If possible, send me a copy of your autobiography
direct to Eilsen (Bückeburg).   I can make good use of it
in connection with the pamphlet which is to be published (in French) in June by Brockhaus.   If your
article on the Zurich theatre has appeared, send it also
to me at Eilsen, where I shall employ my time in reading
and working.   I am most curious to know your views
and practical proposals with regard to theatrical
matters, and I shall be most ready to adopt your ideas
as far as possible.

Draw up occasionally for me a repertory of earlier
and modern works which appear to you most adapted
to further the cause of art.   At present I cannot help
thinking it advisable to make some eclectic concessions
(alas ! alas !) to the existing state of our theatrical
institutions.

Be well and active, dear, splendid friend, and soon
give news to your   F. LISZT.

WEYMAR, *May 17th*, 1851.

61.

BEST OF ALL FRIENDS,

I must reply to you at once about a few things
which you ask me in your letter received yesterday, so
as to let you know how matters stand. First of all (as
is always the case when I have to deal with you), I
must wipe a blush of shame off my face before answering you. Your wishes always concern *me*, and that in
a sense which must flatter me to the very core. You
want a copy of my autobiography in order to make
use of it for your pamphlet. What can I say to that?
I will say nothing, but only reply that in this instance
my vanity is not sufficiently great to make me carry my
biography about with me. I do not possess it, and do
not know where to get it. If you really want to see it,
you might perhaps get it more easily from Weimar, if I
told you exactly where it is to be found. It appeared
in the *Zeitung für die elegante Welt* in the year 1843,
first quarterly issue, month of February, I believe.
But I can scarcely think that you will find much in it
beyond the confirmation of the fact that I too have
erred much in my artistic efforts, not being one of the
elect who, like Mendelssohn, received the only true,
infallible, "solid" food of art, like heavenly manna in
their mouths, and who therefore were able to say, "I
have never erred." We poor earthly worms can get
only through error to a knowledge of truth, which therefore we love passionately, like a conquered bride, and
not with the genteel approval with which we look upon
a spouse selected for us beforehand by the dear parents.
At that time when I wrote my autobiography by Laube's
desire, I had, it is true, finished my *Flying Dutchman*

and sketched the poem of *Tannhäuser,* but only through my *completed Tannhäuser* and my *completed Lohengrin* did I gain perfect clearness as to the direction in which I had been impelled by unconscious instinct. Later on, in connection with the edition of my operatic poems, I shall take occasion to explain the process of development observed in me ; certain it is that nothing of this can be contained in my autobiography. All the more interesting will it be for me to see that direction judged from his own observation by some one else, *i.e.,* some one like you.

Concerning my last letter to you, I must ask you to be assured that I wrote it without ostensible object. To you alone I wanted to speak on a topic started by yourself, because I did not desire to support an opinion in a general way, but to effect something real, viz., the foundation of an *original theatre.* I therefore did not want to address the public—which *quâ* public is quite useless for that purpose—but some one who has the intellect and before all the energy to view distinctly the accomplishment of such an object in given cir-cumstances. If in the actual condition of generally accepted opinion something is to be undertaken which combats and denies that opinion as detrimental to art, this can of course only be done by individuals. We cannot expect a better general condition until the individual has become perfectly strong in itself, for the general must proceed from individuals, and for the present therefore we must be intent upon being ready ourselves and communicating with none but those nearest akin to us. In this spirit I look upon the theatre. If we want to work for a rational condition of

the theatre in all Germany, we shall never achieve anything in the slightest degree rational unless we begin
at some given point, even the smallest. That point I
imagine I have found where an embodiment of genius
and energy is already acting in the right sense. Where
else can you find such things as are done at Weimar?
But through whom is this done? Through *you* alone!
The Court may have the best possible intention; it is
not an artist to realise its intention or even to conceive
a distinct intention, for that in this case none but an
artist can do. This is the reason why I have applied
to *you* alone. I had no other intention. If you think
it useful and appropriate to make a wider use of my
communication, you are quite at liberty to do so. If
you think that a totally independent word of mine as to
the position of poetry and the fine arts, especially in
reference to a given object, may not be wholly without
beneficial influence on many of those concerned, before
all if you think that the object in question may be
furthered by it, I ask you to dispose of my letter as
your property. I, however, cannot undertake its publication. I should defeat my original purpose in doing so,
besides which no journals are open to me. In the
Deutsche Monatsschrift, to which I am now and then
asked to contribute, I do not like on principle to treat
the question in this form; our object would not be
furthered by it. Act therefore entirely according to
your judgment. If you think it useless, leave it alone.
If, however, you print the letter, omit what you think
unfit for publicity. I should not willingly make additions, because they would of necessity have reference to
the " original theatre," and about that I should have to

say a *great deal* to make my idea comprehensible to the general public.

You have probably received my little pamphlet "Ein Theater in Zurich." Much, yea most, in it will not suit you, for the conditions here are too different from those of Weimar; but my idea of the essence of the activity of the "original theatre" the little work will make tolerably clear. In case you ask "whether I wish to exclude altogether *everything extraneous*," I reply in advance, Yes, for the present, and until the main object is attained, but not for the future. The main object is this : that the theatre imagined by me should, by the originality of its work, gain perfect individual independence, should educate itself to be a conscious individual. This object once attained, this individual independence achieved, then, and then only, should it exchange its achievements with those of other equally independent theatrical individualities, and by means of this exchange be fructified to ever greater capability and variety, ex-extending in this manner to wider and generally human circles. This fructifying exchange can be successfully accomplished only when *receiving* means at the same time *giving*; only he who can *give* can *receive* with benefit to himself. At present our theatres are so wholly dependent, so entirely without individuality, that they can do nothing but receive, without having the power of really appropriating what they receive. Our theatres are undeveloped beings, pulpy, pappy molluscs, which can never bring forth a *man*.

I must refrain from saying any more on this head; it might easily lead me to writing another book of four hundred pages, and the writing of books I am deter-

mined to abandon in preference to producing a work of
art.   Only this much I must add : *through you* Weimar
is already in a good way; proceed on that way of
original achievement with *conscious principle*, express
that principle distinctly, and by that means gain more
and more participants in your consciousness; by *that
means* you can easily show how an intention may
gradually become a reality.   Raff's opera has pleased
me immensely ; that is right, and now onwards ! or, to
speak plainly, *it is your turn now.*

Write an opera for Weimar, I entreat you; write it
exactly for the artists who are there, and who through
your work will be elevated, made more noble, more
universal.   Continue, if you like, your plans for the
Italians ; there also, I feel sure, you can do famous and
useful things, but at the same time abide by what is
nearest to you, by what is your present home; where
you are in bodily presence, and with your whole mental
energy, be there also with your productive will; do not
trouble yourself about the other German theatres and
their conditions.   You do not want them in order to
achieve something *beautiful* and at the same time useful.
Candidly speaking, what do you seek *just now*, and with
your *present activity* amongst the Italians, otherwise
than an increase of your fame ?   Very well, but will
that make you happy ?   For *that* you no longer care !
Other conditions are necessary to give *you* happiness.
Do something for *your* Weimar.

Well, I will not entreat you any more for the present;
you must find out for yourself what you have to do.

One thing more, however : work thoroughly for the
culture of your theatrical people.   You will get the

desired artists from nowhere unless you create them
for yourself. Be careful to make your singers first
of all good actors ; how is he to sing who cannot speak
and declaim well ? Nothing can here be done in a
casual manner ; you must proceed on principle and
with expressed intention. (For that reason think of
the Goethe foundation !) To speak plainly, you want
a good stage-manager. Genast is a splendid fellow, but
he has grown old in *routine*; he does not know, and
will never understand, what has to be done. A man
like Eduard Devrient would be of excellent effect for
the training of your actors, for he *knows* what has to be
done. (I admit the difficulty of getting such a man.)
You must further have an able singing master. I
believe that Götze has good qualities for the post, but
he ought to have *power* as well ; people ought to be
compelled to learn from him.

I am aware that a man does not become an artist by
mere training, but he can never become an artist unless
his organic faculties are healthily developed, and that is
what is wanting amongst us almost everywhere. Other
things will be easily set right if you are more careful
in the choice of works selected for performance than is
generally the case amongst us. The coarse mixture of all
genres and all styles is the evil which prevents our actors
from gaining any kind of artistic consciousness. Gluck
to-day, Donizetti to-morrow, Weber to-day, Rossini or
Auber to-morrow, serious to-day, frivolous to-morrow—
what is the result ? That the people can do neither Gluck
nor Donizetti, neither the serious nor the frivolous.
How terrible also are the *translations* ! People get
systematically accustomed to the absolute senselessness

of scenic representations; look therefore to a rational treatment of the translated librettos. Before all, accustom your singers to looking upon their work in the first instance as a *dramatic* task; the accomplishment of their *lyrical* task will after that be an easy matter. Works of the earlier French school are most adapted to the purpose, because in them a natural dramatic intention is most perceptible. Singers who cannot execute well and effectively the *Water-carrier*, by Cherubini, or *Joseph*, by Méhul—how are they to be able to master the (*in that case*) enormous difficulties of, for example, one of my operas? The chief thing, however, will always be new works and such works as are adapted to our set of artists and have been written specially for this theatre. But enough of preaching! If I have been almost impertinent, you must forgive me. To-day is my birthday, and you could not have sent me a better present than your letter of yesterday.

As yet Heaven has not given us fine weather, but I wait for the first bright, sunny day to commence the poem of my *Young Siegfried* with the pen. In my head it is ready. In July I hope to send you the poem.

Your last news has once more made me desirous to write to the Hereditary Grand Duchess. The contact with a sympathetic, noble female nature is to me an infinitely joyful feeling, and that feeling I should like to gain as a blessing for my impending work. If you think that I might permit myself a slight deviation from the ordinary official style towards this lady, I should ask you one of these days to forward a letter from me to her. The official style I cannot manage. Our dear, foolish Zigesar always writes to me, "Ew. Wohlgeboren," etc. I wish he would leave that alone. I am sorry when, in his kindness towards me, I stumble over this kind of powder and pigtail business.

May God bless you, not the "god of Bückeburg." You are right in retiring into solitude now and then; without that men like us cannot exist. Greet the Princess most cordially. I hope she will soon be well again.

Farewell, dearest of friends. I press you to my heart!

Your

RICHARD WAGNER.

ENGE, ZURICH, *May 22nd*, 1851.

62.

DEAREST FRIEND,

Short news from me to-day.

I have quite finished the poem of my *Young Siegfried*. It has given me GREAT joy; it is certainly what I was bound to do, and the *best thing* that I have done so far. I am *really glad* about it. With my violent way of working, I am always considerably tired at the end. I must take some time to recover. I cannot just yet make up my mind to copy it out for you, for many reasons, too long to tell. I feel also some bashfulness in submitting my poem to you without further explanation—a bashfulness which has its reason in *me*, not in *you*. I therefore ask you whether there is not a chance of my seeing you soon. Some time ago you made me think so. How is it now? Can you visit me, or at least appoint a place, accessible to me, for meeting? Please answer this question at once. My longing to see you, dear, splendid friend, again after two years, during which you have been more to me than I can describe, and to spend a few days with you, is greater than I am able to express. Can you fulfil this longing? If we could meet shortly, I should keep my *Young Siegfried*, in order to *read* it to you. This would add to my peace of mind considerably. The written word is, I fear, insufficient for my intention ; but if I could read it to you *viva voce*, indicating how I want to have it interpreted, I should be quite satisfied as to the desired impression of my poem upon you. Write to me at once what my chances are. If, alas ! you cannot come, I shall have a copy made at once and send it you.

One thing more : in my last letters I entirely forgot to mention the Härtel affair to you. By a certain impulse, I applied to Breitkopf and Härtel about *Lohengrin*. I owed them from of old two hundred thalers for a grand pianoforte, and proposed to them to wipe out this debt and to take the copyright of *Lohengrin* in return. At first they entertained my offer as to the pianoforte score, but I insisted again on the *full score* being engraved, telling them that something might be done by subscription, and referring them to your influential help. For a long time I heard nothing, but to-day I have a letter from the H.'s, saying that they accede to my wish and are prepared to print the *full score*. How has this happened ? Now that my demand has been granted, it almost appears fabulous to me that they should publish *the full score of an opera which has* ONLY *been given at Weimar*.

What do you think ? Can I expect this of them ? This, in my opinion, is a nobility of conduct which makes me feel ashamed. I should almost like not to accept the H.'s offer for *Lohengrin* on condition that they engrave the full score of my *Young Siegfried*. This child, which I have engendered and should like to give to the world, is naturally even nearer to my heart than *Lohengrin*, for I want it to be stronger and healthier than he. If the H.'s publish the score of *Lohengrin*, it may be assumed to a certainty that the sale will be so small as to make them wholly disinclined for the engraving of the full score of *Young Siegfried*; and this latter is of course of much greater importance to me. What do you think? Advise me, dear Liszt! Shall I hold their offer over for *Siegfried* and give up *Lohengrin* instead? To get both appears almost impossible to me. Advise me!

Farewell for to-day. My pen will not obey me any longer; I am too excited by many things.

Farewell, and write to me how you are and whether *I shall see you*. Are you well? Greet the Princess! Farewell.

Your
RICHARD WAGNER.

Enge, Zurich, *June 29th*, 1851.

63.

DEAREST FRIEND,

The news of the happy birth of *Siegfried* pleases me much, and I thank you for letting me know at once. How I should like to hear you read it and to visit you at Zurich! But, alas! this year it is quite impossible for me to think of any journey whatever. At the end of this month I hope that the health of the Princess will allow her to start; and in order to make the journey less fatiguing, we shall return slowly by Düsseldorf, Cologne,

Frankfort, and Eisenach. You, dear friend, must need rest and a little country life after the completion of your work. Please do not trouble yourself on my account by making at once a copy of *Siegfried* ; you will send it me on occasion later on at Weymar, where, locked up, still remains *Wiland*, which, to my regret, I have not been able to send you, not having the necessary keys at hand. I have explained this to Uhlig. If he is with you, remember me kindly to him, and excuse me to him once more for my involuntary negligence.

The Härtels are quite *comme il faut* in their personal and business relations. Dr. Härtel came to Weymar to hear *Lohengrin*, and I am delighted to hear that his impression has been confirmed by an *imprimatur*. As you ask my advice about what you had better do, accept his proposition or hold it over till *Siegfried*, so as to make him publish the score of a new work for you, I have no hesitation in saying that, for all manner of reasons, I should think it preferable to publish *now* only the pianoforte score of *Lohengrin*, and to make arrangements with Härtel that the pianoforte score and full score of *Siegfried* should appear soon after the Weymar performance, which probably, and at the latest, will take place in February, 1853, for the fête of H.R.H. the Grand Duchess. *Lohengrin* will lose nothing by waiting *chez nous*.

As I wrote to you before, it will take some time before this glorious work meets with the swans which are to draw its barque to the banks of the Spree and the Elbe. Ganders and turkeys would like to lead it to shipwreck, but do not lose patience, and have confidence in the moderate amount of practical knowledge which your

friend places loyally at your service and disposal. In
the early days of August my pamphlet "*Lohengrin* et
Tannhäuser" will appear; it was written for a purpose
which neither you nor your friends have hitherto been
able to guess, and which it will take me some time
to attain. I am far, however, from despairing of that
attainment, but shall not let you know till the moment
of success, in order to avoid unnecessary words—a habit
which is growing upon me more and more. If you
follow my advice, dear friend, write to H. in the sense
indicated by you; that is, ask him to keep his good
intentions for the engraving of one of your full scores
till after the first performance of *Siegfried*, and to
publish for the present only the pianoforte score of
Lohengrin. Send to me here, please, if you possess
them, the numbers of the *Monatsschrift* of Kollatschek
containing your and Uhlig's articles. Heine in the
same number has thought it necessary to make some of
his rhymed jokes at my expense with his usual spirit.
More than a fortnight ago I subscribed to that magazine
through my bookseller, but as yet it has not reached
me. Farewell, dearest friend. Believe me that I am
truly vexed at not being able to attend the rendezvous
which you propose, and which would have given me
great pleasure—the pleasure of seeing you again and of
having plenty of talk with you.

Always rely upon your

EILSEN, *July 3rd*, 1851.   F. LISZT.

64.

MY BEST FRIEND,

I had just come down from the Alps when I
found your letter, which again has given me the greatest

joy. I thank you with my whole heart for your advice, so speedily given. You agree with me as to Härtel's offer; I expected so much, and it is a confirmation of my right sense in the matter. *The full score of Siegfried* it is to be, then. I feel as safe with you as a child in the mother's bosom; you take such care of me, dearest friend.

Uhlig is here. He has taken every trouble and made every sacrifice to save enough for a visit to me in Switzerland. Considering his cool, quiet, and passionless nature, the faithful attachment and friendship of this young man are of great value to me. As a very young musician he attracted my attention in the Dresden orchestra by his uncommon musical certainty and circumspection. Being struck by traits of unusual force of character and of a firm, manly disposition, I admitted him to intimate intercourse, and found a man who in the poorest circumstances had developed himself entirely out of himself. Thus I gained a friend who subsequently from a distance made it the task of his life, as far as his power extended, to serve me in a manner which,— the inclination being equal in both cases,—has been surpassed only by your brilliant genius.

You wanted to have some numbers of the *Deutsche Monatsschrift*. I happen to possess them, and send them to you, although I do not quite see of what use they can be to you. My book "Oper und Drama," in which I certainly express myself in a decisive, firm, and detailed manner, is passing through the press very slowly, and will probably not be ready before two months. Out of this book I have, by special desire, communicated some articles about modern dramatic poetry to the *Monatsschrift*, but am now sorry for it, for, torn out of their context, they are not particularly clear. I send them to you all the same, although I should almost like to ask you to ignore them. As you will not get the *Monatsschrift*, because it will be discontinued, I send you another number with an article entitled *Wir*, by Solger; it is written so prettily that I should almost like you to read it. So many stupid things have appeared in that *Monatsschrift* that the detached good bits really deserve attention. As to Heine's stupid joke you will probably not be in need of comfort. Lord, how delighted I am with my *Young Siegfried*; he will deliver me once for all from all literature and journalism. This month I require fully to recover my health in order to rush at the music next month. The copy of the poem I shall send you by Uhlig, if not sooner.

May the god who dwells in both of us keep you healthy and happy. With pleasure I see from your letter that the Princess also is recovering. I hope you will both get safely back to Weimar, which is more and more becoming my real spiritual home.

Farewell, and be greeted from the full heart of your

RICHARD WAGNER.

ENGE, ZURICH, *July* 11*th*, 1851.

65.

I am much obliged, dearest friend, for your sending me the *Monatsschrift* of Kollatschek, which I had been unable to get previously. As soon as I have read the articles which interest me I shall return them to you, and perhaps you might send me the numbers which contain the continuation of Uhlig's articles on instrumental music.

To my regret, I shall probably miss Uhlig's visit to Weymar, for I shall not be able to leave here till between the 26th and 30th of this month, and shall travel very slowly by Düsseldorf, Cologne, Frankfort, to Weymar, which I shall not reach till about the 10th of August. But in any case I shall go to see Uhlig at Dresden in the course of the autumn, for I attach real value to the continuance of my friendly relations with him, and I ask you to assure him of this as well as of my sincere and loyal sympathy.

I send you to-day the letter of M. Philipront, of Brussels, and the draft of my answer, by which you can regulate your subsequent correspondence with those gentlemen. For many reasons, I ask you specially not to give way on the *two conditions* of your collaboration in the adjustment of the French words to the music and of your presence at the general rehearsals, which I have mentioned distinctly to M. Philipront as *necessary*, and without which, *entre nous*, *Lohengrin* would run a great risk of being abominably cut and slashed.

I am delighted that you agree with my opinion about the publication of the score of *Lohengrin*. In this, as in other matters, the Härtels have behaved with a tact and good taste for which one ought to be truly thankful, and I feel convinced that the scores of both *Siegfried* and *Lohengrin* will appear at short intervals, and in the course of two years. But, all things considered, I think it advisable to begin with the pianoforte score of

Lohengrin, to be followed by the full score of *Sieg-fried*, and finally that of *Lohengrin*, in 1853 or perhaps sooner.

If Uhlig leaves you before the end of the month, he might inquire at Bückeburg whether I have left Eilsen, for he is obliged to pass through Bückeburg if he takes the railway from Cologne or Düsseldorf, which will be the shortest route to return to Dresden. I have written this to him in my last letter, which should have reached him. I should like very much to see him here, and you will oblige me by giving him a pressing invitation on my account. What has become of your disciple Ritter? Remember me to him when you see him. The manuscript of *Wiland*, which is still locked up in a chest at Weymar, will be sent on demand to Uhlig immediately after my return there.

The Princess, who, God be thanked, has been perceptibly better these last days, charges me with her admiration for you, to which I add only the simple expression of my friendship and true devotion.

F. L.

Draft of my answer to M. Philipront, which, I hope, will *draw* the question of the *Lohengrin* performance at Brussels out of confusion :—

" Sir,—As your letter of July 6th did not find me at Weymar, you will kindly excuse the delay of my answer. When Herr Wagner informed me of the proposal of M. Hanssens to perform *Lohengrin* at the Brussels theatre and asked my opinion of the matter, I advised him to thank M. Hanssens for the hospitality he had offered to that beautiful work and to accept it on two conditions, which seem to me indispensable for its full success. They are that the author should collaborate in the adjustment of the French words to the music, and that the last two rehearsals should take place in his presence. *Lohengrin* belongs by no means to the ordinary run of operas, but is in all respects an exceptional and sublime work ; and it would therefore, in my opinion, be dangerous to attempt a performance which would not be completely identified with the ideas and intentions of the poet-composer. In another fortnight I shall have an opportunity of sending you a copy of my pamphlet on *Lohengrin*, which will appear at the beginning of August (in French, Brockhaus, Leipzig). If, after having read it, you continue in your intention of giving *Lohengrin* at the Brussels theatre and of rendering a double service to dramatic art and the author, you can easily communicate direct with Herr Wagner as to the arrangements for carrying out the two conditions made and insisted upon by him.

"I am, Sir, etc.,

"F. Liszt.

"Eilsen, *July* 16th.

"The theatre of Weymar not being able to part with its one copy of the score of *Lohengrin*, in consequence of the frequent performances of that work, it is out of my power to send it to you ; but Herr Wagner will, no doubt, send you either the original manuscript or a copy, specially made for Brussels.

"The address of Herr Wagner is 'Abendstern, Enge, Zurich.'"

66.

Dear Liszt,

Two words only. You have understood *Lohengrin* aright ; Stahr has not. I withdraw my consent to his opinion ; it was given in haste. You will soon hear more from me, best of all men !

Your

Richard Wagner.

August 23rd, 1851.

67.

My Dear Friend,

At last I am able to break my long silence. The contents of this letter will show you with regard to how many and comparatively important matters I had to come to a clear decision before I could write to you in the definite manner which has now become possible.

My silence was to a large extent caused by my weak state of health. For more than two months I have been using a water cure, and during that time I found it quite impossible to write to you at such length as I felt more and more every day that I ought to do. A most cogent reason for writing to you arose to me from reading your pamphlet on my two operas, which I received at the hydropathic establishment. Your rare friendship for me, your energetic love of my works, your restless zeal in making propaganda for those works, and, before all, the splendid enthusiasm, the spirit, the subtlety, and boldness with which your zeal inspired you, moved me too deeply and powerfully to allow me to express my gratitude in the excited state in which I was. I had to leave this to a time when better health and a more collected mind would make it possible for me to communicate with you at greater length. I hope now to have got so far, and must tell you first of all that the sacrifice of the most beautiful affection which you have again offered me has moved me to the heart and has made me very glad and happy. You have moved me most deeply in all those parts where you had come to a perfect agreement with me, for the reason that this agreement was not a ready-made thing, but a discovery new to both of us. Most specially were my attention, sympathy, and eagerness awakened when I saw my original intention newly reflected in the mirror of your individual conception; for here I was able to realise fully the impression I had been fortunate enough to produce on your fertile artistic receptivity.

What you have been to me I tried recently to explain in a public manner, and having to write for publicity, I did so as soberly as possible, limiting myself entirely to the facts of our relations which I wanted to explain to those who perhaps could not understand such a friendship nowadays. I did this, being irresistibly impelled by my heart, in a "Mittheilung an meine Freunde," which I prefixed as an introduction to my three operatic poems. In the same place I stated plainly that I had despaired of ever again undertaking an artistic task, and that to *you* and your active sympathy it was solely due if I once more had gathered sufficient courage and energy for an artistic enterprise, which I should dedicate to you and to those of my friends comprised in "the local idea: Weimar." The timidity of Messrs. Härtel, the publishers of the book, has taken exception to certain passages in that preface to which I did not wish to have any demonstrative intention attributed, and which I might have expressed just as well in a different way; and the appearance of the book has in consequence been much retarded, to my great annoyance, for special reasons.

For the public declaration as to the intended destiny of my next dramatic work would, owing to my latest resolution, require an essential modification if it were to be quite in accordance with actual circumstances. But, although the preface, written at the beginning of last August, appears in the present circumstances too late, the aforesaid declaration will be given to the public without any change; and if I cannot fulfil the promise given in it in the manner there stated, it may at least serve you and my Weimar friends as a proof of the genuine sincerity of the intention then held by me. I should also be glad to think that in that public declaration I have furnished a sign of my gratitude for the sympathy they have shown to me, even if, as I said before, I cannot prove that gratitude in the exact manner there promised.

To you, my dear Liszt, I am now compelled to confess that my resolution of writing a new opera for Weimar has been so essentially modified as scarcely to exist any longer in that form.

Hear then the strictly veracious account of the artistic enterprise in which I have been engaged for some time, and the turn it had of necessity to take.

In the autumn of 1848 I sketched for the first time the complete myth of the *Nibelungen*, such as it henceforth belongs to me as my poetic property. My next attempt at dramatising the chief catastrophe of that great action for our theatre was *Siegfried's Death*. After much wavering I was at last, in the autumn of 1850, on the point of sketching the musical execution of this drama, when again the obvious impossibility of having it adequately performed anywhere prevented me in the first instance from beginning the work. To get rid of this desperate mood, I wrote the book

"Oper und Drama." Last spring your article on *Lohen-grin* inspired me to such a degree that for your sake I resumed the execution of a drama quickly and joyously ; this I wrote to you at the time : but *Siegfried's Death*—that, I knew for certain, was in the first instance impossible. I found that I should have to prepare it by another drama, and therefore took up the long-cherished idea of making the young Siegfried the subject of a poem. In it everything that in *Siegfried's Death* was either narrated or more or less taken for granted was to be shown in bold and vivid outline by means of actual representation. This poem was soon sketched and completed. When I was going to send it to you, I for the first time felt a peculiar anxiety. It seemed as if I could not possibly send it to you without explanation, as if I had many things to tell you, partly as to the manner of representation and partly as to the necessary com-prehension of the poem itself. In the first instance it occurred to me that I still had many and various things to communicate previous to my coming before my friends with this poem. It was for that reason that I wrote the long preface to my three earlier operatic poems, of which mention has already been made. After this I was going to begin the com-position, and found, to my joy, that the music adapted itself to these verses quite naturally and easily, as of its own accord. But the very com-mencement of the work reminded me that I should ruin my health entirely if I did not take care of it thoroughly before yielding to my impulse and finishing the work at a stretch and probably with-

out interruption. When I went to the hydropathic
establishment, I felt compelled at last to send you
the poem; but, strangely enough, something always
seemed to restrain me. I was led to hesitate, because I felt as if your acquaintance with this poem
would place you in a certain awkward position, as
if you would not exactly know what to make of it,
whether to receive it with hope or diffidence. At
last, on mature consideration, my plan in its logical
sequence became clear to me. Listen to me :—

This *Young Siegfried* also is no more than a frag-
ment, and as a *separate* entity it cannot produce its
proper and sure impression until it occupies its
necessary place in a *complete* whole, a place which
I now assign to it, together with *Siegfried's Death*, in
my newly designed plan. In these two dramas
a number of necessary relations were left to the
narrative or even to the sagacity of the hearer.
Everything that gave to the action and the character
of these two dramas their infinitely touching and
widely spreading significance had to be omitted in
the representation, and could be communicated to
the mind alone. But, according to my inmost conviction since formed, a work of art, and especially a
drama, can have its true effect only when the poetic
intention in all its more important motives speaks
fully to the senses, and I cannot and dare not sin
against this truth which I have recognized. I am
compelled therefore to communicate my entire myth in
its deepest and widest significance with the greatest
artistic precision, so as to be fully understood. Nothing in it must in any sense be left to be supplied

by thought or reflection; ,the unsophisticated human mind must be enabled by its artistic receptivity to comprehend the whole, because by that means only may the most detached parts be rightly understood.

Two principal motives of my myth therefore remain to be represented, both of which are hinted at in *Young Siegfried*, the first in the long narrative of Brynhild after her awakening (Act III.), the second in the scene between Alberich and the Wanderer in the second act and between the Wanderer and Mime in the first. That to this I was led not only by artistic reflection, but by the splendid and, for the purpose of representation, extremely rich material of these motives, you will readily understand when you consider the subject more closely. Think then of the wondrously fatal love of Siegmund and Siegelinde, of Wotan in his deep, mysterious relation to that love, in his dispute with Fricka, in his terrible self-contention when, for the sake of custom, he decrees the death of Siegmund, finally of the glorious Valkyrie Brynhild, as, divining the innermost thought of Wotan, she disobeys the god, and is punished by him; consider this wealth of motive indicated in the scene between the Wanderer and the Wala, and at greater length in the above-mentioned tale of Brynhild, as the material of a drama which precedes the two Siegfrieds; and you will understand that it was not reflection, but rather enthusiasm, which inspired my latest plan.

That plan extends to three dramas: (1) *The Valkyrie*; (2) *Young Siegfried*; (3) *Siegfried's Death*. In order to give everything completely, these three dramas must be preceded by a grand introductory play : *The Rape of the Rhinegold.* The object is the complete representation of everything in regard to this rape : the origin of the Nibelung treasure, the possession of that treasure by Wotan, and the curse of Alberich, which in *Young Siegfried* occur in the form of a narrative. By the distinctness of representation which is thus made possible, and which at the same time does away with everything of the nature of a lengthy narration, or at least condenses it in a few pregnant moments, I gain sufficient space to intensify the wealth of relations, while in the previous semi-epical mode of treatment I was compelled to cut down and enfeeble all this. I mention only one thing :—

Alberich ascends from the depth of the earth to the three daughters of the Rhine ; he persecutes them with his loathsome wooing ; rejected by one, he turns to the other ; laughing and teasing, they all refuse the gnome. Then the Rhinegold begins to glow ; Alberich is attracted ; he inquires as to its meaning ; the girls tell him that they use it as a bright plaything, and that its splendour lights up the depth of the waves with blissful glow, but that he might work many wonders, might gain power and strength, wealth and dominion, through means of the gold, who could weld it to a ring. But only he *who renounces love* can do this. They tell him that to prevent any one from robbing the gold they have been appointed its warders, for he who approaches them would certainly not desire the gold ; Alberich at least is not likely to do this, as he is so much in love with them. Again they laugh at him.

Then the Nibelung grows furious, he robs the gold, and takes it with him into the depths.

But enough of these particulars. Let me tell you my plan for the practical execution of the whole.

Of a separation of the materials of this great whole I cannot think without destroying my object at the outset. The entire cycle of dramas must be represented in rapid sequence, and their external embodiment can be thought of only in the following favourable circumstances. The performance of my Nibelung dramas will have to take place at a great festival, to be arranged perhaps especially for the purpose of this performance. It will have to extend over three consecutive days, the introductory drama to be given on the previous evening. If a performance in such circumstances has been accomplished, the whole may in the first instance be repeated on another occasion, and after that the single dramas, being complete in themselves, may be given separately *ad libitum*; but in any case the impression of a continuous performance must have gone before.

Where and in what circumstances such a performance may become possible I must not for the present consider, for first of all I have to complete my great work, and that will take me at least three years if I have any regard for my health.

A fortunate turn in the affairs of my intimate friends the R. family has had the effect that for that time and for the rest of my life I may attend to my artistic creations quietly and undisturbed by material cares. When once I have finished my great work, means will, I hope, be found of having it performed according to my design. If Weimar is still standing then, and if your efforts at doing something fine there have been more fortunate than at present, alas ! seems likely, and more than likely, we shall see how the matter can be managed.

However bold, extraordinary, and perhaps fantastic my plan may appear to you, be convinced that it is not the outgrowth of a mere passing whim, but has been imposed upon me by the necessary consequences of the essence and being of the subject which occupies me wholly and impels me towards its complete execution. To execute it according to my power as a poet and musician is the only thing that stands before my eyes; anything else must not trouble me for the present. Knowing your way of thinking, I do not doubt for a moment that you will agree with me and encourage my purpose, although it will frustrate for the moment your flattering wish soon to produce another work of mine.

After this I may confess that the definite alteration of my plan relieves me of an almost painful difficulty : the difficulty of having to demand the performance of *Young Siegfried* of the Weimar theatre. Only now, together with this explanation, do I send you the poem of *Young Siegfried* with a light heart, for I know that now you will read it without the anxiety which the thought of its completion and of its performance at the Weimar theatre, such as it is and cannot help being, would necessarily have caused in you. Let us have no illusions on this subject. What you, and *you alone*, have done for me at Weimar, is astonishing, and was all the more important for me, as without you I should have been entirely forgotten. Instead of this you have used all the means which you alone could have brought together in drawing towards me the public attention of lovers of art with such energy and such success that your efforts on behalf of me and my reputation are the only thing which enables me even to think of the execution of such plans as the one I have just communicated to you. This I see with perfect clearness, and I call you openly the creator of my actual position, which may perhaps lead to great things in the future.

I further ask, What expectations have you still of Weimar? With sad candour I must tell you that, after all, I consider your trouble about Weimar to be fruitless. Your experience is that as soon as you turn your back the most perfect vulgarity springs luxuriantly from the soil in which you had laboured to plant the noblest things; you return, and have just ploughed up once more half of the soil, when the tares begin to sprout even more impertinently. Truly I watch you with sadness. On every side of you I see the stupidity, the narrow-mindedness, the vulgarity, and the empty vanity of jealous courtiers, who are only too sadly justified in envying the success of genius.

But enough of this disgusting matter. For *my sake* I care no longer about it, for I have quite made up my mind as to it, but I care about it for *your sake*. I hope you will arrive at my opinion before it is too late for your good humour.

It is quite touching to me to have in a manner to take leave of our amiable Zigesar; I must write to him and at the same time pay my debt to him. This last is one of the most painful features of the explanation which will be necessary.

You are aware that I had determined upon writing a new work for *you* before the pecuniary arrangement between Zigesar and me was made. That such an arrangement was made and was offered to me by our friend with such obvious pleasure and satisfaction was of the greatest value to me.

This I have confessed to him candidly. It would appear almost trivial, mean, and in a certain sense offensive on my part to repay the sum already received on account of that agreement, for it was given to me, not in order to place me under any " obligation " towards you and Zigesar, but with the friendly desire to relieve me as far as possible of domestic cares during the composition of an opera. Nevertheless this agreement has still anothe meaning, which appears all the more serious at this moment because Zigesar has, temporarily at least, a successor in the management of the theatre. Towards this successor I am simply in the position of a debtor; and as I am not able to execute the commission I had accepted, I am bound formally and materially to dissolve a contract which cannot exist any longer. Fortunately I am in a position not to cause you any disagreeable difficulty as to this point.

After all these explanations, I send you, my dear friend and brother, the poem of my *Young Siegfried*, such as I designed and executed it when I still thought of its separate performance. In connection with the other dramas it will naturally have to undergo many alterations, and especially some beneficial abbreviations in the narrative portion. Many things will strike you in it, notably its great simplicity and the few characters amongst whom the action is distributed; but if you think of this piece as placed between the *Valkyrie* and *Siegfried's Death*, both of which dramas have a much more complicated action, you will, I have little doubt, in accordance with my intention, receive a peculiar and sympathetic impression from this forest scene, with its youthful, fearless solitude. As I told you before, I can now send you this poem willingly and without fear, for you are no longer required to glance from it anxiously towards your public. You need, for example, no longer trouble about what will be thought of the "woman" by people who see in "woman" only their own wives, or at the outside some girl, etc., etc. From this anxiety also I know you to be free, and am glad that I can disclose to you my artistic intention without fear of a real misunderstanding. Could I but succeed in engaging your favour and sympathy for my plan whenever and wherever it may be accomplished! I firmly hope for a future realisation, for there is too much creative impulse in me not to nourish hope along with it. My previous continual anxiety about my health has also now been relieved by the conviction I have since gained of the all-healing power of water and of nature's medicine; I am in the way of becoming and, if I choose, of remaining a perfectly healthy man. If you wretched people would only get a good digestion, you would find that life suddenly assumes a very different appearance from what you saw through the medium of your digestive troubles. In fact, all our politics, diplomacy, ambition, impotence, science, and, what is worst, our whole *modern art*, in which the palate, at the expense of the stomach, is alone satisfied, tickled, and flattered, until at last a corpse is unwittingly galvanised—all this parasite growth of our actual existence has no soil to thrive in but a ruined digestion. I wish that those could and would understand me to whom I exclaim these almost ridiculously sounding but terribly true words !

But I notice that I am straying from one thing to another, and therefore will conclude at last. I ask you fervently, my dear Liszt, to write me soon and fully what you think of this letter and parcel. May I always find in you the kind friend and protector that you have been and are to me, and whom at all times I shall embrace with grateful, fraternal love.

Your deeply obliged

RICHARD WAGNER.

ALBISBRUNN, *November 20th,* 1851.

When you receive these lines, I shall be back in Zurich, where my address will be " Zeltweg, Zurich."

68.

Your letter, my glorious friend, has given me great joy. You have reached an extraordinary goal in your extraordinary way. The task of developing to a dramatic trilogy and of setting to music the Nibelung epic is worthy of you, and I have not the slightest doubt as to the monumental success of your work. My sincerest interest, my warmest sympathy, are so fully secured to you that no further words are needed. The term of three years which you give to yourself may bring many favourable changes in your external circumstances. Perhaps, as some papers state, you will soon return to Germany; perhaps by the time you finish your *Siegfried* I shall have other resources at my disposal. Go on then and do your work without care. Your programme should be the same which the Chapter of Seville gave to its architect in connection with the building of the cathedral: "Build us such a temple that future generations will be obliged to say, 'The Chapter was mad to undertake so extraordinary a thing.'" And yet the cathedral is standing there at the present day.

I enclose a letter from Herr von Zigesar, the contents of which I know, but have by no means inspired. Zigesar is a sure, excellent, sterling character, and you may always count upon his friendship in that capacity. I hope that as soon as his painful disease of the eyes will allow him he will resume the management, probably by next spring.

Your well-accounted-for and justified fears as to my Weymar activity I pass by without reply; they will be proved or disproved by facts during the few years that you dwell amongst your Nibelungs. In any case I am prepared for better or worse, and hope to continue quietly in my modest way. Raff has finished a thick volume of preparatory studies for the composition of his new Biblical opera *Simson* (pronounce *Schimmeschon*). The opera itself will be finished next year. Cordial thanks, dear friend, for sending me *Young Siegfried.* Unfortunately I was last week in such a turmoil of business that I could not find a quiet hour to read the book. Can you let me keep it till Christmas? When will your three dramas *Flying Dutchman, Tannhäuser,*

and *Lohengrin* appear? Have you rewritten the preface?
H. promised it to me, but up till now I have received
nothing. Have you perhaps changed your publisher?
Let me know about it on occasion through B.,
who is writing to you at the same time with this.
Farewell, and live, if possible, in peace with the upper
world and with your lower stomach, to which in your
letter you attribute many things not quite pertaining
to it. People may think as they like, I cannot get rid
of the definition " L'homme est une intelligence servie
par des organes," and that your organs serve you
excellently well is proved by your writing the Nibelung
trilogy with prologue.

May the living God bless you and have you in His
keeping!

Your cordially devoted friend,

F. Liszt.

Weymar, *December 1st,* 1851.

69.

My Dearest Friend,

To-day only a few lines of thanks for your last
letter, which has rejoiced me unspeakably. I showed
it to every one who is in the least near to me, and told
them, " Behold, I have such a friend!"

The full and unconditional approbation with which
you receive my new plan is the best proof to my mind
that I have hit upon the right thing. To be understood
by you, and in the peculiar circumstances, in an undertaking which, besides thwarting your personal wish, can,
on account of its unmeasured boldness, be understood
by almost no one but him who is impelled to it by inward

necessity—this, my dearest Liszt, makes me as happy as if my plan had been successfully accomplished. To Herr von Zigesar also I ask you to express my most cordial thanks for the very kind manner in which he has received and replied to my last communication. He has by that means laid me under a new obligation, and I can only wish that I may be able to show my gratitude.

As far as I am concerned, I am still occupied in resting from the finally somewhat powerful effect of my cure. I shall not undertake much this winter, but shall get everything out of the way, so that the whole poem may be ready by the beginning of summer.

How could you think that I had sent you *Young Siegfried* only to look at? The copy which you have has been made specially by me for you, and I ask you to accept it, although it is not written as beautifully as might be. One thing I must ask you to do for me: send me your medallion, so that I may give it to myself as a Christmas present. I had wanted a long time to ask you for this; and now that, after a prolonged fugitive state, I begin to be a little settled in my small but cheerful dwelling, I want you amongst my Penates in one form or another. If you have a really good portrait, I should like to have that too. You need not be ashamed of hanging on my wall; at present I have there only Beethoven, besides the Nibelung design by Cornelius.

"Oper und Drama" has long been published, as you probably know. The three operatic poems, with a communication to my friends, will appear at the end of this month, together with the pianoforte score of

Lohengrin. Please order a copy at once; you are nearer to it than I. I bet that the preface will interest you very much. The conclusion I have recently altered a little, but in such a manner that everything referring to Weimar remains unchanged.

Farewell, dear friend, and let me very soon again hear from you.

Your

RICHARD WAGNER.

ZURICH (ZELTWEG), *December* 14*th,* 1851.

70.

DEAREST FRIEND,

I am very late in telling you how we have all been delighted and enlivened by your splendid work. How can we thank you for it? How can I more especially express my gratitude? B. and Br. have written to you that the sixth performance of your *Lohengrin* has been, comparatively speaking, a satisfactory one. What I wrote to you at once after the very feeble and faulty first performance has actually happened. The comprehension and interest of the actors, together with those of the public, have increased with every performance; and I feel convinced that the seventh performance on Saturday, January 24th, will be even more successful. Next season we shall without delay attack your *Flying Dutchman*, which, for local reasons explained to B., I did not propose this winter. We shall then probably be able to add and improve several things in regard to the scenery, etc., of your *Lohengrin.* You may firmly rely upon me for bringing your works at Weymar more and more up to the mark, in the same measure as our theatre in the course of time gets over divers economic considerations, and effects the necessary improvements and additions in chorus, orchestra, scenery, etc. Excuse my bad German style; I am better at *doing* a thing than at writing about it.

Cordial thanks for your splendid gift of *Siegfried*. I took the liberty of arranging a recital of it for the Hereditary Grand Duke and his wife at Zigesar's. Zigesar, who had previously read your poem, is in a state of enthusiasm about it, and the small circle of about fifteen persons whom he assembled on that evening was selected exclusively from the most zealous Wagnerites—the real *crême de la crême*. I am very curious as to how you are going to execute the work musically, what proportions the movements will have, etc.

Go at it as soon as possible. Perhaps you will be able to complete the whole work in less than three years. As regards the performance, we shall manage to arrange it somewhere by strictly observing your orders and indications. With all the genius of your fancy, you are so eminently experienced and practical that you will of a certainty write nothing unpractical. Difficulties are necessary—in order to be overcome. If, as I do not suppose, you should not be back in Germany by that time, I charge myself with the whole thing, and shall only trouble you to give me an exhaustive programme of all that you desire and expect in the performance of this gigantic work. To that I shall strictly adhere. Persons and things shall be provided somehow. But I look forward to the pleasure of enjoying your Nibelung

trilogy more quietly from a stall or a seat in the
balcony, and I invite you for four consecutive days to
supper after the performance at the Hotel de Saxe,
Dresden, or the Hotel de Russie, Berlin, in case you
are able to eat and drink after all your exertions.

Of the conclusion of the preface to the three operatic
poems I say nothing. It has hit me in my heart of
hearts, and I have shed a manly tear over it.

My portrait I shall send you through H.; the medallion I must order from Paris, as there are only galvano-
plastic copies in Germany.

The Princess has written a few words to you after
the performance of *Lohengrin*, which I enclose.

Farewell, and live as tranquilly as possible, my
glorious friend. Let me soon hear something of
you.

Your

F. LISZT.

WEYMAR, *January* 15*th*, 1852.

71.

Just returned home, with my eyes still moistened
by the tears brought to them by the moving scenes of
Lohengrin, to whom should my thought turn at this
moment but to you, sir, with the desire that you could
have witnessed the effect produced by your beautiful
work, better understood as it is every day by executants
and spectators ? I cannot tell you with how much zeal
the former endeavour to respond to the efforts of Liszt
for the worthy interpretation of your drama. Having
been ill and absent from Weymar for a year, I was this
evening able to judge how indefatigable Liszt has been

in his instruction, recommenced again and again, and becoming ever more fruitful. You would certainly be satisfied with the progress they all make at each new representation.

Fräulein Fastlinger having left our theatre, Frau Knopp Fehringer takes the part of Ortrud. The former having been generally successful, both as a singer and an actress, opinions are divided as to the latter ; and you, as the creator of the part, can alone decide which of them is really preferable. The former had the undoubted advantage of eighteen years, a pretty face, a slim, tall figure, which qualities, as they placed her in age and in beauty near to Elsa, suggested the idea of secret rivalry between woman and woman. One thought that she not only desired to win the throne of Brabant, but was also jealous of Frederick and of the charms of her from whom she had torn him away. The timidity natural to so young an artist gave to her movements the restraint which is characteristic of youth and of the instinct of a rival. Frau Knopp has over Fräulein Fastlinger the advantage of consummate and very impressive dramatic talent, but she is not very beautiful, in spite of regular features, and not in her first youth, besides which her figure is rather thickset. Her action indicated every *nuance* with admirable eloquence ; she rendered the disdain, the hatred, the rage, which alternately inspire her with gestures and pantomimic actions of such striking reality that she might be compared to the greatest artists in the most famous parts. But she could not be more than an ambitious woman. Between her and Elsa the spectator's mind could not see any comparison or rivalry, and this has no doubt put

out many of the audience without their being able to
account for the reason, for nothing could have been
more admirable than the acting of Frau Knopp, infinitely
more energetic, more richly coloured, more living, more
certain, more bold, than that of Fräulein Fastlinger.

It is then for you, sir, to say whether in general it
is better to give the part to a young and beautiful
artist, whose acting is naturally less experienced and
more subdued, or to a woman of mature talent, who gives
us an Ortrud less young, but more inflamed and devoured by the secret flames of the hatred of one who is
vanquished and the revenge of one who is oppressed.
As to myself, I cannot say which of these two conceptions produces the greater impression; the second has
certainly something more sombre, more inexorable, about
it. One trembles in advance for Elsa on seeing that
such hands will fashion her destiny; one is inclined
to say that the premeditation of a whole life gives
more grandeur to the struggle between ambition and
innocence.

Pardon, sir, this long digression; it will show to
you how much your poetic conceptions occupy us
here. I must not close these lines without telling you
how I have been touched by the manner in which you
speak of him whose glorious name I am soon to bear.
Who could fail to speak of his spirit, of his genius, of
his intelligence? But one must have a high-toned and
delicate soul to understand the *infinite tenderness* of his
soul, which so few can feel or divine. He will, no doubt,
write to you soon. This evening, after the close of the
performance, he accompanied some people who had
come from Leipzig to hear your *Lohengrin*.

Good-bye, dear sir.   Permit me to thank you for all
the rare pleasures we owe to you by the contemplation
of your beautiful works, and accept the expression of
my distinguished esteem.

CAROLYNE.

WEYMAR, *January 4th,* 1852.

72.

MY DEAR FRIEND,

Accept my cordial thanks for your last kind letter,
and for the beautiful performance of *Lohengrin* which
you have again accomplished; according to all accounts,
it must have realised my wishes in a high degree.   In
such circumstances my longing increases to enjoy my
work, of which hitherto I have only felt the pains of
giving birth to it; and my grief at being condemned to
the fate of a blind and deaf man towards my own artistic
creations begins to have a more and more depressing effect
upon me.   The existing impossibility of seeing and hearing my works makes the inspiration for new creations
so grievously difficult, that I can only think with sorrow
and with an unspeakably bitter feeling of the execution
of new works.   I tell you this for the sake of truth, and
without accompanying my complaint by wishes which,
as no one knows better than I, must remain unfulfilled.

As regards my Nibelung drama, you, my good,
sympathetic friend, regard my future in too rosy a
light.   I do not expect its performance, not at least
during my lifetime, and least of all at Berlin or Dresden.
These and similar large towns, with their public, do not
exist for me at all.   As an audience I can only imagine
an assembly of friends who have come together for the

purpose of knowing my works somewhere or other, best of all in some beautiful solitude, far from the smoke and pestilential business odour of our town civilization. Such a solitude I might find in Weimar, but certainly not in a larger city.   If I now turn to my great work, it is done for the purpose of seeking salvation from my misery, forgetfulness of my life.   I have no other aim, and shall think myself happy when I am no longer conscious of my existence.   In such circumstances my only joy is to know at least that I may benefit my friends by my art; in their sympathy with my works lies the only enjoyment I find in them.   For that reason I am very pleased that you are thinking of performing the *Flying Dutchman*, and I hope that those who love me will reward you for your trouble.   As to the representation, and especially the scenery, I shall come to an agreement with you in due time ; in Kassel it is said to have been not unsatisfactory, and some communication with the scenic artist there as to the arrangement of the ships, etc., would therefore seem desirable.   Do not begin the copying of the orchestral parts until I have sent to you from here a copy of the score, in which, in accordance with my more recent experiences of orchestral effect, I have revised the instrumental parts.

As regards *Tannhäuser*, I am glad to learn that you think of complying with my wish to have it given in the form on which I have fixed as the best.   On that condition only a permanent success of that opera at Weimar can be of interest to me.   I had not the slightest fault to find with you for thinking certain omissions necessary when you first rehearsed *Tannhäuser* at Weimar.   You did not do this because you objected to the omitted

parts, but because the artistic resources which were *then*
at your disposal filled you with natural diffidence. I
know in particular that in this manner arose the large
cut in the finale of the second act which displeased me
so much when I attended the rehearsal at Weimar.
This is the scene where Elizabeth throws herself in
front of the knights to protect Tannhäuser. In scenes of
this kind, before all others, my feeling for the perfect
truth and nature of things impels me to use all the
means of art which are within my grasp, and the
grandeur of the situation can only be rendered if not
the slightest of its essential parts is wanting. In this
scene it is necessary that those who rush at Tannhäuser
should not be driven away from him like children. Their
wrath, their fury, which impels them to the immediate
murder of the outlaw, should not be quelled in the turning of a hand, but Elizabeth has to employ the highest
force of despair to quiet this roused sea of men, and
finally to move their hearts to pity. Only then both
fury and love prove themselves to be true and great ;
and just in the very gradual calming down of the
highest excitement, as represented in this scene, I
discover my greatest merit in the interest of dramatic
truth. After you have in *Lohengrin* solved much more
difficult problems of representation, it becomes—I tell
you so openly, dear friend—your duty to give this scene
completely, and I know that success will reward you.
It is the same with all other things. In Tannhäuser's
narration (Act III.) the trombones in the reminiscence of Rome cannot produce the right impression
unless this theme has before been heard completely
and in fullest splendour, as I give it in the instru-

mental introduction to the last act, etc.   I ask you
therefore to adhere strictly to the full score which I had
sent to you from Dresden with all my marks ; and I
will only add that the song of Tannhäuser in the first
act should be sung in its entirety (the three verses) :
the real climax, especially in its effect upon Venus, is
otherwise totally lost.

Concerning the new conclusion of the last act, I was
very angry that it was not given at Weimar from the first,
as I assumed at the time that it would be.   Even then
I did not want a new public to know the first version,
which was caused by a misapprehension on my part of
the essence of the scene, as to which unfortunately only
the first performance at Dresden enlightened me.   Nothing that lies within the possibilities of representation
on the stage should be only thought or indicated, but
everything should be actually shown.   The magical
illumination of the Venusberg was, however, no
more than an indication ;   the magic event becomes
reality only if Venus herself appears and is heard.
This is so true that the afterthought of this situation
brought me great wealth of music ; consider the scene
with Venus in the last act, and you will agree with me
that the previous version stands to it in the relation of
an engraving to an oil picture.   It is just the same
with the appearance of the body of Elizabeth.   When
Tannhäuser sinks down by the side of that body, and
sighs, " Holy Elizabeth, pray for me ! " that is realised
which was formerly only indicated.

As I said before, if the performance of *Tannhäuser*
in Weimar cannot be a *complete* one, it loses all value
for me, for in that case I shall not have drawn the

public up to me, but shall have accommodated myself to the public, and that I do not care to do any longer.

Through B. I hear that the *Liebesmahl der Apostel* is on occasion to be given at Weimar. I call your attention to the fact that the orchestration of this work was designed for a vast space (the Frauenkirche of Dresden) and for a chorus of a thousand men. For a smaller room and a less numerous chorus the brass orchestra should be reduced to the usual limits, and especially the four trumpets should be reduced to two. That reduction will have no great difficulties, and B., if I ask him, will be quite able to perform the task well.

To Princess Wittgenstein, who has delighted me with a very friendly letter, I ask you to express my best thanks for her kindness. The deep interest which she has again shown in my *Lohengrin*, particularly at the last representation, is of priceless value to me. Her intelligent remarks on the character of Ortrud attracted me especially, as well as the comparison she makes between the efforts of the previous and the actual representative of that part. To which side of the question I incline your valued friend will recognize at once when I explain to her my view of the character by simply saying that Ortrud is a woman *who does not know love*. By this everything that is most terrible is expressed. Politics are her essence. A political *man* is repulsive, but a political *woman* is horrible. This horror I had to represent. There is a kind of love in this woman, the love of the past, of dead generations, the terribly insane love of ancestral pride which finds its expression in the hatred of everything living and actually existing. In man this love is ludicrous, but in woman it is terrible, because a woman, with her strong natural desire for love, *must* love something; and ancestral pride, the longing after the past, turns in consequence to murderous fanaticism. In history there are no more cruel phenomena than political women. It is not therefore jealousy of Elsa perhaps for the sake of Frederick which inspires Ortrud, but her whole passion is revealed only in the scene of the second act where, after Elsa's disappearance from the balcony, she rises from the steps of the minster, and invokes her old, long-forgotten gods. She is a reactionary person who thinks only of the old and hates everything new in the most ferocious meaning of the word; she would exterminate the world and nature to give new life to her decayed gods. But this is not merely an obstinate, morbid mood in Ortrud; her passion holds her with the full weight of a misguided, undeveloped, objectless feminine desire for love: for that reason she is terribly grand. No littleness of any kind must occur in this representation; she must never appear simply malicious or annoyed; every utterance of her irony, her treachery, must transparently show the full force of the terrible madness which can be satisfied alone by the destruction of others or by her own destruction.

She of the two actresses who approaches this intention most nearly must therefore be thought the better of the two.

Once more, dear friend, my best compliments to the Princess, and my warmest thanks for her communication.

Permit me to recall to your memory the medallion I asked you for ; it will give great pleasure to me.

Farewell, best of friends, and make me soon happy again by a few lines from you.

Wholly thine,

RICHARD WAGNER.

ZURICH, *January* 30*th*, 1852.

73.

DEAREST FRIEND,

I send you enclosed an explanation of my *Tann-häuser* overture, written for our public here, which, I have reason to hope, will soon hear a very good performance of that composition. When I had finished this programme, I read over once more what you have written about this overture, and had again to give way to the utmost astonishment. Herwegh has had the same experience with regard to your work. Only he can fail to understand your style who does not understand the music either ; to see how you express precisely and keenly in words the feelings which music alone can evoke in us fills every one with delight who himself experiences those feelings without finding words for them. This perusal, which really filled me with astonishment, has once more roused in me the wish, expressed to you some years ago, that you might become your own poet. You have the necessary qualities as much as any one. Write French or Italian verse ; in that direction you might produce something quite new and cause a great revolution. Let me hear about this from you, dearest friend.

Of my health B. probably gives you news occasionally; he writes to me more frequently now, and I always reply to him. That B.'s article about the S. has caused such a disastrous sensation amongst you confirms my opinion of the deep decay of our artistic and public conditions.

One thing grieves me: that the Goethe foundation had applied to the S.; and one thing pleases me: that her assistance came to nothing, and that a complete breach with the spurious element was thus effected.

My letter to you about the Goethe foundation will, with your permission, be published; many things are said in it which had to be said at this moment, and which, if I had wished to say them in a new and different form, would have withdrawn me again from my artistic projects. I *will* have nothing more to do with literature. As soon as the air grows a little warm and clear the poem will be begun.

Let me hear from you again.

Wholly thine,

RICHARD WAGNER.

ZURICH, *March 4th*, 1852.

74.

How are you, most excellent of men? It is too long since I heard from you. The rehearsals of *Cellini*, many visits from abroad, several pieces and transcriptions for the pianoforte, have much occupied my time during the last month. Of the performance of Berlioz's opera H. gives a most detailed account in Brendel's paper. This much I may add: that the motives which made me select this opera proved to be right and favourable to the further progress of my work here. "Why *Cellini* at Weymar?" is a question which I need not answer to the first comer, but the practical solution of which will be such that *we* may be satisfied with it. Perhaps you yourself did not at first look upon the thing in the practical light in which it will appear to you later on. In any case I believe that you will agree with me, unless you are inclined to aim at thin air. I have just been positively informed that you have handed in your petition for a free pardon at Dresden. How is this? Write to me as to this point, in perfect reliance on my discretion. I might possibly be of service to you in the matter.

A few days ago I saw here Madame B. D. She looks very well; and her husband is a handsome, decent gentleman. Amongst other things, she told me that she had been unable to understand the part of your preface which referred to her, and that her husband, after reading the passage several times, had remained in the same state of ignorance. As to the rest, she speaks well of you, and wishes very much to see *Lohengrin* here. Unfortunately Fräulein Fastlinger has left for Dresden, and Frau Knopp is continually ill, so that there is little hope of an immediate performance of that opera, for which even those are *longing* who formerly were of the opposition. Moreover, the deep court mourning in consequence of the death of Duchess Bernhard leaves me little hope that a performance of *Lohengrin* will be given *by command*. For next season, in February at the latest, the *Flying Dutchman* is set down.

It would be a beautiful and gladsome thing if by that time you were back in Germany. We should then sing your finale of *Tannhäuser*, " Er kehrt zurück," with seven times seventy-seven throats and hearts. Have you any particular instructions for your *Liebesmahl der Apostel*? I think of producing it here in the course of the summer. At the next concert of the Gesang-verein we shall have your *Faust* overture.

Farewell. Be as much as possible at peace with yourself and others, and write soon to your cordial and devoted friend,

F. LISZT.

WEYMAR, *April 7th*, 1852.

75.

My best thanks, dearest friend, for your last letter, which came to me quite unexpectedly, for you have weaned me from expecting letters from you, so seldom do you write to me. H. also has again been owing me an answer some time.

I feel so-so ; the beautiful spring weather cheers me after a somewhat dreary winter, and I shall begin my poem again. If I lived in Naples, or Andalusia, or one of the Antilles, I should write a great deal more poetry and music than in our grey, misty climate, which dis-poses one only to abstraction. I am in the midst of rehearsing my *Flying Dutchman*. Some of my friends here would not leave me in peace ; having heard my *Tannhäuser* overture, they wanted absolutely to have a taste of one of my operas. I allowed myself at last to be talked over, and am now about to introduce to the imagination of my friends a travesty of my opera, as closely resembling it as possible. Everything as re-gards scenery and orchestra is done to help that resemblance; the singers are not a bit better or worse than everywhere else; so I shall find out what can be done by the best intentions and a fabulous faith in me. So much I am confident in saying, that the performance would not be uninteresting to you, and therefore I invite you quite seriously, after receipt of this letter, to get leave for a week, trust yourself to the railway, and visit me at Zurich. The first performance takes place Wednesday, April 21st, and between that and May 1st there will be two repetitions. Are you no longer capable of this piece of folly? I am sure that you can if you will, and you would rejoice in the *joy* which your visit would give to me. Nothing else you could do in these days would compensate you for it. Do come! To Germany I shall not return; I have no hope and no wish for it. There are too few people whom I should care to see again, and those few I should like to see anywhere but in Germany. You, my dearest friend, for example, I should like to see in Switzerland. Please contradict most positively the rumour that I have pleaded for grace; if it were to spread and to be seriously believed, I should feel compelled to make a *public* declaration, which, for *every* reason, I should like to avoid.

Leave this matter alone; if the return to Germany were open to me, I should certainly use it only to make perhaps an *incognito* visit to you at Weimar.

Apropos! Ernst was here, and gave concerts, and he told me that the hope of seeing the *Flying Dutchman* had induced him to remain in Switzerland till the end of this month. You would therefore see him too.

Bring the Hereditary Grand Duchess along with you.

As you are going to give the *Flying Dutchman* at Weimar, you would be interested to see the scenic arrangements which I have made for a small stage.

What is this you have heard about me in connection with your performance of *Cellini*? You seem to suppose that I am hostile to it. Of this error I want you to get rid. I look upon your undertaking as a purely personal matter, inspired by your liking for Berlioz; what a beast I should be if I were to criticise that liking and that undertaking! If every one would follow the inner voice of his heart as you do, or, better still, if every one had a heart for such a voice as you have, things would soon be changed. Here again I must rejoice in you. But where a pure matter of the heart is submitted to speculative reason, I must find that mistakes creep in which a third person can perceive. In the consequences which, as I am told, you expect from the performance of *Cellini*, I cannot believe; that is all. But can this my unbelief in any way modify my judgment of your action? Not in the least. With my whole heart I say, you have acted rightly, and I wish that I could say as much to many people.

I am sorry that you have not produced *Lohengrin* again; you were in the right swing with it this season. What a pity that only a single performance should have been possible! This shows of what use half a year may be.

That Madame D. and her husband were unable to understand the passage in my preface proves their exceedingly fine tact. This was, no doubt, the best way for them of saving themselves a painful impression, and I am glad that they were able to do this, for it was

really and truly far from my mind to annoy them.   Ah,
I wish I could this summer make at last a beautiful
journey, and that I knew how to set about it!   To
this sigh only my own voice replies as echo from the
wall of leather which surrounds me.   This longing for
a journey is so great in me that it has already inspired
me with thoughts of robbery and murder against
Rothschild and Co.   We sedentary animals scarcely
deserve to be called men.   How many things we might
enjoy if we did not always sacrifice them to that
damnable "organ of sitting still."

Alas! this "organ of sitting still" is the real law-
giver of all civilized humanity.   We are to sit or at best
to stand, never to walk, much less to run for once in a
while.   My hero is the "bold runner Achilles."   I would
rather run to death than sit still and get sick.   That is
your opinion also, is it not? and therefore I may expect
you for the *Flying*, not the lying-down, *Dutchman*.

We shall see.   Live gloriously and well!

Wholly thine,

RICHARD WAGNER.

ZURICH, *April* 13*th*, 1852.

76.

That I was unable to fly to your *Flying Dutchman*
was not my fault; how genuinely glad I should be to see
you again, and what beautiful enjoyment your splendid
work would give me, I need not tell you, most excellent
friend.   The news I received from various sides as to
the performances of the *Flying Dutchman* could not but
greatly please me.   Next winter you shall have news
of our performance at Weymar, for we must not delay

it any longer, and hope that it will be a success on the part of the artists, for as to the work itself there can be no question. Be kind enough to let me have as soon as possible the exact alterations, additions, and omissions you have made in the score, for I want to have the copies made at once. Quite lately I again expressed the principle that our first and greatest task in Weymar is to give the operas of Wagner exactly *selon le bon plaisir de l'auteur.* With this you will, no doubt, agree, and in consequence we shall, as before, be bound to give *Lohengrin* without cut and to study the whole finale of the second act of *Tannhäuser,* with the exception of the little cut in the adagio. This will be done at our next representation. Send me therefore the necessary instructions about the study of the *Flying Dutchman,* and be assured that I shall not deviate from them by a hair's breadth.

For your kind offer of the designs I thank you, and accept it eagerly. Send them to me soon ; we have here a very clever young scene-painter and engineer, Herr Händel, late of the Hamburg theatre, who will take every care to comply with your demands. I have advised Baron von Beaulieu-Marconnay, the intendant, of the impending arrival of your designs, and the honorarium (five louis d'or) will be sent to you by the end of August. If you would rather have this small sum at once, I will remit it by return.

I have asked B. to tell you of the *crime* committed by me during the visit of his Majesty the Emperor of Russia. *Tannhäuser* had been announced for the evening, when it was hoped that his Majesty would visit the theatre. Knopp and Milde were unable to sing a note, and Frau von Milde also was hoarse. It was impossible to give a whole opera, so I coolly took the first act of *Tannhäuser* as far as the end of the Pilgrims' Chorus, closing in G major, then after a pause commenced again in G major with the prelude to the third act of *Lohengrin*, and so continued with the whole act to the end of the duet, winding up the performance with the overture "Carneval Romain" and the second act of *Benvenuto Cellini*, omitting the baritone air.

Fräulein Fromann was present, and has probably written to you about it.

By the end of this month the Empress of Russia is expected, and *Tannhäuser* is again announced for the 31st. Beck takes the part of Tannhäuser, and the entire finale of the second act will be sung. The new close, however, must unfortunately wait till next season, for a new scene is being painted for it, which cannot be finished ; everything else is ready and copied out.

For next season we have Spohr's *Faust*, with new recitatives, and shall give Schumann's *Manfred* at the beginning of June. Of the Ballenstedt Musical Festival, with the *Tannhäuser* overture, and the *Liebesmahl der Apostel*, you have probably heard.

Your *Faust* overture made a sensation, and went well.

Farewell, and have a go at *Siegfried*.

Your
F. L.

77.

DEAREST FRIEND,

To-day I write only a few hurried lines in order to avoid a misunderstanding.

Herr C. has made the sketches for the *Flying Dutchman*; but, as I look at his work, it weighs heavily on my heart that you are to pay five louis d'or for it, which, according to my inmost conviction, it is not worth. (The man is altogether extremely mediocre, and the only thing that attracted my attention towards him was that he became acquainted with the subject under my own extremely painstaking direction, and in accordance with my most special intentions.) I have told him that the management at Weimar had a good scene-painter, and that you would only make occasional use of his sketches; if he would send them to you, you could offer him no more than the small remuneration of fifty francs.

If he sends the sketches, please make Herr von Beaulieu acquainted with this arrangement, so that he may reply to him in the sense above indicated and send him the honorarium to his own address.

Pardon me, but I could not make up my mind to allow you to pay five louis d'or for this trifle. About everything else I shall write to you at greater length within the next few days.

Farewell.

Your

RICHARD WAGNER.

ZURICH, *May 24th*, 1852.

78.

DEAREST FRIEND,

In addition to my last hurried lines, I write to you to-day a little more comprehensively. First of all, I must thank you for the news of the continued activity which you employ in the propaganda of my works.

Expressions of praise on that account I omit once for all, for you are far above praise. Of the performance of the *Faust* overture I had heard nothing beyond your own brief notice. I cannot be angry with this composition, although many detached things in it would not now flow from my pen; especially the somewhat too plentiful brass is no longer to my mind. If I knew that the Härtels would pay me a nice sum for it, I should be almost inclined to publish the full score, together with a pianoforte arrangement, which H. would have to make ; but I should like to be warmly persuaded to this, for on my own account I do not care to propose such things.

Am I really going to figure at the next Musical Festival ? People say that I am a famous " *made* " man ; if that is true, who is the maker ? Do not forget to add to the programme the explanation of the *Tannhäuser* overture which I wrote last winter for the Zurich performance, and which I consider indispensable, because it gives briefly a condensed picture of the poetic subject, which is conceived in the overture quite differently from what it is in the opera itself. (In that sense you are quite right in saying that this overture is altogether a work by itself.) A copy of my explanation you probably possess ; if not, Uhlig has plenty.

I really cannot understand why our numberless male choir festivals, etc., have never yet produced the *Liebesmahl der Apostel*. But so many things are now to me inconceivable and yet quite conceivable. In a large room, and with a strong chorus, you may leave the instrumentation as it is ; but I call your attention to the fact that at Dresden I was compelled,

after certain important divisions of the composition, to
have the key indicated by *two harps* : the larger the
chorus, the more inevitable is the dropping of the pitch
from time to time ; but of this you would probably
have thought yourself.

Concerning the (future) *complete* performance of
Tannhäuser I have still many things on my heart, of
which I do not find it easy to unburden myself.   First,
certain minor matters.   I do not know exactly whether
Walther von der Vogelweide in the contest of the
minstrels sang his song with you in the original B flat
major or in C major.   There is here some inconsistency.
I am aware that B flat does not agree with the rest of
the somewhat high-lying part, and a singer who has the
voice for the whole part cannot make much effect in B
flat, for which reason I was compelled at Dresden to
transpose the piece to C.   But this C major is altogether out of relation to the other songs of the singers'
contest, and more especially it destroys the transition to
the bright tone of the ensuing song of Tannhäuser, who,
with his C major, is supposed to go beyond Walther.
Apart from this, the song of Walther loses by means of
this higher C major much of the calm dignity which is
its character.   The dilemma can be solved only by the
part of Walther being sung by a *low* tenor and that of
Heinrich der Schreiber by a *high* tenor.   The two parts
therefore must be rewritten, and in *all the ensembles*
Walther should sing the notes which in the score are
assigned to Heinrich der Schreiber, and *vice versâ*.
Only in the first finale Walther retains all the *solo passages*.   This is what I should like.   I further hope that
you will give the scene between Venus and Tannhäuser

in its entirety. The necessity of *three* verses of the Tannhäuser song I have, I believe, already pointed out to you.

But now comes the principal thing; *i.e.*, the great adagio of the second finale. When at Dresden, after the first performance of *Tannhäuser*, I made the cut in this adagio, I was in complete despair, and in my heart cut every hope of *Tannhäuser* as well, because I saw that T. could not understand, and therefore much less represent, the part. That I had to make this cut was to me tantamount to abandoning altogether the purpose of making my *Tannhäuser* really understood. Kindly look at the omitted passage, dearest friend, and realise what it contains. While previously everything was grouped round Elizabeth, the peacemaker, she being the centre, and all the others listening to her and repeating what she said and sang, Tannhäuser here recognizes his terrible crime, and breaks down in the most terrible repentance. When he once more finds words for his emotion, which he can scarcely utter, because he lies on the ground in a state of semi-consciousness, *he* suddenly becomes the principal person, and the whole scene is grouped round him, just as before it was round Elizabeth. All else is thrown into the background, and in a manner only accompanies him as he sings :—

> "Zum Heil den Sündigen zu führen,
> Die Gottgesandte nahte mir :
> Doch ach ! sie frevelnd zu berühren
> Hob ich den Lästerblick zu ihr !
> O ! du, hoch über diesen Erdengründen,
> Die mir den Engel meines Heil's gesandt :
> Erbarm' dich mein, der ach ! so tief in Sünden
> Schmachvoll des Himmels Mittlerin verkannt !"

In this stanza and in this song lies the whole significance of the catastrophe of Tannhäuser, and indeed of
the whole essence of Tannhäuser; all that to me makes
him a touching phenomenon is expressed here alone.
His grief, his sad pilgrimage of grace—all this springs
forth from the meaning of these lines; without hearing
them, and hearing them in this place, the spectator sees
in Tannhäuser an inconceivable, arbitrary, wavering,
miserable creature.   (The commencement of his tale in
the last act comes too late to make up for that which
here must penetrate our mind like a thunderstorm.)   Not
only the close of the second act, but the entire third act,
and in a sense the whole drama, receive their true significance only when the centre of the whole drama, round
which it develops itself, as round its kernel, becomes
perfectly clear and lucid in that particular passage.
And that passage, the keynote of my whole work, I
was compelled to cut at Dresden.

This I declare: no representation of *Tannhäuser*
answers my purpose if *that passage* has to be omitted.
For its sake I will, if need be, consent to the cut in the
allegro of the finale, which contains what is really the
continuation of that passage—I mean the place where
Elizabeth takes up the B major theme as *canto fermo*,
while Tannhäuser at the same time gives passionate
vent to his wild despair.   If at some future time a
performance of this opera were wholly to satisfy me,
Tannhäuser would have to sing this passage also in
such a manner that it would not appear long.

You will ask me, "What are we to do? How can we
expect a minor singer to do what T. failed to accomplish?"   I reply that T., in spite of his voice, failed to

accomplish many things that were not beyond much less gifted singers. At the *Tannhäuser* rehearsal which I attended at Weimar the invalided Götze brought out passages and interpreted intentions in respect of which T. remained my debtor. This latter has nothing but either brilliancy or tenderness in his voice ; not a single true *accent of sorrow*. The singer of the *Flying Dutchman* here did a great deal more than those at Dresden and Berlin, although they had better voices. Try what you can do with Herr Beck, and explain to him what is the important part. Only in case this passage comes out well the Weimar public will see what the whole is about. (I add a technical remark : If the singer in this passage is quite sure, let him take the tempo freely ; all the others must go with him : he rules alone.)

If a performance of *Tannhäuser* were to be quite perfect, the last finale of the opera would have to be given as it stands in the new edition of the pianoforte score, *including* the song of the younger pilgrims. Your score of the *Flying Dutchman* you can send to Uhlig, who possesses a newly revised score, and will arrange yours in strict accordance with it.

When the time for the rehearsals comes, I will let you have some further details. For the present I shall be satisfied if the parts are copied in accordance with Uhlig's score and if the scenery is painted after the sketches which I hope C. will send you.

The *Flying Dutchman* has made an indescribable impression *here*. Philistines who never go to a theatre or concert attended each of the four performances in one week, and are supposed to have gone mad. With the *women* I have made a great hit. The pianoforte scores sell by the half-dozen. I am now in the country, and feel tolerably cheerful. My work also pleases me again; my Nibelung tetralogy is completely designed, and in a few months the verse also will be finished. After that I shall be wholly and entirely a "music-maker," for this work will be my last poem, and a littérateur I hope I shall never be again. Then I shall have nothing but plans for performances in my head; no more writing, only performing. I hope you will help me.

Are you going to make a trip this year? How about the rendezvous which you made me look for as long ago as last summer? Are we never to meet again?

H. also ought to write to me again. Is he so busy with his compositions? Of the Imperial Russian *Tannhäuser-Lohengrin-Cellini* theatre bill he told me nothing.

Are you going to have *Tannhäuser* the day after to-morrow? Good luck to you! Make my compliments to the sovereign lady of all the Russias. I hope she will send me an order, or at least travelling money for Italy, where I should like to roam beyond anything. Tell her so. I hear those people throw plenty of ducats out of window just now. I am sorry to think that you will not be able to manage *Lohengrin* for such a long time; the pause is too long. As a punishment I shall dedicate the score to you when it appears in print. I do not ask you whether you accept the dedication or not, for punishment there must be.

I must ask you to send me the score of my *Faust* overture ; I do not possess a copy.

Farewell, and be greeted with all my heart.

Your

RICHARD WAGNER.

ZURICH, *May 29th*, 1852.

79.

DEAREST FRIEND,

I have a favour to ask.

I am hard at work and eager to finish the poem of my *Valkyrie* in a fortnight. Some recreation after that will be a necessity ; I want the change of travelling, and should especially dislike to finish my last poetic work, the great introductory play, here, where the monotony of my accustomed surroundings oppresses me, and where troublesome visitors put me generally in a bad temper. I want to go to the Alps, and should like at least to have a taste of the frontier of Italy, and to make a short sojourn there. Such extravagances I cannot afford from my ordinary income. For next winter I expect some extraordinary incomings (*Tannhäuser* at Leipzig and presumably at Breslau). But, before all, I reckon upon the money which you will get me for the *Flying Dutchman* at Weimar. This latter I may calculate at something like twenty to twenty-five louis d'or. Could you get any one to advance me that sum ?

Unless Zigesar is again at the head of affairs, I should think it inadvisable to apply to the theatrical exchequer for this advance of honorarium, but perhaps some benevolent private person might be found who would not refuse to disburse this sum for me. You would at the same time furnish the best guarantee that the money would really be forthcoming, for your zeal secures the performance of the *Flying Dutchman* at Weimar during the winter. This advance would give me great satisfaction, but I should want the money by the end of June at the latest. Kindly see how you can arrange this.

My *Valkyrie* (first drama) turns out terribly beautiful. I hope to submit to you the whole poem of the tetralogy before the end of the summer. The music will be easily and quickly done, for it is only the *execution* of something practically *ready*.

Farewell, and let me soon have news of you. Did the Imperial Russian *Tannhäuser* come off? You are in the midst of great Musical Festival troubles, are you not? Much luck and joy to it!

Wholly thine,

RICHARD WAGNER.

June 16th, 1852.

Do you know anything about *Tannhäuser* being contemplated for Munich next autumn? *I* know nothing. It would be nice of Herr Dingelstedt to think of such a thing.

80.

Herewith I send you a bill for one hundred thalers, and cordially wish you good luck and a good mood, fine weather externally and internally, for your Alpine trip. Let all be well with you, my glorious friend, and proceed bravely with the completion of your tetralogy. When do you think it will be ready? Is there a possibility of thinking of its performance in the months of August and September, 1854 ?   Do not allow other undertakings or claims to detract or detain you from this great enterprise, the task of your life.

For the dedication of *Lohengrin* I thank you most cordially ; I am delighted with it.

The *Flying Dutchman* will most certainly be performed here next February.   Send me the designs *soon,* so that all may be prepared in good time.   Zigesar will probably resume the management before long, at which I am very glad.

Beaulieu has taken leave officially, and is gone to Kreuznach.

The *Liebesmahl der Apostel* was satisfactorily given by the Pauliner choir of Leipzig, under the direction of its conductor, Langer.   I was truly delighted with it, and mean to repeat the splendid work as soon as there is a good opportunity.   Although external success and a certain (very uncertain) *pleasing quality* are a secondary consideration with me in the case of works which are decidedly *above* the public, it was agreeable all the same to see that success and that *pleasing quality* as fully confirmed as one could have desired.

The chorus was not very numerous (about a hundred and twenty), but well balanced, and the whole sounded beautifully.   Milde and his wife sang the duet from the *Flying Dutchman*, which was much applauded, and the *Tannhäuser* overture went splendidly, and was repeated by desire at the close of the Musical Festival on the second day.   The orchestra and the public were unanimous in their enthusiasm, as indeed must be the case wherever the performance is adequate.

Long accounts of the Musical Festival you will find

in Brendel's *Neue Zeitschrift* (Brendel himself was at Ballenstedt), the *Signale*, *Rheinische Musikzeitung*, and Berlin *Echo*.

Your

F. Liszt.

June 26th, 1852.

Perhaps you can spare a few minutes before starting on your journey to write a few friendly lines to Langer about the performance of the *Liebesmahl* at Ballenstedt. He has behaved as excellently as might have been expected, and the chorus of students is splendid. Without it the performance would have been impossible, because the other singers were only just sufficient to strengthen the chorus. Send your letter to Brendel, who will give it to Langer, and let me have without delay the designs for the *Flying Dutchman*.

81.

Cordial thanks, best of friends, for sending me the money, in connection with which I am troubled by one thing only : you do not tell me that the hundred thalers have been advanced on account of the honorarium for the *Flying Dutchman*. I asked for the sum on that understanding, and no other, and only if I may assume that no one has been inconvenienced in this manner will it give me pleasure to spend the money on a trip of recreation. That trip, on which I start to-morrow, has come just in time; uninterrupted work has again strongly affected me, and the nerves of my brain are so overwrought that even these few lines put me in a state of violent excitement, wherefore I must ask you not to be angry if I make them very short. I feel that I am still capable of doing good things, but only by keeping very strict diet, and especially by frequently interrupting my work and entirely diverting my thoughts before going on again.   The *Valkyrie*, the poem of which I finished on July 1st, I wrote in four weeks ; if I had spent eight weeks over it, I should now feel better.   In future I must adopt this course, and cannot therefore fix a term for the completion of the whole, although I have reason to suppose that the music will not give me much trouble.

I am surprised that you ask me for the *designs for the " Flying Dutchman,"* because I have left the whole matter to the designer, Herr C.   This man, with whom I do not care to have any further dealings, because he has a passion for borrowing from a poor devil like me, wrote to me lately to say that he had applied by letter to Weimar in this matter, but had as yet had no reply. If you care to have the designs, all that is necessary will be for the management to reply to C.'s letter, and I ask you therefore to see that this is done.

Uhlig will arrange the score for you as soon as he receives your copy.

A thousand thanks for all you have again done for my works lately.   I was not able to read the account of the Ballenstedt Musical Festival with anything but deep emotion.   I am sure that by these performances you have again won many new friends for me, and I have no doubt that if ever I come to the fore it will be your doing.

Farewell, and be happy !

Your

RICHARD WAGNER.

82.

MOST GLORIOUS FRIEND,

You have once more given me real, God-sent joy by your dedication of *Lohengrin*. Accept my most cordial, most fervent thanks in return, and be convinced that it will be the task of my life to be worthy of your friendship.   The little that so far I have been able to do for *you* and through you for the honour of art has chiefly this merit : that it encourages me to do still better and more decisive things for your works in the future.   But what do you mean by occupying yourself with the bad jokes which have been circulating in a few newspapers, and by even accusing me of having been the cause of them ?   The latter is quite impossible, and H. has probably told you already that the manuscript of *Siegfried* has not been out of his hands for months. Some time ago I lent it, by your desire, to Fräulein Fromann alone, and the reading that took place at Zigesar's at the beginning of last year for the Hereditary Grand Duke cannot very well have originated the bad joke in the *Kreuzzeitung*.   However, that joke is quite harmless and insignificant, and I ask you urgently to ignore totally this kind of gossip once for all.

What can it matter to you whether people indulge their silliness in connection with you and your works ? You have other cats to flog—" d'autres chats à fouetter," as the French proverb has it.   Do not therefore hesitate on your account or on my account to publish the Nibelung tetralogy as soon as it is finished.   Härtel spoke to me about your letter in connection with this affair about two months ago ; and, in my opinion, you cannot do better than give the poem to the public while you finish the score. As to the definite performance of the three operas we must have a good talk when the time comes. If in the worst case you are not then back in Germany (and I need not tell you how I wish that this worst case should not happen), I shall stir in every possible way for the production of your work. You may rely on my practical talents for that purpose and have implicit confidence in me. If Weymar should prove too mean and poor, we shall try somewhere else ; and even if all our strings snap (which is not to be expected), we may still go on playing if you give me full power to organise an unheard of music or drama festival, or whatever the thing may be called in any given place, and to launch your *Nibelungen* there.

You finish your score! and in the meantime let Härtel or some one else publish the poem as a forerunner.

How about the performance of *Tannhäuser* at Berlin ? I quite approve of your exceptional demand of 1,000 thalers for the same reasons which induced you to make that demand, and I thank you cordially for the artistic confidence with regard to the preparations which you have placed in me. Although a journey of Berlin would in existing circumstances be somewhat inconvenient, I am quite at your disposal, with the sole condition—which alone would make my journey useful and serviceable to *Tannhäuser*—that the *Royal management asks me* to come to Berlin by your desire and to settle with that management and with the other persons concerned the necessary preparations for the best possible success of your work.

In any other circumstances I should be in an awkward and useless position at Berlin, without achieving the slightest thing. If you consider the matter, you will certainly agree with me, and see that this is the only way in which I perhaps might be of use to you.

As you know already, the *Flying Dutchman* is announced for the next birthday of H.I.H. the Grand Duchess : February 16th, 1853. Care will be taken that the opera is properly mounted. Zigesar is full of enthusiasm for your genius, and will work with a will. The corrected score has been sent at once to the copyists, and in six weeks the work will be rehearsed *comme il faut.*

The theatrical season begins with Verdi's *Hernani,* after which Spohr's *Faust,* with new recitatives, will follow soon. By the middle of November I expect Berlioz, whose *Cellini* (with a considerable cut) must not be shelved, for, in spite of all the stupid things that have been set going about it, *Cellini* is and remains a remarkable and highly estimable work. I am sure you would like many things in it.

Raff has made great changes in the instrumentation and arrangement of his *Alfred,* and probably the opera in its new form will have better effect even than before, although the three or four first performances were much applauded. Altogether I look upon this opera as the ablest work that has been written by a German composer these ten years. You of course are not included; you stand alone, and can be compared with no one but yourself.

I am very glad you have taken this trip. The glaciers are splendid fellows, and in the years of my youth I, too, had struck up a friendship with them. The tour round Mont Blanc I recommend you for next year; I made it partly in the year 1835, but my travelling companion was soon fatigued, and fatigued me still more.

Farewell. Be at peace with yourself, and soon publish your Nibelung poem, in order to prepare the public and put it in the proper mood. Leave all manner of *Grenzboten, Wohlbekannte, Kreuzzeitungen*, and *Gazettes Musicales* on one side, and do not bother yourself with these miserable scribblings. Rather drink a good bottle of wine, and work onwards, up to eternal, immortal life.

Your cordially grateful and truly devoted

F. LISZT.

WEYMAR, *August 23rd*, 1852.

83.

DEAREST FRIEND,

A thousand thanks for your last letter. Unfortunately I cannot reply to it as I should like to do; the nerves of my brain are once more in a state of great suffering, and for some time I ought to give up all writing and reading, I might say all mental existence. Even the shortest letter wearies me terribly, and only the most perfect quiet (where and how shall I find that ?) may or might restore me. But I do not wish to complain, only to explain to you why it is that to-day I must limit my communication to stating briefly what is absolutely necessary. Do not be angry with me for not writing with that joyful expansion which is intended to make up for the impossibility of personal intercourse.

As to Berlin nothing is settled yet. Hülsen considered my demand as a vote of want of confidence in his personal intentions, and this error I had to dispel by laying my most perfect confidence as a weight on his conscience. All I want him to do now is to acknowledge in a few words that he perfectly understands my difficult position with regard to *Tannhäuser* at Berlin, and that he undertakes the performance with the desire of conquering that difficult position. The whole subject of honoraria I leave to him. One thing has recently calmed my anxiety: I have written tolerably comprehensive instructions for the performance of *Tannhäuser*, and have had them printed as a pamphlet and sent a sufficient number of copies to the theatres which had bought the score. I hope this will be of use. I send you herewith half-a-dozen copies. There will not be much that is new to you in the pamphlet, because I have discussed most things with you by letter; still it might be useful to you, because it will materially assist you in your purpose of restudying *Tannhäuser* if you will give it to the stage-manager and the singers. This therefore I would ask you to do. The work has been a perfect torture to me. This eternal communication by letter and in print is terrible to me, especially when it is about things the significance of which has for a long time lain far behind me. In fact, if I still trouble myself about these earlier operas, it is only from the necessity of circumstances, not from any desire to hark back. This leads me to Berlioz and Raff. Candidly speaking, I am sorry to hear that Berlioz thinks of recasting his *Cellini*. If I am not mistaken, this work is more than twelve years old. Has

not Berlioz developed in the meantime so that he might
do something quite different ?   It shows poor confidence
in himself to have to return to this earlier work. B.
has shown quite correctly where the failure of *Cellini*
lies, *viz., in the poem* and in the unnatural position in
which the musician was forcibly placed by being
expected to disguise by purely musical intentions a
want which the poet *alone* could have made good.
This *Cellini* Berlioz will never put on its legs.   But which
of the two after all is of more importance, *Cellini* or
Berlioz ?   Leave the former alone, and help the second.
To me there is something horrible in witnessing this
attempt at galvanizing and resuscitating.   For heaven's
sake let Berlioz write a *new opera* ; it will be his greatest
misfortune if he fails to do this, for only one thing can
save him, the *drama*, and one thing must lead him
to ever deeper ruin, *his obstinate avoidance of this sole
refuge*: and in this latter he will be confirmed by
occupying himself again with an old attempt, in which
he has been deserted by the *poet*, for whose faults he
will try once more to make up by his music.

Believe me, I *love* Berlioz, although he keeps apart
from me in his distrust and obstinacy; he does not
know me, but I know *him*.   If I have expectations of
any one, it is of Berlioz, but not in the direction in
which he has arrived at the absurdities of his *Faust*.
If he proceeds further in that direction, he must become
perfectly ridiculous.   If ever a *musician* wanted *the
poet*, it is Berlioz, and his misfortune is that he always
prepares this poet for himself, according to his musical
whim, arbitrarily handling now Shakespeare, now
Goethe.   He wants a poet who would completely

penetrate him, who would *conquer* him by delight, who
would be to him what man is to woman.   I see with
dismay that this exceedingly gifted artist is perishing in
his egotistic solitude.   Can I save him ?

You do not want to have *Wiland*.   I believe it to
be a beautiful poem, but am no longer *able* to execute
it for myself.   Will you offer it to Berlioz ?   Perhaps
Henri Blaze would be the man to treat it in French.

How about Raff ?   I thought he was writing a new
work, but no ; he is remodelling an old one.   Is there no
LIFE in these people ?   Out of what can the artist *create*
if he does not create *out of life*, and how can this life
contain an artistically productive essence unless it
impels the artist continually to creations which
correspond to life ?   Is this artificial remodelling of old
motives of life real artistic creativeness ?   How about
the source of all art unless new things flow forth from
it irresistibly, unless it is wholly absorbed in *new*
creations ?   Oh, ye creatures of God, do not think that
this *making* is artistic creating.   It betrays no end of
self-complacency, combined with poverty, if we try to
prop up these earlier attempts.   If Raff's opera, as you
tell me, has pleased, he ought to be satisfied ; in any
case he had a better reward than I had for my *Feen*,
which was never performed at all, or for my *Liebesverbot*,
which had *one* abominable performance, or for my
Rienzi, of the revival of which I think so little that I
should not permit it if it were contemplated anywhere.
About the *Dutchman, Tannhäuser,* and *Lohengrin* I
trouble myself with disgust, and only for the reason
that I know that, on account of imperfect representations,
they have never been perfectly understood.   If they

had had their due anywhere, I should care devilishly little about things that I have outlived.

Good people, do something *new*, *new*, and once more *new*. If you stick to the old, the devil of barrenness holds you in thrall, and you are the most miserable of artists.

Well, this is off my heart; he who charges me with insincerity will have to answer Heaven; he who charges me with arrogance is silly.

I can write no more; do not be angry; my head is bursting. Only let me say the warmest farewell that is in my heart. Love me as before, and write soon to

Your

RICHARD WAGNER.

ZURICH, *September 8th,* 1852.

84.

DEAREST FRIEND,

After my last letter you will think that I am quite mad. Lord knows how I wrote myself into such a fury. To-day follows something very sober, a troublesome thing for you.

Frau Röckel sent me the letter of her poor husband, without giving me his address. I ask you therefore to forward her the enclosed letter, also two parcels, which I have posted to you to-day—(1) two little pamphlets; (2) a score of *Lohengrin*—both meant for Röckel, and to be sent through his wife. H. was really to have the score, but must resign it to the poor prisoner. He must do this for the love of both of us, and Heaven will find him another copy sooner or later.

As I have once begun asking favours, I go on. Be kind enough to send me two things :—

1. My *Faust* overture. I hope that, if you want it still, you have had a copy made. I have a mind to rewrite it a little and to publish it through H. Perhaps I shall get a little money for it. B. must do the pianoforte arrangement, according to his promise to me.

2. My instructions as to the performance of *Lohengrin* which I sent to you from Thun by letter in the summer of 1850. I want particularly to have my beautiful designs of the scenery. I intend to have new designs for the scenery, according to my indications made by a Dresden friend or through his intercession, so as to have them in readiness for such theatres as want to undertake *Lohengrin* in future. If the Weimar management or any other persons desire to keep my originals, they shall be faithfully restored to its or their possession.

Have I troubled you enough ? When are you going to send me some of your compositions ? I see nothing of them here, and, in fact, learn scarcely anything about music. Think of me occasionally.

H. also is once again reticent. Uhlig complains of him and of a hostile feeling on his part. What is the meaning of this ? Let each go his own way without snarling at the other who goes a different way.

Shall I soon hear from you again ? How delighted I should be !

Farewell, and think of me lovingly.

Wholly thine,

RICHARD WAGNER.

ZURICH, *September 12th*, 1852.

The parcel will probably arrive a day after this.

At Berlin things now tend towards the non-performance of *Tannhäuser*. The performance has been postponed. As, according to my calculation, it could not have been produced before the end of January, and as my niece Johanna leaves Berlin at the end of February, I was compelled to stipulate that ten performances of the opera should be guaranteed for this winter. Otherwise there was the danger that this opera too would have disappeared after three or four performances, as was the case with the *Flying Dutchman* and *Rienzi*, which for that reason were cried down as *failures*. If this guarantee is refused, I have given instructions that the score shall be withdrawn.

85.

DEAREST AND BEST OF FRIENDS,

Set my mind at rest by a few lines telling me that I did not offend you some time ago. I live at such a distance from my friends, that I always have a thousand anxieties, especially when I do not receive news from them for long. Tell me, for heaven's sake, have I written to you anything about Berlioz or Raff which you might have misunderstood in the sense that I had something against them? I have spoken as best I could from a distance; and, especially with regard to Berlioz, my intentions are the best. Therefore—a few lines, please! About Berlin everything is now settled, but *Tannhäuser* will not be fully rehearsed till about December. Considering this delay of the matter, I do not want to trouble Herr von Hülsen with new conditions just yet; but when the time comes, I shall ask you to let me

know once more whether you can afford the sacrifice
of going to Berlin.

Belloni, as you know, is here; he has again talked
much to me about Paris, and, to my astonishment, I
hear that you still have plans of world-conquest for me
in your head. You are indefatigable indeed! To
the translation of *Tannhäuser* I have no particular
objection, especially as in Roger I might expect the
best Tannhäuser that I could think of. In addition to
this, Johanna—I confess it would not be amiss.
Herwegh also is doing something for the Paris performance. He proposes to make a richly coloured
prose translation of the poem; however, I cannot yet
think seriously of it.

My instructions as to the performance of *Tannhäuser*
have already induced the Leipzig people to abandon
the opera—a very modest sign of acknowledgment ot
ill-will on their part. I am pleased to hear, on the
other hand, that Schindelmeisser in Wiesbaden, after
reading my pamphlet, has again begun the rehearsals
from the beginning. Did you like the pamphlet? As
you think of studying *Tannhäuser* again, I assume that
it will be useful to you for that purpose with the
stage-manager; the singers also may derive excellent
and much-needed service from it. But why has B.
become silent once more?

Gradually my solitude here is becoming unbearable;
and if I can afford it, I shall go to Paris for the winter.
How delighted I should be to hear something from my
Lohengrin played to me by a good orchestra! Confess
that I know how to bear much.

My nerves are not in the best condition, but I have

begun again to work at my poem for an hour or so every day. I can find no rest till it is ready, and I hope it will be soon.

Farewell, best of all men. Let me hear from you soon, and before all that you still love me. Farewell.

Wholly thine,

RICHARD WAGNER.

ZURICH, *October 3rd*, 1852.

About the *Dutchman* I must write to you at length some day. Have you forgotten the *Faust* overture and the designs for *Lohengrin* for which I asked you ?

86.

You are quite right, dearest friend, if you attribute the weakness of Berlioz's mode of working to the poem, and my opinion perfectly coincides with yours on this point ; but you have been erroneously led to believe that Berlioz is rewriting his *Cellini*. This is not the case ; the question at issue is simply as to a very considerable cut—nearly a whole tableau—which I have proposed to Berlioz, and which he has approved of, so that at the next performance *Cellini* will be given in three tableaux instead of four. If it interests you, I will send you the new libretto together with the old, and I think you will approve of the change and of the combination of the two last tableaux in one. I thank you cordially for your offer to let Berlioz have *Wiland*, and shall talk to him about it on the occasion of his presence in Weymar. Unfortunately it must be feared that the Parisians will not relish it, and Henri Blaze is in any case not the man who could treat such a subject in a poetic manner and do justice to it. Above all, dearest, best friend, do not imagine that I could place a bad construction on any utterance of yours about one man or the other. My sympathy for you and my admiration of your divine genius are surely too earnest and genuine to let me overlook their necessary consequences. You can and must not be different from what you are; and such as you are, I esteem, understand, and love you with my whole heart.

Your *Faust* overture you will receive by to-day's post. A copy of it exists here, and I shall probably give it again in the course of this winter. The work is quite worthy of you; but if you will allow me to make a remark, I must confess that I should like either a second middle part (at letter E or F) or else a quieter and more agreeably coloured treatment of the present middle part :—

The brass is a little too massive there, and—forgive my opinion—the motive in F is not satisfactory; it wants *grace* in a certain sense, and is a kind of hybrid thing, neither fish nor flesh, which stands in no proper relation or contrast to what has gone before and what follows, and in consequence impedes the interest. If instead of this you introduced a soft, tender, melodious part, modulated *à la* Gretchen, I think I can assure you that your work would gain very much. Think this over, and do not be angry in case I have said something stupid.

Lohengrin was given last night in honour of the
Prince and Princess of Prussia. The theatre was
again crowded, and Fräulein Fromann, who had
been specially invited by the Princess, has probably
written to you about it. Our further performances of
Lohengrin and of *Tannhäuser* will greatly benefit by the
influence of our new artistic director, Herr Marr. I
have given him your pamphlet about the performance
of *Tannhäuser*, and we shall both do our best to satisfy
your demands. I am very glad you have published that
pamphlet, and advise you strongly to do the same thing
for *Lohengrin* and the *Flying Dutchman*. I have not yet
succeeded in discovering your designs and instructions
for *Lohengrin* ; I gave them at the time to Genast, and
they made the round of the theatre here. If possible, I
shall send them to you, but I can make no definite
promise, for the rage for autographs may have gone so
far that I shall not be able to get them back again.

Concerning Berlin, I repeat to you what I said
before, viz. :—

If you are convinced that I can be of service to the
public and still more to your works by my presence in
Berlin, I am prepared to perform this duty of art and
of friendship. My efforts, however, can lead to a good
result only if Herr von Hülsen gives me his perfect
confidence and asks me to settle the necessary steps for
the rehearsals and performance of *Tannhäuser*. As
mouche du coche I cannot go to Berlin, and should in
that capacity be of little service to you. Your works,
it is true, are above *success* as at present understood,
but I will bet ten to one that *Tannhäuser* or *Lohengrin*,
rehearsed and placed before the public in a proper

manner, will have the most decided success. Wherever this does not happen the fault lies exclusively with the inadequate performance. If, therefore, you wish to send me to Berlin as your plenipotentiary, I am at your disposal, and give you my word that the whole world, with the exception of envious and inimical persons, who will be reduced to a small minority, shall be content. But before I consent to this it is absolutely necessary that Herr von Hülsen should give me an invitation to Berlin black on white, and also invest me with the powers which my responsibility will make possible and desirable. In my opinion, it behoves Berlin to find room for your three works *Tannhäuser*, *Lohengrin*, and the *Flying Dutchman*, and I have not the slightest doubt of a complete success if the thing is managed properly. Herr von Hülsen will, no doubt, be of the same opinion soon ; but in the ordinary way and with the old theatrical routine an extraordinary thing of this kind cannot be done.

Send me soon your instructions for the *Flying Dutchman*. I should like you to write a few lines to Marr, so as to gain his goodwill completely for your cause and to induce him to undertake the stage-management of the *Flying Dutchman*. Eduard Devrient paid me a visit last month. We talked a great deal about you, and I hope he will do something useful in Carlsruhe later on.

You are good enough to ask for some of my compositions, but you must allow me to delay this communication till we meet. I hope to visit you, unless you visit Weymar next summer, and shall then play many things to you.

Of my orchestral pieces I might sooner or later send you *Prometheus*, but would rather not think of it till I have done other things. Unfortunately I have been much detained from working latterly, but I shall not tell you of my pains and sorrows; you have more than enough of your own. Let us stand bolt upright and trust in God. When shall I have your poems? How long do you think that the four scores will approximately occupy you? Can you expect to be ready by the end of 1854?

Of a Paris performance of *Tannhäuser* we must not think for the present; and extraordinary as is my confidence in your extraordinary work (although personally I like *Lohengrin* still better), I cannot fail to take into account my experience of operatic performances in Paris and to think that the incompatibility of *Tannhäuser* with the operatic tricks now in vogue might interfere with its success. Germany, first of all, must take the lead, for you have the advantage and the misfortune of being an arch-German poet and composer. As far as I know your works, I still think that *Rienzi* would be most adapted for a French version, but do not vainly trouble your mind about it. Write your *Nibelungen*, and care about nothing else. All other things will arrange themselves of their own accord when the time comes.

Farewell, and be as happy as I wish you to be with all my heart.

Your

F. Liszt.

Weymar, *October 7th,* 1852.

87.

My Dearest, Best-beloved Friend,

For your last letter, and especially for your remark about the *Faust* overture (which has delighted me!), I owe you a regular long letter, and must wait till I am in a good mood for it; for I know that only in that case my answer can give you real pleasure. To-day I write you two hurried lines to say that I have accepted your generous offer and, relying upon your kindness, have asked Herr von Hülsen in a decided manner that you should be invited to Berlin to take my place at the performance of *Tannhäuser.* I have, I think, left nothing untried in order to induce Hülsen to get over any possible difficulties in connection with his own conductors there; I have made it a matter of personal feeling between him and me, just as it is between you and me. I hope that if Hülsen consents, his invitation will find you in a good and favourable mood. I know how great this new sacrifice is which I expect of you and how difficult you will find it to make but your friendship makes me venture upon anything. Hülsen, who probably will not write to me himself, is to answer me through you; and you also must tell me that you do it willingly for my sake.

Of the great success of *Tannhäuser* at Breslau you have probably heard.

But no more to-day. Weary as I am, I should only produce halting things.

Soon I shall write better and more.

My best regards to H. Farewell, and do not lose your temper with   Your old plague,

Zurich, *October 13th,* 1852.   Richard Wagner.

88.

MY DEAR FRIEND,

I have to write to you, and am so annoyed about what I have to write to you that I would rather not take pen in hand any more. Hülsen has declined; I enclose his letter. He has no notion of what the matter is about, and it will never be possible to give him a notion of it. This Hülsen is personally a well-disposed man, but without any knowledge of the business under his care. He treats with me about *Tannhäuser* just as he might with Flotow about *Martha*. It is too disgusting. I see fully that I have made a great mistake. From the beginning I ought to have made it the first and sole condition that everything concerning the performance of *Tannhäuser* should be left wholly and entirely to *you*. I can explain to myself how it happened that I did not hit upon this simple method: The first news from Berlin about *Tannhäuser* only frightened me. I had no confidence in anything there, and my instinct advised me to decline the thing altogether. It is true that you occurred to me at once as my only guarantee, but I had first to secure your consent to undertake *Tannhäuser* in Berlin. In order, as it were, to gain time, I sent to Berlin the demand for 1,000 thalers, so as to keep them going, and at the same time I applied to you, with the urgent, impetuous question whether you would see to this matter. Simultaneously with your answer in the affirmative I received from Berlin the news of the delay and postponement of *Tannhäuser* till the new year. Being under the impression that my niece would leave Berlin at the beginning of February, I thought the *Tannhäuser* performance

would have to be given up altogether, and instructed
my brother to get the score back unless Hülsen could
guarantee me *ten* performances this winter. I thought
the matter ended, when I was told in reply that my
niece would stay till the end of May and that Hülsen
would undertake to announce the opera six times during
the first month. Thus the possibility of a performance
of *Tannhäuser* at Berlin, wholly given up by me, was
once more restored.

From all the letters of Hülsen and my brother I
could in the meantime see perfectly well that these people
were without any understanding of what was to me
essential and important in this matter; that in all their
views they were so totally incapable of leaving the
grooves of *routine* that I should have to fear they would
never understand my desire to invite you to Berlin.
I confess that I had some anxiety on the point, but
at last I wrote to Hülsen myself as clearly, warmly,
cordially, and persuasively as was in my power; I at
once called his attention to the fact that the hostility of
the very insignificant Berlin conductors would be as nothing compared with the favourable influence which you
would exercise on every side ; in short, I wrote in such
a manner that I could not believe in the possibility of
an unfavourable answer. Read that answer, and take
notice that I have once more met with my usual fate:
the fate of calling out to the world with my whole soul
and of having my calls echoed by walls of leather. I
am now discussing with myself what I shall do. To
give up everything and simply demand my score back
—that would be most agreeable to me. As yet I
have not replied with a line to either Hülsen or X.

What do you think ?   Or shall I look on indifferently, amuse myself when I can make a hundred thalers, buy champagne, and turn my back upon the world ?   It is a *misery*.

I am going from bad to worse every day, and lead an *indescribably worthless* life.   Of real enjoyment of life I know nothing ; to me " enjoyment of life, of *love*," is a matter of imagination, not of experience.   In this manner my heart has to go to my brain, and my life becomes an artificial one ; only as an " artist" I can live ; in the artist my whole " man" has been sunk.

If I could visit *you* in Weimar and see a performance of my operas now and then, I might perhaps still hope to recover.   I should there find an element of incite-ment, of attraction for my artistic being ; perhaps a word of love would meet me now and then ;—but here !   Here I must perish in the very shortest space of time, and everything—everything will come *too late*, *too late* !   So it will be.

No news can give me pleasure any more ; if I were vain and ambitious, it would be all right ; as I am, nothing " written" can attract me.   All this comes—too late !

What shall I do ?   Shall I implore the King of Saxony, or perhaps his ministers, for mercy, humble myself, and confess my repentance ?   Who can expect *that* of me ?

You, my only one, the dearest whom I have, you who are to me prince and world, everything together, have mercy on me.

But calm ! calm !   I must write to you about the *Faust* overture.   You beautifully spotted the lie when

I tried to make myself believe that I had written an "Overture to *Faust*." You have felt quite justly what is wanting; the woman is wanting. Perhaps you would at once understand my tone-poem if I called it *Faust in Solitude*.

At that time I intended to write an entire *Faust* symphony; the first movement, that which is ready, was this "solitary Faust," longing, despairing, cursing. The "feminine" floats around him as an object of his longing, but not in its divine reality, and it is just this insufficient image of his longing which he destroys in his despair. The second movement was to introduce Gretchen, the woman. I had a theme for her, but it was only a theme. The whole remained unfinished. I wrote my *Flying Dutchman* instead. This is the whole explanation. If now, from a last remnant of weakness and vanity, I hesitate to abandon this *Faust* work altogether, I shall certainly have to remodel it, but only as regards instrumental modulation. The theme which you desire I cannot introduce ; this would naturally involve an entirely new composition, for which I have no inclination. If I publish it, I shall give it its proper title, *Faust in Solitude*, or *The Solitary Faust*, "a tone-poem for orchestra."

My new poems for the two Siegfrieds I finished last week, but I have still to rewrite the two earlier dramas, *Young Siegfried* and *Siegfried's Death*, as very considerable alterations have become necessary. I shall not have finished entirely before the end of the year. The complete title will be *The Ring of the Nibelung*, "a festival stage-play in three days and one previous evening : previous evening, *The Rhinegold*; first day, *The Valkyrie*; second day, *Young Siegfried*; third day, *Siegfried's Death*." What fate this poem, the poem of my life and of all that I am and feel, will have I cannot as yet determine. So much, however, is certain : that if Germany is not very soon opened to me, and if I am compelled to drag on my artistic existence without nourishment and attraction, my animal instinct of life will soon lead me to *abandon art* altogether. What I shall do then to support my life I do not know, but I shall not write the music of the *Nibelungen*, and no person with human feelings can ask me to remain the slave of my art any longer.

Alas ! I always relapse into the miserable key-note of this letter. Perhaps I commit a great brutality in this manner, for perhaps you are in need of being cheered up by me. Pardon me if to-day I bring nothing but sorrow. I can dissemble no longer ; and, let who will despise me, I shall cry out my sorrow to the world, and shall not conceal my misfortune any longer. What use would it be if I were to lie to you ? But of one thing you must think, if nothing else is possible : we must see each other next summer. Consider that this is a *necessity*; that it *must* be ; that no god shall prevent you from coming to me, as the police (make a low bow !) prevent me from coming to you. Promise me for quite certain in your next letter that you will come. Promise me !

We must see how I shall be able to exist till then.

Farewell. Bear with me. Greet H., and be of good cheer. Perhaps you will soon be rid of me.

Farewell, and write soon to

Your

RICHARD WAGNER.

ZURICH, *November 9th*, 1852.

89.

MY DEAR FRIEND,

I wait with great longing for a letter from you.

For to-day one *urgent* request. Send *at once* the scores of the *Dutchman* after which that of Weimar was corrected to Uhlig at Dresden. In Breslau they have very long been waiting for a copy to be arranged in the same manner. Please, please see to this *at once*. Next week you will receive my remarks on the performance of the *Flying Dutchman*. Farewell, and remember lovingly

Your

RICHARD WAGNER.

December 22nd, 1852.

90.

DEAREST FRIEND,

If through any delay the model score of the *Flying Dutchman* has not yet been sent to Dresden, these lines may serve to inform you of the great difficulty in which I have to-day been placed towards a second theatre—that of Schwerin—because I cannot supply it with the score which they urgently demand. I am truly sorry that I have to plague you with such "business matters;" but who else is there in Weimar?

I wait with indescribable longing for a letter from you. Farewell.

Wholly thine,

RICHARD WAGNER.

December 24th, 1852.

91.

December 27th, 1852.

Pardon me, dearest friend, for my long silence. That I can be so little to you and to your interests is a great grief to me. Your last letter, of about six weeks ago, has made your whole sorrow and misery clear to me. I have wept bitter tears over your pains and wounds. Suffering and patience are unfortunately the only remedies open to you. How sad for a friend to be able to say no more than this. Of all the sad and disagreeable things which I have to suffer I shall not speak to you; do not think of them either. To-day I will, before all, tell you something pleasant, viz., that I shall visit you in the course of next summer, probably in June. I shall not be able to stay in Zurich long, where there is nothing but you to attract me. It is possible—*but this must not yet be spoken of*—that on my way back I may conduct a kind of festival at Carlsruhe. Can you by that time prepare an orchestral work for the purpose? —perhaps your *Faust* overture—for I should like to produce a new work by you besides the *Tannhäuser* overture.

Eduard Devrient wrote to me some days ago that the Court Marshal, Count Leiningen, who is a friend of mine, had spoken to him of the plan for a musical festival, to be conducted by me. It may be predicted that considerable means will be at hand in Carlsruhe, but as yet the public and the papers are to know nothing of it. Write to me when convenient about some pieces which you could recommend for the programme. I think, amongst other things, of the *Missa Solemnis* (D major) by Beethoven, but should not like to have again the ninth symphony, so as not to repeat the Ballenstedt programme *in extenso.*

The rumour reported by several papers that I am about to leave Weymar and settle in Paris is quite unfounded. I stay here, and can do nothing but stay here. You will easily guess what has brought me to this maturely considered resolution. In the first instance I have faithfully to fulfil a serious duty. Together with this feeling of the most profound and constant love which occupies the faith of my whole soul, my external life must either rise or sink. May God protect my loyal intention.

How far have you got with your *Nibelungen*? It will be a great joy to me to grasp your creation through your immediate aid. For heaven's sake, let nothing distract you from this, and continue to *weld your wings* with steadfast courage!

All is perishable, only God's word remains for ever, and God's word is revealed in the creations of genius.

Yesterday your *Tannhäuser* was given apart from the subscription nights, before an *overcrowded* house. A new scene had been painted for the revised conclusion of the piece, and for the first time we have given the entire finale of the second act (a splendid, masterly finale!) and the entire prayer of Elizabeth in the third act without any cut. The effect was extraordinary, and I think you would have been pleased with the whole performance. I celebrated on this occasion a perfect triumph in your cause, for now that the success has been so decided, I may tell you candidly that no one here cared for the troublesome study of the finale or for the execution of the revised close, and that the talking backwards and forwards about the change lasted several months. "Why," it was said, "do we want a different *Tannhäuser* from the one we are accustomed to?" Several people who had seen *Tannhäuser* in Dresden declared decidedly that our performance was much better, and that it would lose by the new close and by the restoration of the entire finale, etc., etc. To all these excellent arguments I had but one answer: "For Weymar it is a duty to give Wagner's works when and as far as it is possible in accordance with the wishes and intentions of the composer."

And, behold! in spite of all the previous chatter, the decisive success of yesterday has been wholly in favour of my assertion.

Herr von Zigesar has to-day written to Tichatschek to ask him to sing *Lohengrin* here on February 26th, and has offered him a fee of fifty louis d'or, an unheard-of sum for Weymar. I sent Tichatschek the part soon after the first performance of *Lohengrin* here, and hope that he will give us the pleasure of complying with our request. I wish you could write to him direct on this matter, or else induce him to come here through Uhlig or Fischer.

With the performance of *Lohengrin* I am in parts
still very much dissatisfied. The chief evil lies, as you
say, in the as yet unborn representative of the chief
part. For the performance of February 26th a new
scene is being prepared for the second act, for the one
hitherto used is miserable. The question of cuts, as
you know, arose only in connection with the second
performance ; at the third I again produced the entire
work unmutilated. With Heine and Fischer, who
attended the last performance, I had much talk about
this glorious drama, to me the highest and most perfect
work of art. If Herr von Hülsen had invited me to
Berlin, I should probably have persuaded him to give
Lohengrin first ; and I repeat that in Berlin I will lay
any wager on the colossal success of *Lohengrin*, provided it is given faithfully and enthusiastically, to do
which would not be excessively difficult in Berlin with
goodwill and true understanding.

That Herr von Hülsen hesitates to call me to Berlin
does not surprise me, but as you have honoured me
with your confidence, I am sorry I cannot justify it
in a brilliant manner. During his last visit here the
Prince of Prussia spoke to me about my participation
in the study of *Lohengrin* at Berlin. The Prince has
a high opinion of you as a poet and musician, and
seems to take an interest in the success of your
works at Berlin. Beyond this I can unfortunately
have no influence in the matter, and must quietly
wait to see how they are going to cook up *Tannhäuser*
there. In any case do not trouble yourself about the
future and contemplate the course of events in an
objective mood. When you hear particulars about

the *Tannhäuser* performances at Berlin, write to me, for I hear from time to time the most contradictory rumours of *pourparlers*.

Have you received the book about *Tannhäuser* by X. ? The dedication was quite unexpected to me, because for several months I have not had the old friendly intercourse with the author. I shall, however, call on him to-morrow, and am quite willing to forget many disagreeable things which he has caused me for your sake. The *Flying Dutchman* will go to Uhlig to-morrow. I was unable to send it sooner, because the copying here is done with the most troublesome slowness. It is therefore no fault of mine that this return has been delayed so long, for I have pushed it on every day. The two first pianoforte rehearsals of the *Flying Dutchman* I have already held, and can guarantee a successful performance on February 16th. After the second on the 20th *Tannhäuser* is to be given, and on the 26th *Lohengrin* will follow. Let me ask you once more to persuade Tichatschek not to leave us in the lurch at the latter. I have special hopes for this performance of *Lohengrin*, and should not like to let it be spoiled on account of our small means. I can assure you, however, that the interest of the public in *Lohengrin* is in the ascendant; at every performance the strangers in our theatre increase in number, and you are very popular at the various hotels in Weymar, for on the days when one of your operas is performed it is not easy to find a room.

One other favour. I have recently made a pianoforte arrangement of the *Tannhäuser* march and of the wedding procession (I don't know how to name the

piece) in the second act of *Lohengrin* (E flat major),
and should like to publish these two pieces.   Tell me
whether Meser has still the copyright of the melodies
of *Tannhäuser*, and whether I must ask his permission
to publish this piece, together with the other from
Lohengrin, with Härtel.   As Kistner has already printed
the *Evening Star*, I do not anticipate any particular
difficulty in letting Härtel publish the *Tannhäuser*
march ; at the same time, I should like to be safe
from any possible discussion afterwards, and therefore
inquire of you how the matter stands.

Joachim goes on the 1st of January to Hanover as
concert-master.   A very able violinist, Ferdinand Laub,
has been engaged for our orchestra.

I am glad that my marginal notes to your *Faust*
overture have not displeased you.   In my opinion, the
work would gain by a few *elongations*.

Härtel will willingly undertake the printing; and if
you will give me particular pleasure, make me a present
of the manuscript when it is no longer wanted for the
engraving.   This overture has lain with me so long,
and I have taken a great fancy to it.   If, however, you
have disposed of it otherwise, do not mind me in the
least, and give me some day another manuscript.

Au revoir then in a few months !   I look forward to
the moment with joy.   My pen is getting too horribly
blunt to write to you.   One single chord brings us
nearer to each other than any number of phrases :—

Continue to love me, even as I am cordially devoted to you.

F. L.

Your pamphlet on the rendering of *Tannhäuser* I have read with much interest, and, let us hope, with some benefit for our representations. I am glad to see that in several indications of tempo I had guessed your meaning, and that many of your intentions had been realised here in advance. H. will soon write to you about yesterday's performance.

92.

BEST OF FRIENDS,

Have not in your version the overture and *the close of the last finale* of the *Flying Dutchman* been rearranged in accordance with a special score written by me last year? The close of the overture especially has been entirely changed in the instrumentation. The score containing *this* change *I sent a year ago to Uhlig*, and he wrote to me that he had sent it to Weimar, together with a *second* score containing the changes in the remainder of the instrumentation. Please ask H. B.; you *must* have received two scores. Look also in *your* score at the theatre. If in that the close of the overture has been considerably changed, and if especially at page 43 a new bar has been inserted, then your score must have been arranged after that *second* one sent to you, and the model copy *must* still be with you, for in the Dresden score the close of the overture had been only very slightly changed (a little in the violins). Two things I have to ask you: if the *second* score is with you, send it *at once* to Dresden, addressed to Choir director W. Fischer; if it does not exist at Weimar, Uhlig having forgotten to send it to you, and if therefore in your score at the theatre the *close* of the overture has not been changed *much* (in the instrumentation), and no *new bar* inserted at page 43, then let Fischer know at once, so that he may send you the materials for making this important alteration. I shall send him the score which is at the theatre *here*, and in which I hope the matter has been corrected.

To your most important kind letter recently received I shall soon send an answer which, I hope, will please you. To-day only this business in great haste.

Farewell.

Ever thine,

RICHARD WAGNER.

ZURICH, *January 8th*, 1853.

93.

DEAREST FRIEND,

After many inquiries, thoughts, and searches the affair of the *Flying Dutchman* scores has turned out to be as follows :—

The score containing the corrected close of the overture and of the finale of the opera is the same which you left me here as a present. I never thought of using it for our performance, and therefore wrote to Uhlig (whose death has affected H. and me painfully) shortly before his death that he had made a mistake in demanding back two theatre scores, as one of them we necessarily required here, while the other had already been returned to him. Uhlig does not seem to have

known that one of the three scores which were here
for some time was my personal property; and I, on
my part, could not admit his justification in describing my copy as a score belonging to the theatre. The
confusion which had previously happened in connection
with the *Dutchman* score, sent from and returned to
Dresden, made me assume that Uhlig had made a
second mistake. Your letter to-day explains the matter;
and I promise you that by to-morrow evening the
theatre score shall be carefully corrected after my copy,
and that my copy, containing the newly corrected close
of the overture, etc., will be sent to Fischer the day
after to-morrow. You need not trouble yourself about
it, and may dispose of this score as you like.

Kindly excuse these delays. Musikdirektor Götze,
who had to make these alterations in the score, has
been much detained from his work, and only your letter
explained the matter to me in the sense that you wish
to dispose of my copy, which is cordially at your service.   *Nunc et semper.*

Your truly devoted

F. LISZT.

January 12th, 1853.

Your remarks about the rendering of the *Flying
Dutchman* have safely reached me, and I have already
communicated them to the singers. Farewell, and be
God's blessing upon you.

94.

MY DEAR LISZT,

The real answer to your last great letter you do
not receive to-day; I hold it over for a good reason.

But I must tell you something at once. Yesterday I heard from my niece at Berlin that *Tannhäuser* there could not be thought of for the present, because the *Feensee* and Flotow's *Indra* had first to be given. (The last thing that Hülsen had said was that *Tannhäuser* should be put in rehearsal after the Queen's birthday, November 13th, 1852.) I have let them know that I look upon this cavalier treatment as an insult, and consider all previous transactions finished, demanding at the same time the immediate return of my score. This has eased my heart, and by Hülsen's fault I have been released from all previous concessions.

Now, dearest friend, comes the principal thing. I accept your generous offer, and place all my further relations with Berlin in *your* hands. Hülsen may reply to me what he likes ; he may offer to produce " *Tannhäuser* " *at once*. I am determined to answer that in my present condition I am unable to take a leading part in so important a matter as the performance of my operas at Berlin, and that therefore I refer him *once for all*, and concerning *everything* in connection with the performance of my works at Berlin, to *you*, who have unlimited power to do or leave undone in my name what seems good to you. Let it be settled in this way, and I ask you to act in the matter quite according to your own opinion. I should think it most advisable if you had nothing further to do with Hülsen, who is merely an instrument without a will of his own. You will, I think, prefer to keep up communication solely with the Prince and Princess of Prussia. I was very glad to learn that even the Prince of Prussia understood at once that your *personal direc-*

tion was inseparable from an important performance of my operas.

This then is the only basis on which a performance, be it of *Tannhäuser* or of *Lohengrin*, will henceforth be possible in Berlin. Without your direction I should not consent to such a performance, even if you were to ask me. Our motto therefore must be " Patience ! "

It is true that the hope of good receipts for next Easter had made me a little soft towards the Berlin project. Lord knows, I poor devil, should have liked to have a few thousand francs in my pocket, so as to divert my thoughts and cure myself of my terrible melancholy by a journey to Paris or Italy. However, I must bear this and remain in my old state of *resignation* and *want*. For all that I thus remain in want of, the unspeakable joy of seeing YOU at last in the summer will compensate me; believe me, THAT will make up for all.

But let us stick to the point. Time will be needed, but perhaps you will succeed in obtaining through the Prince and Princess for next winter the invitation and commission to perform my *two* last operas in Berlin. You will then probably begin with *Tannhäuser*. This would appear to me a more natural order of things : perhaps in the first half of the season *Tannhäuser* and soon afterwards *Lohengrin*. It is true that you cannot count upon my niece, who will be in Paris next winter. But there is little harm in this, for Elizabeth is not of the first importance, and as regards *Lohengrin* I am in a dilemma which it would perhaps be difficult to solve. Six years ago I intended Elsa for my niece ; now she would have served me better as Ortrud.

Therefore—just as you decide ; I am content with

everything. From this day I shall have no further transactions with Berlin.

The Leipzig people also have eaten humble-pie; they have capitulated to me through Härtel. The performance there will probably take place soon. Could you occasionally look after it a little?

At Frankfort they will begin next Saturday. The conductor writes to me that he hopes for a good success. We shall see.

I have written to Lüttichau and asked him not to perform *Lohengrin* at present, because I have not sufficient confidence in any of his conductors.

I am sorry to say I cannot write to T. He is very angry with me on account of my instructions for the rendering of *Tannhäuser*. Of course he cannot understand me.

Do arrange that about the close of the overture to the *Flying Dutchman*. In case the *one* score should have been lost (a rather serious loss to me), let Fischer know, and he will send the new close to you; but do not give the overture without this change.

Herewith I send you another alteration; you will see where it belongs. The effect of the brass and the kettledrums was too coarse, too material; the spectator should be terror-struck by the cry of Senta on seeing the Dutchman, not by kettledrum and brass. God bless you. You will soon have news from me again.

Farewell, and remember kindly your

RICHARD WAGNER.

ZURICH, *January* 13*th*, 1853.

95.

DEAREST FRIEND,

I cannot thank you for your more than royal present otherwise than by accepting it with the deepest, most heartfelt joy. You are best able to feel yourself how I was affected by the receipt of your splendid presents, how I greeted the three scores with plentiful tears. The Florentines carried the Madonna of Cimabue round the city in triumphal procession, amidst the ringing of bells. I wish it were given to me to arrange a similar festival for your works. In the meantime the three scores will repose in a particular niche near me ; and when I come to see you, I will tell you more.

First of all, the three works must be performed here in a proper manner. All the changes in the score of the *Flying Dutchman* have been carefully copied into the parts, and I shall not forget the *pizzicato* you sent last.

Tichatschek has accepted Zigesar's offer, but Lüttichau cannot give him leave for the end of February. In consequence we must wait for another opportunity, and Beck will sing Lohengrin and Tannhäuser. Brendel and some other papers will probably notice these performances. The *Flying Dutchman* presents no great difficulties to our well-drilled artists, and I look forward to a better performance, comparatively speaking, than of either *Tannhäuser* or *Lohengrin*. The latter, however, goes much better than at the four first performances, and upon the whole one need not be dissatisfied. By the middle of May the newly engaged tenor, Dr. Liebert, will arrive here, and I shall not fail to study the three parts properly with him and to sing them to him. I hear that he has a splendid voice and the best intention to join in our movement.

Till the end of May I must in any case remain in Weymar, much as I long to see you again. The wedding festivities for the marriage of Princess Amalie (daughter of Duke Bernhard, brother of our Grand Duke) with Prince Henry of the Netherlands (brother of the reigning King of Holland and of our Hereditary Grand Duchess) are to take place in May, when probably *Lohengrin* or *Tannhäuser* will be given again, besides a grand orchestral concert in the hall of the castle.

The honorarium for the *Flying Dutchman* you will receive immediately after the first performance (about February 20th). How about Berlin? Has Hülsen replied to your last letter, and to what effect? In case the whole matter is settled, as you indicate to me, you may wholly rely and count upon me. Your annoyance at the delay of the performance of *Tannhäuser* is quite comprehensible; and, in my opinion, you were right in demanding back the score. Whether they will comply with your demand is a different question. We must now see how we can achieve our purpose in the quietest and safest manner. I need not repeat to you that I desire with all my heart to justify the honour of your confidence, but I earnestly hope that I shall be able to prove this practically as soon as possible.

Once more I thank you with all my soul, and remain immutably

Your sincerely devoted

F. Liszt.

96

My Dearest Friend,

Herewith you receive a whole heap of new stuff. You perceive that my poem is ready, and although not yet set to music, at least set in type, and printed at my own expense, and in a few copies only, which I shall present to my friends, so that they may have my legacy in advance in case I should die during the work. He who knows my position will again think me very extravagant in the face of this luxurious edition; let it be so; the world, properly so called, is so stingy towards me, that I do not care to imitate it. Therefore, with a kind of anxious pleasure, I have secretly (in order not to be prevented by prudent counsel) prepared this edition the particular tendency of which you will find stated in an introductory notice. Only a few copies have been struck off, and I send you herewith a parcel of them, asking you to dispose of them in the following manner. Of the three copies in a *de luxe* binding you must accept the *first* as a present from me. The *second* I have destined for the Grand Duchess on her birthday. Tell her I have heard that she is indisposed and will probably be unable to appear on her birthday in public. As therefore she will not hear the *Flying Dutchman* at the theatre, I ask her to cast a glance at my latest work. Tell her that, if it did not please her throughout, I still thought I might assure her that *woman* had never yet received such a tribute as every one who understood it must find in my poem. The *third* copy *de luxe* forward to the Princess of Prussia. Fortunately I have been able to get the type, printing, and binding done in good time, and I assume therefore that you will be in a position to present the gift on the 16th. Of the other copies sent herewith, I ask you to keep two in your own possession to lend them out according to your discretion, and you will oblige me particularly by thinking soon of A. Stahr, to whom I wish to be kindly remembered. He was the first littérateur who ever paid attention to me as a poet. A *third* copy please to forward in my name, with cordial greeting, to Herr von Zigesar. Apart from this I send the following parcels :—

1. For B., containing two copies : one for himself, the other for my poor friend Roeckel.

2. For Herr F. M., whose title I have unfortunately forgotten, and my answer to whom, in return for his kind present, I have held over till to-day.

3. For A. F., who has just written to me that she is going to Weimar for the festival ; kindly give the parcel to her as to the others.

If you further find that you can dispose of some other copies where they will be well and thankfully received, kindly let me know soon ; for that and similar emergencies I have kept back a small number of copies.

About the poem itself I cannot, and do not care to, say anything more to you ; when you find leisure to read it sympathetically, you will say to yourself all that I could tell you. I shall never again write poetry.

But I am looking forward with much delight to setting
all this to music. As to form, it is quite ready in my
mind, and I was never before so determined as to
musical execution as I am now and with regard to this
poem. All I want is sufficient *charm of life* to get into
the indispensable cheerful mood from which motives
spring forth gladly and spontaneously. As to this I
once before made bitter moan to you ; I desired
salvation from the killing circumstances in which I am
placed at Zurich; I inquired as to the possibility of
being permitted to make a trip to Germany now and
then, so as to witness a performance of my works,
because otherwise I should perish here for want of
encouragement. To your great grief, your answer had
to be in the negative, and you admonished me to have
—patience.

Dear, noble friend, consider that patience is only just
sufficient to preserve bare life, but that the vigour and
fulness which enable one to enrich life and employ it
creatively no man has ever yet drawn from patience,
i.e., from absolute *want*. Neither can I succeed in this.
Listen to me ! You are very reticent as to the point in
question. Let me know whether anything has been
done from Weimar in order to obtain for me at Dresden
permission to return to Germany, also what impediments
have been found in the way. If everything has not
already been tried, I should make the following suggestion : The Weimar court invites me to visit Weimar for
a few weeks, and sends me a passport for four weeks ;
it then inquires, through its minister at Dresden,
whether they object, and would be likely to demand my
extradition to Saxony. If the answer were satisfactory

—somewhat to this effect: that the prosecution instituted against me four years ago would be suspended for that short time—I might be with you very quickly, hear my *Lohengrin*, and then return straight to Switzerland and wait for *your visit* (I might also read my poem at court). See what can be done in this. I must hear *Lohengrin* ; I will not and cannot write music before.

The German theatres do not cause me much delight ; there is a hitch everywhere, and I confess candidly that I often feel great repentance at having consented to any performance outside Weimar. Even two years ago I was conscious of myself, clear, and firm, while I allowed myself no thought of the further expansion of my work. Now I am torn to pieces, wavering, uncertain, and exposed to every breath of wind, because I have to read now one thing, now another, but never an intelligent judgment about my works in the newspapers. I am much lowered in my own eyes. How disgustingly dirty was again this Leipzig affair ! The manager makes sacrifices, enlarges the orchestra, reconstructs the same, etc. ; he hopes soon to recover his outlay, and raises the prices as for an extraordinary thing ; the enthusiastic public—stops away and leaves the second performance empty. Oh, how different I am from such *canaille* ! But what a bad, disgusting scandal this is ! I am never to enjoy my life again.

You thought the score would not be returned to me from Berlin at my demand ; this time you were mistaken. The score was returned at once, and neither from Hülsen nor from any one else have I had a line about it. Disgusting as such conduct is, showing as it does how they felt in Berlin towards *Tannhäuser*

I must yet be glad at this issue, first because it proves
that in such circumstances the opera, if it had been
performed, would have been lost, and second because
now *tabula rasa* has been made, and everything has been
committed to your faithful care.   The Berlin affair has
herewith taken an entirely new form ; no obligation
exists, and your hand is henceforth perfectly free, provided that I may place the matter once for all in your
hands, while I have no longer anything to concede or
refuse, and am towards Berlin as one of the dead.
Cassel has asked for the score of *Tannhäuser*, and
there, I presume, the matter ends ; I do not count upon
any other theatre.   I can now therefore sum up my
gain from this glorious undertaking ; very slender it is,
and I must thank God that the R. family continue to
assist me.   Otherwise I should (after buying a few
commodities for house and body, of which we were
very short) have reached once more the bare rock of
my existence, and this through the noble sympathy of
that splendid Germany.

I have no hopes at all for the further spreading of
my operas.   To theatres like those of Munich and others
I should have to refuse them, because the conductors
there would have nothing better to do than to ruin me
thoroughly.   Once more I have to regret that I yielded
to a sanguine hope.

How long I shall endure this terrible joylessness I cannot tell.   About the middle of last month, I was on the
point of succumbing, and thought that I should soon have
to follow my poor Uhlig.   I was persuaded to call in a
doctor, and he, a careful, considerate, and conscientious
man, takes much trouble with me.   He visits me nearly

every other day, and I cannot but approve of his treatment. Certain it is that if I do not recover, it will not be *his* fault. The isolation of my position is too great; all my social intercourse has died away; I was fated to survive and cast from me everything. I stand in a desert, and feed on my own vitals; I *must* perish. Some people will be sorry for this one day, perhaps even the King of Saxony.

What nonsense am I talking! Let us leave it alone; we cannot alter it; it has always been so.

Much luck to the *Flying Dutchman*! This melancholy hero is never out of my head. I always hear

"Ach möch-test Du, blei-cher See-mann sie fin-den!"

With the

"Doch kann dem blei-chen Manne Er-lö-sung ein-sten noch wer-den!"

all is over. For me there is no salvation but *death*. Would that it found me in a storm at sea, not on a sick-bed! Yea, in the fire of Valhall I should like to perish. Consider well my new poem; it contains the beginning and the end of the world.

I shall have to set it to music, after all, for the Jews of Frankfort and Leipzig; it will just suit them.

But stop; my epistle is getting wild and wilder; therefore I must conclude. Adieu, my Franciscus, the first and only one who stands before me like the heart of a giant! You indefatigable one, farewell. When they play the ballad to-morrow, think of me. I am sitting alone on the sofa, staring at the lamp and brooding over my good fortune in having gained *you* from this miserable world. Yes, yes, it is that which supports me.

Farewell, my friend. My affectionate regards to you !

Your

RICHARD WAGNER.

ZURICH, *February 11th,* 1853.

97.

BEST OF FRIENDS,

H. sent you yesterday a long account of the first performance of the *Flying Dutchman.* The rendering was satisfactory, and the reception such as I had reason to expect—decidedly warm and sympathetic. The two Mildes did their very best to give to the parts of the Dutchman and of Senta their full significance, and they were completely successful. The overture raged and crashed superbly, so that, in spite of the usual custom not to applaud on the fête-day of the Grand Duchess, they clapped their hands and called "Bravo !" with enthusiasm. Our orchestra is now on a good footing; and as soon as the five or six new engagements which I have proposed have been made, it may boast of being one of the most excellent in Germany.

Enclosed I send you the honorarium for the score of the *Flying Dutchman,* about which Herr von Zigesar has also written to you yesterday. At the performance of the day before yesterday the following princely personages, strangers here, were present: the Duke of Coburg, the Duke of Mecklenburg-Schwerin and his wife, Prince Charles of Prussia, the Hereditary Prince

of Meiningen and his wife, Princess Charlotte of
Prussia, the son of the Prince of Prussia, heir-pre-
sumptive to the throne, the Prince of Sondershausen;
also several ambassadors from Dresden, General
Wrangel, and Prince Pükler-Muskau.

In a few weeks the King of Saxony is expected
here.

Write to me soon what titles I am to give to the
Tannhäuser march and the *Lohengrin* procession
(E flat, Act II.), which I have arranged for H. for
drawing-room use. H. has forwarded you two letters:
one from Count Tichkiewitz, who is said to be a
passionate admirer of your genius (he wrote to me
soon after the appearance of my *Lohengrin* article a
very enthusiastic letter, and has now caused the
Tannhäuser overture to be played at Posen; his
family belongs to the higher aristocracy of Poland);
the other letter, from S. in H., I merely wanted to
communicate to you without wishing to influence your
decision in this matter. I made the acquaintance of
S. in Weymar in a very casual manner . . . and . . .
so on. . . .

I call your special attention to the postscript with
regard to Gotha which H. has added to his letter of
yesterday by my desire.

The time has not yet come for explaining the details
of this matter to you, and probably nothing further will
come of it. In any case I ask you, if they should
apply to you direct from Coburg-Gotha, to give me
exclusive power to carry on this little transaction,
without troubling you with it.

My most cordial thanks to you, best of friends, for

all the pleasure your *Dutchman* gives me; this summer
we will have another chat about it.   Write soon to

>Your faithful
>
>F. LISZT.

WEYMAR, *February 18th,* 1853.

98.

DEAREST FRIEND,

 I have just received the incredible news from
the Prague manager that, after the censorship had
authorised the performance of *Tannhäuser,* permission
was suddenly withdrawn by a higher personage, in
other words that the opera was forbidden.   There
must surely be some personal stupidity at work here.
I should like to assist the man; and thinking it over,
I hit—as I always do when there is need—on you.
You have influence everywhere, and, as far as I know,
can say a word to some very influential persons at
Vienna.   Kindly consider to whom you could apply,
so as to win over some one who would interest himself
in the withdrawal of this absurd prohibition.   If it is
not too much trouble, I ask you specially to arrange
this also for me.   You can do so many things.

 Adieu, dearest!   Shall I soon hear from you?

>Your
>
>RICHARD WAGNER.

February 19th, 1853.

 At Riga, in Russia, the performance has been permitted.

99.

 You are truly a wonderful man, and your
Nibelungen poem is surely the most incredible thing

which you have ever done. As soon as the three performances of the *Flying Dutchman, Tannhäuser,* and
Lohengrin are over I shall lock myself in for a few
days to read the four poems; as yet I have been unable
to get a free hour for it. Excuse me therefore for not
saying more to-day than that I rejoice in the joy which
the printed copies have given to you.

The one intended for the Grand Duchess I have
presented to her, and that for the Princess of Prussia
I have given to her brother, the Hereditary Grand
Duke. The others also have been forwarded to their
respective owners. If it is possible, send me about
three copies more; I can make good use of them.

Your letter I have not put on the shelf, and hope to
be able in about six weeks to give you a definite and
(D.V.) a favourable answer concerning your return.
I am extremely sorry that hitherto I have had to be so
"*reticent,*" but you may be sure that I have not omitted
to do all that appeared to me opportune and was in my
power. Unfortunately I have nothing but very timid
hopes; still they are hopes, and all timidity and lukewarmness must be far from me in my endeavour to
gain you back for yourself. Rely upon my warmest
friendly love in this as in other matters.

The Berlin affair you have arranged in the best
possible manner, and it is probable that, if henceforth
you leave it entirely to me, you will be satisfied with
the final result. Whether *Tannhäuser* and *Lohengrin*
are given in Berlin a year sooner or later matters little
to you; the chief question is *how* and in what manner
they are given: and as long as you are not back in
Germany, I believe that in our actual musical cir-

cumstances I can offer you the only perfect security on this point. Moreover, Berlin is the *most important* field for your works, and on the success of those works there your whole position depends in the most decisive manner. However, the performances at Frankfort, Breslau, Schwerin, Leipzig, etc., are in themselves very desirable, because they keep the matter warm and facilitate the conquest of Berlin. They have also tended to place the artistic question which has arisen through your means in a clearer light than was previously possible.

Before all, regain your health, dearest friend. We shall soon take some walks together, for which you will want good steady legs. I do not mean to drink *tisane* with you at Zurich; therefore you must take care that I do not find you a hospital patient. The Prague affair can, I hope, be arranged, and I am willingly at your service. A very reasonable and intelligent man, whom I used to know very well at Lemberg, Herr von Sacher, is now commandant of Prague, and I shall apply to him in this matter. Write to me at once, by return of post, from what quarter and when the prohibition of the *Tannhäuser* performance was issued, and send me the letter of the Prague manager, so that I may be able to explain the matter properly. Apart from this, I can knock at another door in Prague.

But, before all, I must be more accurately informed of the actual state of things.

Your

F. Liszt.

Weymar, *February 20th,* 1853.

The Princess read your *Ring of the Nibelung* the first

day from beginning to end, and is full of enthusiasm for it.

100.

BEST OF FRIENDS,

Please let me have two words to say *whether you have received a parcel, sent from here on February 11th, and containing several copies of my new poem, " The Ring of the Nibelung."*

I had hoped that it would reach you before the 16th, but your letter makes no mention of it. I am very anxious about this, because it has spoiled a great pleasure to me. Therefore one word, please! If it has not arrived, I must apply for it at the post-office.

All the rest I shall answer later on.

Your

R. W.

ZURICH, *February 28th,* 1853.

101.

MY DEAR FRIEND,

I send you to-day, immediately on receipt of your kind letter, the epistle from the Prague manager announcing the prohibition of my *Tannhäuser.* This is all I know of the matter. It would be an excellent thing if you could succeed in having this interdict withdrawn. It annoys me specially on account of the manager, who in the whole affair has behaved energetically and charmingly. We should both be very grateful to you.

In order not to forget your question as to the titles, I will answer it at once, as best I can. Nothing occurs to me but "Two Pieces from *Tannhäuser* and *Lohengrin*."

1. Entrance of the guests at Wartburg.
2. Elsa's bridal progress to the minster.

This, in my opinion, would best indicate the character of the pieces in accordance with the events represented. I am looking forward to your pianoforte arrangement of these pieces in the ingenious manner peculiar to you ; and, above all, I am most agreeably flattered by it. I myself nurse the plan of calling a good orchestra together here next May in order to give to the people who would like to hear some of my music a characteristic selection (not dramatic, but purely lyrical) of pieces from my operas. I have composed the following programme. *By way of introduction* :

The March of Peace from *Rienzi.*

After that—

I. *Flying Dutchman.*

    A. Ballad of Senta.
    B. Sailors' song (in C).
    C. Overture.

II. *Tannhäuser.*

    A. Entrance of the guests at the Wartburg.
    B. Tannhäuser's pilgrimage (*i.e.*, introduction to the third act complete and with programme) ; then, joining on immediately, the song of the returning pilgrims (E flat major).
    C. Overture.

III. *Lohengrin.*

    A. Instrumental prelude.

    B. The whole scene for male chorus commencing with the song of the watchman on the tower, which enters in D major immediately after the great prelude in A major, and thus leads from the heights to the earth. This is followed (after a transition specially written) by Elsa's bridal progress (with a close, specially written in E flat).

    C. Wedding music (introduction to Act III.); bridal song; then wedding music in G major repeated. This makes the conclusion.

I undertake the whole thing only to hear something out of *Lohengrin*, and would willingly abandon this substitute if I could *once* hear the real *Lohengrin*.

Well, you have at least hopes. I sigh on your and my own account when I hear you say so.

But all this leads me beyond the purpose of these hasty lines.

To Zigesar I hope to write to-morrow; I have to thank him for his unusually rich gift for the *Dutchman*. To my disgrace, I must confess that it came very conveniently, although it curiously reminded me of the fact that last year I visited the islands of the Lago Maggiore at the expense of friend Liszt. Lord knows, I shall always remain a disreputable fellow. Why do you have anything to do with me?

(In the spectre scene of the third act of the *Flying Dutchman* you might have made cuts without hesitation.)

I am much obliged to the Princess for her zeal in making acquaintance with my new poem; if I could only read it to you both, I should have no fear.

The three copies I shall send you before long.

Farewell for to-day, you dear, good friend.

Your

RICHARD WAGNER.

ZURICH, *March 3rd*, 1853

102.

MY DEAREST FRIEND,

As to *one* thing I must ask you seriously not to misunderstand me.

If your gigantic perseverance of friendship should succeed in opening my return to Germany, be assured that the only use I should make of this favour would be to visit Weimar now and then, take part for a short time in your activity, and witness an important performance of my operas from time to time. This I want; it is a necessary of life to me, and it is this which I miss so cruelly. I should derive no other benefit from it; I should never permanently settle in Germany, but should retain as the scene of my life, or rather work, calm, beautiful Switzerland, endeared to me by nature. How little I am able to endure the permanent excitement which would be involved in my frequent public appearances I know full well; after each explosion, such as I want them now and then, I should require the most perfect quietude for my productive labour; and this I can have here without stint. A permanent position I therefore could never resume in Germany, and it would not fall in with my views and experiences. On the other hand, temporary outings for the purposes already indicated are, as I said before, indispensable to me; they are to me the rain which I require unless my plant is to wither and to die; I can only live in extremes—great activity and excitement and—most perfect calm.

I have already contemplated what my position would be, for example, towards Berlin in case my return were granted, and have, after mature consideration, come to the conclusion that even then I should ask you earnestly to undertake the performances of my operas there.

Twice I have produced an opera of my own at Berlin, and have been unfortunate each time; this time I should therefore prefer to leave the undertaking wholly to you; at the utmost I should enjoy your doings *incognito*. In any case you alone would be able to influence in my favour the circumstances and personal relations which are indispensable; I should again spoil everything. This therefore is *prudence*. Moreover, I cannot express to you how my heart rejoices at the thought that I might look on from a hidden corner while you instilled my work into the Berliners; this satisfaction to my feelings I must live to see!

But enough for to-day. Of your visit to Zurich I dream every day, and make earnest preparations for being able to dispense with my *tisane*. Don't come too late.

Write to me soon how you like my poem; in the summer I shall read it to you. If all goes well, there will also be musical sketches, but before the middle of May I cannot really set to work.

A thousand warm greetings from your

R. W.

March 4th, 1853.

103.

Bach's Passion Music will be performed this evening, which will account for my extraordinary note-paper.

I have forwarded your letter to the D. of C., and he has replied in a very friendly and amiable manner. Finally he says to me, " On verra ce qu'on pourra faire pour lui plus tard," and this point I shall not fail to discuss with the D. on occasion. You have of course not the slightest doubt as to my view of this matter ; otherwise, my dearest friend, I should have to think that you had gone out of your mind. Excuse the word ! You could not have possibly seen the matter in any other light from what you have done, and for the same reason I had to remain perfectly passive and neutral. For heaven's sake, keep as well as you can, and do not be annoyed by the inevitable *stupidity* and malice which are opposed to you so frequently from different quarters.

The affair at Prague appears to me somewhat complicated. Laub, who has taken Joachim's place in our orchestra, wrote to me from Prague yesterday that the prohibition of *Tannhäuser* must be a theatrical trick of St.'s, the director of police (President Sacher) having informed him that he knew nothing of that prohibition. I have asked Laub in consequence to ferret out the matter carefully and to ask St. to write to you or me plainly and precisely. Before taking an official step, one must know by whom and in what manner the prohibition has been issued, and on whom the withdrawal thereof depends. I mentioned to you President Sacher as the director of police in Prague because in the Austrian monarchy similar orders are made by that official. If he declares that "he knows nothing about it," I know still less where the difficulty lies and at what door I should have to knock. On April 4th the *Tannhäuser* overture will be played at Prague, and until then I wait for further information from Laub. In the meantime I think it advisable that you should write a *friendly* letter to St., asking him *in what manner Tannhäuser* has been prohibited at Prague, and to whom one would have to apply in order to get rid of this difficulty. It is of course far from my wish to inspire you with suspicion against St. ; but it is necessary for us to sift the matter thoroughly, and after so many experiences it may be permitted to anticipate different and even contradictory possibilities.

Your

F. LISZT.

LEIPZIG, *March 25th*, 1853.

104.

MY DEAREST FRIEND,

I hear much too little of you. This is not a reproach, but merely a complaint. That you work for me daily and always, I know ; in return I live almost entirely with you, and from my place of abode here I am always absent. I live here a perfect dream life ; when I awake, it is with pain. Nothing attracts or holds me, or rather what attracts and holds me, is in the distance. How can I avoid being deeply melancholy ? It is only the post that keeps me alive ; with the most passionate impatience I expect the postman every morning about eleven. If he brings nothing or brings something unsatisfactory, my whole day is a desert of resignation. Such is my life ! Why do I live ? Often I make unheard-of efforts to get something from abroad ; lately, for instance, I had my new poem printed, to give a strong sign of life. I sent it to all the friends who, I might assume, would take an interest in me, and in this manner I hoped to have compelled people to vouchsafe me a sign. What is the result ? Franz Müller in Weimar and Karl Ritter have written to me ; no one else has thought it worth while even to acknowledge receipt.

If it had not been for a few enthusiastic women at Weimar, I should have heard nothing of the third opera week. Even the most unheard-of efforts which you make on my behalf become an empty breath of air to me. I am condemned to perish amidst leather and oppressive dulness.

Would it not be possible to leave all this and begin an *entirely* new life ? How absurd it is on your part to worry yourself in order to help me ! Alas ! no, you cannot help me in this manner, only my "fame," and that is something entirely different from *me*. Nothing on paper can be of any use to me, and yet my whole intercourse with the world is entirely through paper. What can help me ? My nights are mostly sleepless ; weary and miserable, I rise from my bed to see a day before me which willbring me not *one* joy. Intercourse with people who torture me, and from whom I withdraw to torture myself! I feel disgust at whatever I undertake. This cannot go on; I cannot bear life much longer.

I ask you with the greatest urgency and decision to induce the Weimar court to take a definite step, in order to ascertain once for all whether I have sure and immediate expectations of having the return to Germany opened to me. I must know this soon and for certain. Be perfectly open with me. Tell me whether the Weimar court will take this step; and if it takes it, and takes it soon, let me know the result. I am not inclined to make the slightest concession for the sake of this wish; I can assure *you* that I shall take no part whatever in politics, and any one who is not absolutely silly must see that I am not a demagogue with whom one must deal by police measures. (If they wish it, they may place me under police supervision as much as they like.) But they must not expect of me the disgrace of making a confession of repentance of any kind. If on such conditions a temporary return could be granted to me, I do not deny that it would be a lift to me. If, however, it is not possible, and if a definite negative answer is given, let me know at once and without any prevarication; *then I shall know where I am.* Then I shall begin a different life. Then I shall get money how and where I can; I shall borrow and steal, if necessary, in order to *travel*. The beautiful parts of Italy are closed to me unless I am amnestied. So I shall go to Spain, to Andalusia, and make friends, and try once more to live as well as I can. I should like to fare round the world. If I can get *no* money, or if the journey does not help me to a

new breath of life, there is an end of it, and I shall then
seek death by my own hand rather than live on in
this manner.

I must forge myself artificial wings, because everything round me is artificial, and nature everywhere is
torn and broken. Therefore hear and grant my prayer.
Let me know soon, and know for certain, whether I
may come back to Germany or not. I must take my
decision accordingly.

After this language of despair, I cannot find the tone
which I should have to assume in writing to you about
other matters which I might wish to communicate to
you. Most of these would be effusions of thanks, as
you know. Good Lord, that also drives me wild : that
I always have to *write* this to you. My impatience
to see you grows into a most violent passion ; I can
scarcely wait for the day of your arrival. " Write" to
me definitely about what date you will be here. Let
it not be too late. Can you come in May ? On May
22nd I shall be forty. Then I shall have myself re-
baptised ; would you not like to be my godfather ? I
wish *we two* could start straight from here to go into
the wide world. I wish you, too, would leave these
German Philistines and Jews. Have you anything else
around you ? Add the Jesuits, and then you have all.
" Philistines, Jews, and Jesuits," that is it ; no human
beings. They write, write, and write ; and when they
have " written " a great deal, they think they have done
something wonderful. Stupid fools ! do you think our
heart can beat for you ? What do these wretched
people know about it ? Leave them alone, give them
a kick with your foot, and come with me into the wide

world, were it only to perish bravely, to die with a light heart in some abyss.

Let me soon have news of you ; and, before all, let me know when you are coming.   Farewell, farewell, longingly waited for by

Your

RICHARD WAGNER.

ZURICH, *March* 30*th*, 1853.

105.

DEAREST FRIEND,

Your letters are sad ; your life is still sadder. You want to go into the wide world to live, to enjoy, to luxuriate.   I should be only too glad if you could, but do you not feel that the sting and the wound you have in your own heart will leave you nowhere and can never be cured ?   Your greatness is your misery ; both are inseparably connected, and must pain and torture you until you kneel down and let both be merged in *faith* !

" *Lass zu dem Glauben Dich neu bekehren, es gibt ein Glück;* " this is the only thing that is true and eternal. I cannot preach to you, nor explain it to you ; but I will pray to God that He may powerfully illumine your heart through His faith and His love.   You may scoff at this feeling as bitterly as you like.   I cannot fail to see and desire in it the only salvation.   Through Christ alone, through resigned suffering in God, salvation and rescue come to us.

I had already indicated to you that I did not expect an answer from Dresden before my departure from here.   If you accuse me of negligence and lukewarmness, you are unjust to me, but I can forgive you. If, in accordance with your desire, I made your affair dependent on an immediate "Yes" or "No," I should greatly compromise it. Our court here is very favourably inclined towards you, and you may feel sure that every possible step is being taken to open your return to Germany. A few days ago I spoke about it to our Hereditary Grand Duke, who positively assured me that he would actively intercede for you. This you must not mention anywhere; but it would be well if you were to write a letter to the Hereditary Grand Duke, telling him that you have been informed through me of his magnanimous disposition and asking him not to forget you altogether. Do not write too diplomatically, but give vent to the feelings of your heart, and send me the letter, which I will hand him at once. In spite of all, I hope to find you in a good mental and physical condition when I visit you at the end of May. By then you must turn out your whole hospital, and I promise you to leave mine *en route* to take it up again on my way back. As the wedding festivities of Princess Amalie and Prince Henry of the Netherlands will not take place till after the middle of May, I shall not be with you before the first days of June. Seven or eight weeks must therefore still elapse.

The *Tannhäuser* overture was received with enthusiasm and encored at Prague, as Laub told me, who was present at the performance.

As regards the performance of *Tannhäuser*, the real state is very nearly what I wrote to you. The tenor St., brother of the manager, will shortly leave Prague, and there will then be no singer for the principal part. I also hear that there is no Elizabeth, and until you give me further information in the matter I am not inclined to put down the non-performance of *Tannhäuser* to a fictitious order of the police while such real theatrical impediments are in the way. Has St. replied to you?

From Laub I hear that the supposed difficulties have been discussed in high circles (Count Nostitz, Princess Taxis, etc.) in a manner not favourable to St. I should, however, not like to accuse St. till we have sufficient proof of his bad conduct. If you write to him in the sense indicated in my letter to you from Leipzig, we shall soon get to the bottom of the matter. Kittl is at present at Frankfort-on-Main, where his "operatic wants" are being supplied by *Die Franzosen bei Nizza.* The work is to be given on April 11th. Probably he will stay here for a day on his way back, and through him I mean to get more accurate information as to the Prague complications.

Kossak's critique of *Indra* has amused me. If you have not read it, I shall send it to you.

Brendel has grand schemes, which he will probably communicate to you. He is coming here for the next performance of Raff's opera *King Alfred*, in order to talk to me about the new paper which he would like to bring out in the course of the summer. The enterprise is in itself good enough, but I have still my doubts as to the means at disposal. What do you mean by Raff's *confidential* letter against the *Tannhäuser* notice in the *Grenzboten*?

Do not be offended, dearest friend, because I have not yet written to you about the *Ring of the Nibelung* at greater length. It is not my business to criticise and expound so extraordinary a work, for which later on I am resolved to do everything in my power in order to gain a proper place for it. I have always entreated you not to abandon the work, and am delighted by the perfection of your poetic workmanship. Almost every day the Princess greets me with the words—

> "Nicht Gut, nicht Geld,—noch göttliche Pracht;
> Nicht Haus, nicht Hof,—noch herrischer Prunk;
> Nicht trüber Verträge trügender Bund,
> Noch heuchelnder Sitte hartes Gesetz:
> Selig in Lust und Leid, lässt—die Liebe nur sein!"

Counsellor Schöll will shortly read the four dramas at the Altenburg to a small circle which I shall invite for the purpose; and when I come to Zurich, you must be good enough to go through the whole with me, so that we may exchange heart and soul on the occasion.

S. wrote me a longish letter, in which he plainly says that the poem is a total mistake, etc. I have not sent you this letter, because I think it useless, and shall never be of his opinion. By word of mouth I shall let you know about various opinions which in the meantime I listen to without comment or discussion.

Your truly devoted

F. LISZT.

WEYMAR, *April 8th*, 1853.

106.

Herewith, dearest, best of friends, I send you the answer of the Prague manager, containing particulars as to the prohibition of *Tannhäuser*. If you have time and care to do so, co-operate in this affair also, in accordance with the love you bear me.

I long for a letter from you, and am curious to hear from yourself what truth there is in your rumoured breach with Weimar.

I live in the expectation of your visit; surely you have not abandoned it.

Adieu. A thousand greetings from your

R. W.

Zurich, *April 11th*, 1853.

107.

[Fragment.]

How ever could you think that I should "scoff" at any of your magnanimous effusions? The forms in which we endeavour to gain comfort in our miserable circumstances depend wholly upon our nature, our wants, the character of our culture and of our more or less artistic sensations. Who could be heartless enough to believe that to him alone the true form has been revealed? Only he could think so who has never fashioned for himself such a form of his hope and faith, but into whose dull mind it has been instilled from outside as some one else's formula, who therefore does not possess sufficient inner power to preserve his own empty existence by dint of vital instinct, and who thus again communicates the formula received from others as a formula for others. He who himself longs and hopes and believes will surely rejoice in the hope and faith of others; all contention about the true form is mere empty self-assertion. Dear friend, I also have a strong faith, on account of which I have

been bitterly scoffed at by our politicians and sages of
the law. I have faith in the future of the human race,
and that faith I draw simply from my inner necessity.
I have succeeded in observing the phenomena of nature
and of history with love and without prejudice, and the
only evil I have discovered in their true essence is *lovelessness*. But this lovelessness also I explain to myself
as an *error*, an error which must lead us from the state
of natural unconsciousness to the *knowledge* of the
solely beautiful necessity of love. To gain that knowledge is the task of history; and the scene on which
that knowledge will be practically shown is none other
than our earth, than nature, in which there are all the
germs tending to this blissful knowledge. The state of
lovelessness is the state of suffering for the human
race ; the fulness of this suffering surrounds us now, and
tortures your friend with a thousand burning wounds ;
but, behold, in it we recognize the glorious necessity
of love : *we* call to each other and greet each other with
the power of love, which would be impossible without
this painful recognition. In this manner we gain a
power of which man in his natural state has no idea,
and this power, expanded to the power of all humanity,
will in the future create on this earth a state of things
from which no one will long to fly to a hereafter henceforth become unnecessary; for all will be happy, will
live and love. Who longs to fly from this life while he
loves ?

Well, well, we suffer *now*. We *now* should despair
and go mad without faith in a hereafter; I also believe
in a hereafter, and have just shown you this hereafter.
If it lies beyond *my life*, it does not lie beyond that

which I can feel, think, conceive, and comprehend; for I believe in mankind, and require nothing further.

I now ask you, Who at the bottom of his heart shares my faith more than do you, who believe in me, who know and demonstrate love as no one else has proved and practised it yet? You *realise* your faith in every moment of your life; I *know* deeply and inly what you believe; how then could I scoff at the form from which such a miracle springs? I should not be as much of an artist as I am if I did not joyfully understand you.

Let us bravely fight and struggle; then all whims will disappear. That I must remain so far from my battlefield is what makes me complain so often.

Well, my highest hope will be fulfilled:

I shall see you again.

This implies everything that can give joy to me; and I am sure that at your arrival, and through means of it, you will find me so *elated* that you will take my present and past complaints for pure hypocrisy. My nerves, it is true, suffer a great deal, and for a very natural reason. But I am now in hopes of strengthening them thoroughly; for that I shall want a little "life:" the medical cure alone will not be sufficient. That "life" you will bring to me, and I promise you that you will find me hale and hearty.

I am almost glad that you are *not* coming to my musical performances here, which will take place May 18th, 20th, and 22nd; we shall afterwards be more by ourselves, belong to each other more. Oh, how I REJOICE IN THE THOUGHT!

You will find everything comfortable with me: the

devil of luxury has taken hold of me, and I have arranged my house as pleasantly as possible. When the real thing is wanting, one does what one can to help one's self. Well, come; you will find me half mad; you, you, you, and no one else!

What further shall I say in reply? I find I have taken to chatting on the main thing.

S.'s judgment of my poem satisfies my vanity—I mean, because it proves *my* judgment. *In spite of all*, I took S. from the beginning for a confirmed littérateur whom you for a moment had carried away with you, but only for a moment. A littérateur *cannot* understand me; only a complete *man* or a true artist can. Leave it alone; it will be all right. When once I have cast everything aside to dive up to the ears into the fount of music, it will sound so well that people shall hear what they cannot see. We must have a long talk about my further *practical* plans as to the *performance*.

All scribbled things are absolutely distasteful to me, and it is the greatest effort to me to read the musical paper. I wish that all this had no reference to *me*; let the people do for *their own* sakes what they think they ought not to omit; what was necessary *for me* you have done. Dearest, dearest friend, do not think that I meant to *reproach* you when recently again I wrote with furious impatience about my return to Germany. I do this quite at random; I call out when I am in pain, but I accuse no one, certainly you least of all. You are unfortunate in being so near to my heart; for that reason you hear everything that I sigh and complain of violently and painfully. Be not angry, and forgive me cordially.

I will write to the Hereditary Grand Duke, because it gives me pleasure.

Enough for to-day; my fingers are becoming cramped. But how many, many things I shall have to *say* to you. I keep everything for that occasion, and have really not written to you once about your performance of my operas, of which quite recently again I heard such wonders. All that will come *by word of mouth*, if only I do not go mad!

Farewell. Greet the Princess. A thousand kisses from

Your

RICHARD WAGNER.

April 13*th*, 1853.

108.

Bravo, Schöneck! Long live Kroll's theatre! Those people have rational ideas, and work bravely. The fact that you are friendly with Schöneck, and can count upon his goodwill and musical intelligence, gives a favourable turn to the performance of *Tannhäuser* at Kroll's theatre, and I, for my part, do not advise you against it, the less so as you seem to like it. Your citing Mirabeau as *marchand de draps* is quite applicable to *Tannhäuser* at Kroll's theatre; and if Schöneck manages to fill the parts moderately well, the thing will, no doubt, hugely amuse you.

Simultaneously with this I write, by your desire, to Schöneck to compliment him on the impending performances. I have advised him to go to work prudently,

as the whole matter is in his hands.   We may anticipate
a very good result, which will cordially please

Your

Franz Liszt.

I shall write to Prague to-morrow, to President
Sacher ; this matter will probably drag on for some
time.

109.

My Dear Friend,

In the most frightful turmoil of business, I must
send you a few words of enthusiasm. I have been writing
an explanatory programme for my musical performance
here, and was led on that occasion to look once more
through your pamphlet on my opera.   How can I
describe my feelings ?   When has an artist, a friend,
ever done for another what you have done for me ?
Truly, when I should be inclined to despair of the
whole world, one single glance at you raises me again
high and higher, fills me with faith and hope ; I
cannot conceive what I should have done without you
these last four years.   Oh, and how much you have
made of me ; it has been indescribably beautiful for me
to observe you during that space of time.   The idea
and the word " gratitude " cannot contain my meaning !

You say that you do not yet expect to get your leave of
absence !   Do not frighten me, and tell me by return
that you are *coming*, and coming *soon*.

I have engaged Damm.   It was a mad undertaking
to find an orchestra of seventy men when there were
only fourteen competent musicians in the place.   I have

plundered all Switzerland, and all the neighbouring states as far as Nassau. It was necessary to raise the guarantee fund to 7,000 francs in order to cover expenses, and all this that I might hear the orchestral prelude to *Lohengrin*.

I expect you for certain in the first days of June. If only the joy of seeing you again does not drive me mad! Adieu. Come to

Your
R. W.

Zurich, *May 9th*, 1853.

110.

Your splendid programme for the musical performances at Zurich, May 18th, 20th, and 22nd, has made me quite sad, dearest friend. Why can I not be present to make some returns to you for all I owe you? But what is the good of questioning, brooding, and sorrowing? I cannot get away from here before the end of June. To-morrow (the 20th) we have a grand court concert (the programme is of no interest to you), and ten days afterwards the performance of *Moses* by Marx, which I have to conduct. On June 15th takes place the jubilee of the Grand Duke, for which his Majesty the King of Saxony will probably come here, and the 29th is the birthday of the Hereditary Grand Duke. On the 26th or 28th I accompany my mother, who is still half lame, to Paris; and by the middle of July at the latest I shall be with you in Zurich. Till then I must have patience, and need not give you any further explanations.

I talked some time ago with the Princess of Prussia about you. The performance of *Tannhäuser* at Kroll's is variously commented upon.   I am still of opinion that the personal influence and ability of Schöneck are in this matter decisive.   Since my last letter to Schöneck I have heard nothing from him, but I believe I told you of an offer that was made to me to take the Leipzig opera to Berlin and to conduct *Tannhäuser* at the Königsstadt Theatre.   I have naturally declined this offer.

I hope Schöneck will keep his word and bear the responsibility of an adequate performance of *Tannhäuser* honourably, thus justifying your confidence.   When you hear further particulars, ask him to communicate them to me, as I have been questioned on various sides about this matter, and have warmly defended Schöneck's undertaking against the wavering portion of your friends and the public.

Alwine Fromann was here for some days.   I have learnt to love her through you.   Your *Nibelungen* has been read *excellently* on four evenings at the Altenburg by Counsellor Sauppe, director of the Grammar School, who formerly lived for some years at Zurich.   The whole subject of the *Nibelungen* I shall work out with you in conversation; in the meantime only this : that I am *wholly in favour of it*, and ask you urgently to take the musical part seriously in hand.

I hear from Prague that *Tannhäuser* is being prepared there for next autumn.   If this is confirmed, the other step which I contemplated will become useless.   In any case I shall wait a little while to gain better ground for the matter.

Lohengrin will be given at Wiesbaden, and at Schwerin the *Dutchman* is heaving in sight.   Have you finished the *Faust* overture ?   Damm has probably told you that we have given it here several times fairly well. *Apropos* of Damm, tell him that he can stop as long as he likes. I envy the fellow his good time with you.

This afternoon Louis Köhler, from Königsberg, will arrive here to hear your *Lohengrin.* Alas! alas! *Indra,* by Flotow, absorbs all the delicate attentions of our *artistic* direction; and this wretched medley will be given the day after to-morrow as *festival opera.* Did you formerly have intercourse with Köhler? I only know him through some very amiable notices of a few of my pianoforte works. His last letter is a kind of dithyramb about *Lohengrin,* which naturally predisposes me favourably towards the man.

Farewell, you unique man! and may we soon be together.

Your
F. L.

Let me soon have news of your performances at Zurich, and do not forget to send Brendel a notice of them for his paper. About Brendel, who recently visited me here, I have several things to tell you.

Please God, I may have good news to bring you from Dresden; *it is that* which keeps me here till the end of June.

III.

DEAREST,

I feel beaten down and weary. Damm has probably written to you about my musical performances. Everything went off right well, and Zurich was astonished that such a thing could have happened. The

Philistines almost carry me on their hands; and if I cared for external success, the effect of my performances would more than satisfy me. But, as you know, my chief object was to hear something from *Lohengrin*, and especially the orchestral prelude, which interested me uncommonly. The impression was most powerful, and I had to make every effort not to break down. So much is certain: I fully share your predilection for *Lohengrin*; it is the best thing I have done so far. On the public also it had the same effect. In spite of the *Tannhäuser* overture, preceding them, the pieces from *Lohengrin* made such an impression, that they were unanimously declared to be the best thing. For the "Bridal Procession" I had specially written a very effective new close, which I must communicate to you; following upon the "Bridal Song," I repeated the G major prelude (wedding music), after a short transition, and gave a new conclusion to this also. These pieces have had a tremendous popular success; everybody was delighted. It was a real feast for the world around me. All the women are in my favour.

I might have repeated the concerts six times, and they would have been full on every occasion, but I stuck to three performances, because I had enough of it, and was afraid of getting tired. Besides this, I could not have retained the orchestra any longer; many had to go home, especially eight musicians from Wiesbaden, the best of the orchestra there, who had given me great pleasure by coming. I had almost nothing but concert-masters and musical directors—twenty most excellent violins, eight tenors, eight splendid violon-

cellos, and five double-basses. All had brought their
best instruments; and in the acoustical orchestra,
constructed according to my indication, the tone of the
instruments was most bright and beautiful. It is true
that the whole cost 9,000 francs.

What do you think of our citizens raising all that
money? I believe that in time I shall be able to do
unheard-of things here, but for the present it has cost
me unheard-of trouble. During the week preceding
the performances, I read in *my* way, which you will
hear later on, my three operatic poems before a very
large audience in public and gratis, and was delighted
by the powerful impression they produced on my hearers.
In the intervals I studied my choruses with amateurs,
and these tame, four-part people at last sang as if they
had swallowed the devil. Well, I am a little lame and
weary in consequence. It is hard that you will have
to leave me in my loneliness for the whole month of
June.

Why have your festivities been suddenly postponed?
Not till *the middle of July?* Just now you would have
been of infinite benefit to me; I am very lonely.

For the present I must try to pick up a little by a
wandering life; perhaps I shall go for a few weeks to
Brunnen, on the lake of Lucerne, and try to settle down to
work. I shall make excursions from there to the Bernese
Oberland and thus pass the time till your much-desired
arrival. How long shall you be able to stay? In the
second half of July I am to go to St. Moritz, in the
Grisons, to go through a cure there from which they
promise great benefit for my health. Will you follow
me to that beautiful, wild solitude? That would be

splendid! By the end of August, when you have to leave me again, I shall go to Italy, as far as it is accessible to me. (I wish it could be to Naples! The King of Saxony might manage that!) The means I must get somehow, if I were to steal them.

In other respects "business" with me is flat. You have probably heard that the manager of the Berlin court opera has procured an order which prevents the smaller theatres of Berlin, and especially Kroll's theatre, from performing such operas as *Tannhäuser*. From this we see how powerfully even a threat acts upon these people; they are of course ashamed of themselves, and do not wish to incur open disgrace. I have authorised Schöneck to announce *Tannhäuser* as a "Singspiel," but he himself is doubtful whether the thing can be managed. He loses in this manner a fine opportunity of making himself favourably known and of raising himself above his hole-and-corner circumstances. I lose a nice income for this summer, for the undertaking would have brought me in a few thousand francs. But God's, or rather Herr von Hülsen's, will be done. It is quite plain that in our excellent states the "other thing" has nowadays the upper hand; the Princess of Prussia may wish and desire what she likes, she will not be able to conquer *that*, nor Herr von Hülsen either. Good Lord, *I know the thing*.

However, I was peculiarly pleased that you from the first looked upon this Berlin experiment just as I did, and that we quite understood each other. I can quite imagine how the Philistine must have shaken his head. It was equally clear that you were unable to accept the proposal for the Königsstadt Theatre with the Leipzig troupe, and I am only annoyed at their impudence in offering you such a thing. It implies indeed a gross insult, for which one must pardon our dull-headed theatrical mob. " Lord, forgive them, for they know not what they do."

Dearest friend, have you not yet had enough of Weimar ? I must own that I frequently grieve to see how you waste your strength there. Was there any truth in the recent rumour of your leaving Weimar ? Have they given in ?

But all this is idle talk. My brain is a wilderness, and I thirst for a long, long sleep, to awake only when my arms are around you. Write to me very precisely, also whether you are inclined, after a little stay at Zurich, to go with me to the solitude of the Grisons ; St. Moritz might, after all, do you good, dearest friend ; we shall there be five thousand feet high, and enjoy the most nerve-strengthening air, together with the mineral water, which is said to be of beneficial effect on the digestive organs. Think this over, consult your health and your circumstances, and let me know very soon what I may hope for.

Farewell, best and dearest of friends. Have my eternal thanks for your divine friendship, and be assured of my steadfast and warmest love.

Your

RICHARD W.

ZURICH, *May 30th*, 1853.

112.

DEAREST FRIEND,

I have just received the enclosed letter, programme, and newspaper from Prague. If you will write a few lines to Apt, you will please him very much. Also be kind enough to send a copy of your *Nibelungen* to Louis Köhler in Königsberg (care of Pfitzer and Heimann, music-publishers). He deserves this attention from you, and I promised it him during his stay here, when he cordially joined your banner. From Leipzig, after the performance of *Tannhäuser*, he wrote me a letter which I could sign myself, and you are sure to find in Köhler a very zealous, able, and honest champion of your cause in the press.

A little book by him on the *melody* of speech will shortly appear. As a composer for the pianoforte he has done some excellent things. Several years ago an opera of his composition was produced at Brunswick. Köhler is about thirty-two years old, and married.

Marx was here recently. We have become friends, and shall probably approach each other still more closely. His oratorio *Moses* was given fairly well under my direction.

A little court concert was given the day before yesterday in honour of their Majesties the King and Queen of Saxony. Further details I shall tell you when I see you. Unfortunately I must doubt that the steps taken so far will lead to the desired result, but there is yet another hope before my departure, for which I must wait. The Hereditary Grand Duke will soon go to Dresden, and has promised me his intercession in this matter.

In ten or twelve days I shall give you an exact plan of my journey. It is very possible and almost probable that Joachim and Robert Franz will accompany me to Zurich. It is quite understood that I go with you wherever you like, but I shall not be able to stay with you longer than ten days altogether. Whether it will be at the beginning or the middle of July I cannot say for certain, because this journey depends on another much longer one.

Damm has told us wonderful things of your three performances. The poetic indications which I read in the programme, especially those of the introduction to *Lohengrin* and the overture of the *Flying Dutchman,* interested me very much. Before long I may send you a little article about the *Flying Dutchman*; and if you approve of it, it shall be published.

I have been much depressed these last few days by many and various things. These are the days of thunderstorms. With all my heart and soul I shall rejoice on seeing you again. Let us be faithful to one another, though the world go to ruin.

F. L.

June 8th, 1853.

113.

I have nothing to *write* to you, dearest, except that I await you longingly. You might come *before* the middle of July, seeing that you will not be able to give me more than ten days in all. This of course determines me not to expect that you should go to the watering-place in the Grisons with me for a few days only. It would have been different if you could have stayed with me there for some length of time. I suppose you will not be here *this* month, and I may, without fear of missing you, go next week to Interlaken in the Oberland to visit part of the R. family. At the *beginning of July* I shall be back again, and expect you daily.

That Franz and Joachim intend to come too is famous. Franz had already half promised me. I shall be delighted to make their acquaintance. Prague and Königsberg (Köhler) will be attended to.

I read to-day in the *Neue Zeitschrift für Musik* the article by T. in Posen, in which there is a stupid thing, viz., an exaggeration, where he says that I consider "Schöneck one of my *most gifted* disciples." Schöneck as a musician is quite insignificant, and as a man without particular culture ; he is simply a theatrical conductor—at least as far as I know him. I was struck, however, by his uncommon and specific *talent as a conductor*, as well as by his nervous, restless, and very active temperament, combined with a strong turn for enthusiasm. He once saw me study Beethoven's music with an orchestra, and conduct it, and devoured what could be acquired with genuine astonishment, making it his own with so much cleverness that later on at Freiburg he produced the music to *Egmont*, which he had heard me do, with very great success, as competent witnesses have assured me. It was the same afterwards with the *Flying Dutchman*, which he grasped completely as a conductor. But beyond his specific gift as a conductor, I do not think that I have influenced him particularly, and should certainly not like him to be considered my representative, although I may count upon his devotion. If the Berlin plan at Kroll's is, after all, realised—and there is again strong opposition to it now—I must think of having my intentions more specially represented, and have young Ritter

in view for that purpose.   As to this also we must have
a talk.   However, the success of *Tannhäuser* at Posen,
under Schöneck's direction, is again a striking incident.
Within six days they gave it four times, with the
largest receipts.   Only think what trouble I had at the
time with this opera at Dresden.

But enough.   That you, like me, do not seem to be
in good spirits, grieves me very much, but I become
more and more convinced that people like us must
always be uncomfortable, except in the moments, hours,
and days of productive excitement; but then we enjoy
and luxuriate during that time more than any other
man.   So it is!   Soon we shall talk!   I am almost
afraid of this joy!   You will write, will you not?

Adieu, dearest friend.

Your

R. W.

ZURICH, *June 14th,* 1853.

114.

BEST OF FRIENDS,

To-day week—Thursday, June 28th—I start
from here.   At Carlsruhe I shall have to stop till July
1st, in order to look at the localities, and to make some
preparations for the impending Musical Festival there.
On July 2nd I shall therefore hope to be with you at
Zurich.   My time will be very short, but it will be an
unspeakable pleasure to live with you for a few days.

I enclose a few disappointing lines concerning your
affair, which have been sent to me by an unknown
hand.   I hope to be able to tell you better news when
I see you.   I shall go straight from the mail office to
you at Zeltweg, to ask you about the hotel where I shall

stop.   Probably Joachim and Franz will come with me.
If it is not too much trouble, notify my arrival at
Winterthur to Kirchner and Eschmann, whose personal
acquaintance I should like to make.

I have just received from Härtel your portrait, which
seems to me more like than the previous one.   If
there is a decent sculptor at Zurich, you must oblige me
by giving him a few sittings, for him to model a large
medallion in relief of you.   I cannot bear lithographed
portraits; to me they have always a somewhat *bourgeois*
appearance, while sculpture represents a man in a very
different way.

In ten days, dearest friend, we shall wholly possess
each other.   If you like to write to me, address *Poste
restante*, Carlsruhe, where I shall be till July 1st.

Your

F. LISZT.

June 23rd, 1853.

[ENCLOSURE.]

If I venture to trouble you with a few lines, my
motive, I hope, will gain me your kind forgiveness.   In
to-day's number of the *Freimüthige Sachsen-Zeitung* the
old *Steckbrief* (order of arrest) (v. 49) against Capellmeister Richard Wagner has been copied, with the
remark " that it is said that he intends to return to
Germany, and therefore the police are requested to keep
a watchful eye on him, and, in case he is found in
Germany, to arrest him and deliver him here."

Although I know Capellmeister R. Wagner from of
old, I do not know how to communicate this news to
him because it is said that most of the letters sent to

refugees in Switzerland are either opened or never delivered ; and I am not acquainted with any other safe way.

A consultation which I had with some of Richard Wagner's friends led us to determine, as the only means, upon asking Court-Capellmeister Dr. Liszt, one of the most faithful and best-known friends of the great composer, " to acquaint Capellmeister R. Wagner with the above by some sure ways and means."

Asking you once more to pardon me for the trouble I give you, I remain, with the greatest esteem and veneration,

———

115.

DEAREST FRIEND,

    I have just returned from a trip, and find your letter. Thank God, I have not much to *write* in answer beyond expressing my joy that you are coming *so soon.* Saturday, July 2nd, in the morning, or at the latest in the evening, I shall await you at the mail office. You might stay with me, but I am afraid you would not be comfortable, especially if you come with Joachim and Franz. All this we shall settle at once at the office. There is a good hotel, Hôtel Baur. I shall let Kirchner and Eschmann know. Good Lord, HOW GLAD I AM. Not another word by letter !

AU REVOIR.

Your

RICHARD WAGNER.

Could you let me know by telegram exactly when you are coming ?

We have beautiful weather.

116.

You see, dear friend, that I am approaching; and unless official impediments delay me one day, I start the day after to-morrow—Friday, July 1st—by the afternoon train for Basle, and arrive at Zurich by the mail-coach on Saturday, early in the morning. At the latest, I shall be there on Sunday at the same hour. Joachim I expect here; Franz, I am sorry to say, will not be able to come till later on.

Your

FRANZ LISZT.

CARLSRUHE, *June 29th.*

117.

FRANKFORT, *Tuesday, July 12th,* 1853, 6 *p.m.*

UNIQUE FRIEND,

The Musical Festival at Carlsruhe will take place on September 20th, and I write you these few lines in haste to ask you to send me the altered passage in the score of *Lohengrin* at Weymar.

If not inconvenient to you, I should be glad if you could lend me for six weeks your Zurich parts of the overture to *Tannhäuser* and the pieces from *Lohengrin* for use at the Carlsruhe festival; send them straight to Devrient. As the Härtels have not printed the parts, it will not injure their interests; and we shall at least be sure that the parts are correctly copied, as you have already used them at Zurich. From Weymar I shall bring the parts of the *Tannhäuser* overture with me. At the two concerts of the Carlsruhe festival the orchestras and artists of the Darmstadt, Mannheim, and Carlsruhe theatres will co-operate. As the performances take place at the theatre, the trebling of the parts will be

quite sufficient, for the house does not hold more than
fourteen or fifteen hundred people, and an orchestra of
a hundred and ninety and a chorus of something like a
hundred and sixty will consequently have a good effect.
As soon as the programme is settled I shall send it to
you ; for the present I tell you only that the *Tannhäuser*
overture will make the commencement of the first concert
and the *Lohengrin* pieces the close of the second.   In
addition to this, there will be two pieces by Berlioz,
the finale of Mendelssohn's *Loreley*, the Ninth Symphony,
etc.   Frau Heim will, I hope, on this occasion be the
reporter for Zurich, and I shall do my best to put her
in a good temper.   Johanna sings this evening at a
concert in the theatre for the benefit of a local actress.
Tannhäuser will *not* be given to-morrow.   After the
concert I shall see Schmidt, and shall inquire as to particulars. . . . In case J. is still here to-morrow, I shall
pay my most humble respects to her.   She appeared
first as Romeo, and yesterday sang Fides for the benefit
of the Pension Fund.   With E. Devrient I spent a
few hours yesterday at Badenweiler.   He is going
to visit you at Zurich, but can make no certain plans
for the present, as he expects the Prince Regent at
Badenweiler.   His daughter suffers a great deal, and
his wife also appeared to me in very weak health.
Frau Meyerbeer also I met at Badenweiler.   With
Schindelmeisser I shall communicate by telegraph
early to-morrow morning ; and in case *Lohengrin* is
given on Thursday, I shall run over to see it, and
return home to Weymar on Friday.

Through your hat I nearly got into difficulties with
the police at Carlsruhe, because its species and colour

are considered specially suspicious, being accounted red, although grey. I was accidentally advised of this; nevertheless I have got on well so far, and shall always maintain that the hat is *well-conditioned* and *loyal*, because you have given it to me.

Apropos, neither of the two persons to whom I have hitherto talked about it was inclined to believe in your wholly *unpolitical* position and mode of feeling. It will certainly take some time before a more correct opinion of your circumstances and your whole individuality is arrived at.

My best compliments to your wife, and many thanks for the kindness and love she showed me during my stay at Zurich.

Do not forget either my most " *well-conditioned*" hommages to Frau Kumner and her sister. To our Grütly brother and his wife say all the friendly and true things which I feel for them, and to Baumgartner give a good "shake-hand" (translated into musical Swiss) in my name. The days at the Zeltweg remain bright, sunny days for me. God grant that we may soon be able to repeat them.

Your

DOPPEL PEPS,

alias "Double Extract de Peps," or "Double Stout Peps con doppio movimento sempre crescendo al fffff," which latter we shall live to witness at the performance of the *Nibelungen*.

Once more I ask you if possible to grant the *Tannhäuser* and *Lohengrin* parts to the Carlsruhe festival, and kindly to write a few words to that effect to Devrient.

I am off to the concert.

Johanna sings three songs by Schubert ("Wanderer," "Trockne Blumen," and "Ungeduld"), and I sing

 etc

Pardon me if I have put the bars in the wrong places, and whistle it better for yourself. Address Weymar.

118.

DEAR, DEAR FRANZ,

Here I am in the capital of the Grisons; all is grey, grey. I must take rose-coloured paper to get out of this grey, just as a certain tinge of red glimmers through your grey hat. You see I am compelled to take to bad jokes, and may therefore guess at my mood. Solitude, solitude, nothing but horrible grey solitude, since you went away! Wednesday evening my Zurich people tried to dispel this grey solitude with their torches; it was very pretty and solemn, and nothing like it had happened to me in my life before. They had built an orchestra in front of my house in the Zeltweg, and at first I thought they were erecting a scaffold for me. They played and sang, we exchanged speeches, and I was cheered by an innumerable multitude. I almost wish you had heard the speech of the evening; it was very naïve and sincere; I was celebrated as a perfect saviour. The next morning I left in company with St. George; since then rain has fallen incessantly. Last night we found the only mail-coach from Coire to St. Moritz full, and had to make up our minds to stop here for another two nights and one day. Before leaving Zurich I fetched your Frankfort letter from the post-office; alas! it was the last joy which I took with me from deserted Zurich. Be cordially thanked for it, you dear, departed joy!

To-day I inaugurate your new writing-case with a first "written" communication to you. Let me talk of *business*; all else has become too terrible for my pen and ink since I possessed you wholly, heard your noble voice, pressed your divine hand. Therefore to—business!

You shall have the parts; each of them is in a book which contains all the pieces of my Zurich concert; you will therefore have *Tannhäuser* as well as *Lohengrin*. But as your orchestra will be larger than mine, you will have to have them copied out; still I think they will arrive in time if I send them to Devrient not before the middle of August, after my return from St. Moritz; let me know whether you think the same. If you also want the voice parts and think the chorus ought to begin studying *before* the middle of August, I will send you them through my wife before the others; as to this also I want your instructions. The newly written score of the *Lohengrin* pieces, containing all the alterations, will be ready in four weeks at the latest. I therefore prefer to wait till then rather than send you the alterations on detached slips of paper, which would be of little use to you. About the middle of August the entire and properly arranged score will be sent to you at Weimar; but if you insist upon having the alterations separately at an earlier date, write to me, and I will obey.

So, so, so, so! this is the business.

And now what remains? Sadness! sadness! After you had been taken from us I did not say a single word to George. Silently I returned home; silence reigned everywhere. Thus we celebrated your leave-taking, you dear man; all the splendour had departed. Oh, come back soon, and stay with us for a long time. If you only knew what divine traces you have left behind you! Everything has grown nobler and milder; greatness lives in narrow minds; and sadness covers all.

Farewell, my Franz, my holy Franz. Think of the wild solitude of St. Moritz, and send a ray of your life there soon.

My wife read your letter with me, and was delighted. She greets you cordially. George asks me to greet you, and thanks you for remembering him. He will soon be a poet for your sake. Farewell, dear, dear Franz.

Your
RICHARD.

COIRE, *July* 15*th*, 1853.

119.

X. is going to sing in *Tannhäuser* at R. in about a fortnight. She had to leave at once after the concert on July 12th, in order to attend to some starring engagements. I saw her first in her dressing-room at the theatre, where she had kindly invited me to visit her for a quarter of an hour after the concert. That quarter of an hour I employed in doing my duty as a doctor and apothecary in the "well-conditioned" line.

I told her many and sundry things which she was able
to understand.   Before taking leave X. promised me to
sing ORTRUD and Elizabeth at Weymar in the course of
next winter, which I accepted very thankfully.   Papa
X. has some plans for a German opera in London, and
opines that your operas would have a fine effect there.
I replied that the needful and indispensable would first
have to be done for them in Germany.   There is no
hurry about London, and perfect success there is only
possible when the ground in Germany has been firmly
occupied.

To S. and M. I repeated once more that it would be
scandalous not to give *Tannhäuser* on this occasion,
and S. went so far as to promise me that, in case of
difficulties, he would announce *Tannhäuser* with Frau
Anschütz-Capitain in the intervals of the starring
engagement.

Has Schindelmeisser sent you our Wiesbaden *Lohengrin* snuffbox ?   As Ortrud was ill, *Lohengrin* could
not be given this week.   Frau Moritz is a very amiable
and excellent woman and artist.   She is studying Elsa
and Senta, and is quite determined to make active
propaganda for your operas.   Moritz is going to read
your *Ring of the Nibelung* this month at Wiesbaden.

When I go to Carlsruhe, I shall again visit Moritz at
Wiesbaden.

Your letter to C. A. reached me this morning early ;
excellent and worthy of you !   This afternoon I drive
to Ettersburg to pay my respects to the young gentleman, and shall hand him your letter at once.

The Princess of Prussia is here with her mother, and
will probably remain till the end of July.   Whether the

etiquette of court mourning will permit me to have a
talk with her I do not know.

Be happy in the Grisons, you godlike man.   When
you work at the *Nibelungen*, let me be with you, and
keep me within you even as you have received me—in
truth and love.

Your

F. L.

WEYMAR, *July 17th*, 1853.

Enclosed I send you a letter from Köhler, which you
may on occasion return to me.   Have you read his
pamphlet "The Melody of Speech"?   Perhaps you
might write a few words to him.

Do not forget the Carlsruhe scores, and, if possible,
the parts.   Address always Weymar.

[ENCLOSURE.]

HIGHLY ESTEEMED DR. LISZT,

This is my book.   Do not expect to find anything
in it, lest I should have the misfortune of incurring
your censure.

I have sent the book to Wagner, and it makes me
anxious to think that it might displease him; I
wish I knew something definite.   Wagner has given me
infinitely great pleasure by sending me his *Nibelungen*.
I owe this to you ; you were my intercessor.

I am still reading the book.   At first it was strange
to me, but attracted me as something strange does
attract us.   Unconsciously, however, I lost myself in
it, and now feel quite at home in it, with the true joy
fo Valhall.   The work strikes me with a power which

is of a peculiar kind, and I do not care to vex my spirit with reflections. It is such a fine thing if they do not occur of themselves, although, no doubt, the after-effect of the book will lead to reflections. I do not think that for centuries so truly *sublime* a piece of poetry has been created, so powerful, so full of simplicity—simple in diction—there is marrow in every word. Everything in it appears *great*, even in an optic sense; the forms of the gods I see before me large, but endowed with the ideal beauty of force; I hear their voices resound afar, and when they move, the air is stirred. This language is in itself true music, and therefore cannot be " set to music." I have a distinct idea of the actual representation of this work and of its perfection; and I discover a kind of speech melody in the forcibly phrased and vividly grouped verses of Wagner, such as I imagined as the ultimate ideal of dramatic tone-speech when I wrote my book; perhaps you hold a similar opinion, or rather you *know*, as you have been with Wagner. To him I should like to write every day, if only two lines; but Heaven preserve so much occupied a man from my very superfluous words. If Wagner would only let me know ten *vocal* notes from his *Nibelungen*, my mind would be at rest. Wotan is sublime, like a statue in bronze, and yet so humanly conceivable at the same time. The close of the first act of the *Valkyrie* is overpowering. Oh ! how I felt with Siegmund. When I read, my soul seemed to expand as if I were looking from a high point upon a large, new world.

Let me have two brief words about Wagner's intention ; I shall be eternally grateful to you.

I shall always think with delight of my journey and my stay at Weimar. The Altenburg stands daguer-reotyped on my soul.

I still smoke your "Plantages" cigars when I want to reward myself after much working. Your arrangement of the Ninth Symphony for two pianos has filled me with the greatest enthusiasm; it is a marvellous work, which I shall shortly notice in print.

How about new editions? Let me write about them all!

In the *feuilleton* of our newspaper here I wrote three articles about you and Wagner; now, after all, comes S. and writes too, upsetting so many things which I had built up. He is a terribly confused spirit, and the humour of it is that he thinks everybody else confused.

Is Raff working busily at his *Samson*? I hope we shall soon hear something of him. Remember me to him very kindly.

And now I take my leave of you, asking for your forbearance with

Your wholly devoted

LOUIS KÖHLER.

KÖNIGSBERG, *July 3rd*, 1853.

120.

Your splendid letter on rosy paper has cheered me up. The air here feels so thick, so buttery (so like rancid butter). Well, let it be as it may, I do not care; you write your *Nibelungen* and *Delenda Philisterium*!

To the young Grand Duke I gave your letter, and I can assure you that he has fully understood your noble language, your high-toned feeling. I had the honour yesterday of seeing the Princess of Prussia; she is staying here at Belvedere without chamberlain or *dame d'honneur*, simply as the loving and very lovable daughter of her mother, "the Frau Grossherzogin-Grossfürstin" (this is now the official denomination of the Grand Duchess Maria Paulowna). Zigesar, who remains with the latter as acting chamberlain and house-marshal, tells me wonders of the grace and amiability of the Princess of Prussia. I have of course told her many and various things about you.

The Zurich people have acted very well, and we at Weymar have taken cordial interest in your serenade and the torchlight procession. What a pity "Double Peps" was there no longer! He would have drummed and torched with a will.

The day after to-morrow I must start for Carlsbad, and shall stay there till August 15th, wherefore address Carlsbad till middle of August, after that Weymar. The 28th of August (anniversary of Goethe's birthday and of the first performance of *Lohengrin*) is fixed for the " Huldigung " (taking the oath of allegiance to the new Grand Duke). I shall probably be there, and must write a march of about two hundred bars *by command*. Raff is to write a Te Deum for the church ceremony.

For your kind loan of *Tannhäuser* and *Lohengrin* to Carlsruhe I am very thankful to you. You save us time and trouble, and I feel quite safe now.

I expect then that between the 15th and 18th of August (please, not later) all the orchestral and choral parts as well as the scores will be in the hands of Devrient at Carlsruhe, and I shall advise him as to their arrival. A correct and spirited performance of the *Tannhäuser* overture and the pieces from *Lohengrin* I guarantee, and you shall have satisfactory accounts of it.

If not inconvenient, please arrange that I, with several others, may meet you after the Carlsruhe festival (about 24th or 25th September) at Basle. I should like to revive in your company for a few days, which shall be called "*Lohengrin* days." By that time I suppose you will be back from your journey, and a meeting will do good to both of us.

Live happy in the enjoyment of your power, my great, splendid Richard.

Remember me very kindly to George, and let me soon hear from you.

Your

FRANZ.

WEYMAR, *July 25th*, 1853.

Till August 15th address Carlsbad, then again Weymar.

121.

Cordial thanks, dearest friend, for your cheerful letter. I am half ashamed of the dismal mood which prevented me so long from writing to you. I lead here an unbearable, solitary life, in grand but terribly charmless surroundings. At the beginning I made excursions with George to the glaciers and neighbouring valleys, but as this did not agree with my cure, I remained confined to this wretched little place, which, fortunately, I leave the day after to-morrow. Whether the cure has been of use to me the future must show, but upon the whole I am not inclined to repeat it. I am too restless to give up all activity for such a long time. In brief, I am not a fit subject for a cure ; that I perceive. I am now all ablaze to go to Italy, but do not intend to start before the end of August, for they say that only in September Italy becomes comfortable for us. For how long I shall roam about there, Lord only knows. Perhaps I shall not be able to bear it long alone, but the thought of returning to Switzerland so very soon is unpleasant to me. Tell me, dearest Franz, have you quite given up your idea of going to Paris ? Our meeting there would be much pleasanter than at the commonplace Basle. Are you so much tied by time and space ? Of course the hope of seeing *you* once more this year regulates all my plans ; and if you offer me an opportunity for the end of September, I should be a precious fool not to make use of it. See you again therefore I shall in any case ; but I venture to ask that you should make it possible to come to Paris, where I should like to divert my thoughts for a little time before permanently returning to my honest Switzerland. The distance from Carlsruhe to Paris is not greater than to Basle. You get there in one day from Strassburg. Pardon me for pressing this caprice upon you.

The Wiesbaden "*Lohengrin* snuffbox" has had a great effect upon me ; it was forwarded to me here by my wife. Your humour seems to have been excellent, so that Schindelmeisser was no doubt unable to understand it. This snuffbox also shall one day figure in my collection of rarities.

Have you received an invitation from Leipzig ?

Wirsing wrote to me about *Lohengrin*, but I, on my part, wrote to Raymund Härtel asking him to take the matter in hand and to communicate to Wirsing my *conditio sine quâ non*. You perceive that, on the strength of your friendly promise, I have freely taken to sinning.

I hear that at Berlin the scheme of *Tannhäuser* at Kroll's is to be taken seriously in hand in September or October. Schäffer also wrote to me about it.

Young T. wrote to me from Posen that his father had at last permitted him to devote himself to music entirely, and he now prays on his bended knees that I should allow him to live near me at Zurich. This somewhat embarrasses me, for I know that the young man is mistaken in me and Zurich; so I have written to tell him that I am starting on a journey, and that, as he wanted to leave Posen at once, he might first visit you at Weimar, where I would announce him to you. After that he might go with you to Carlsruhe and from there proceed to Zurich, where I should be willing to be of service to him as long as he could stand the place. Do not be angry with me for having put him too on your shoulders; you will soon get rid of him.

I always have an anxious feeling that I might have lost something in your eyes since our meeting, probably because I feel how much you have gained in mine— *gained*! as if there had been anything left for you to gain! What a fool I am!

The parts, etc., I shall send next week to Carlsruhe.

St. George is still very lazy, but he *shall* work. He sends best regards.

Farewell. I must not write more. Tell me soon whether you have not yet had enough of me.

Give my best respects to the Princess. We shall soon meet again !

Farewell, farewell, best of human beings.

Your

R. W.

St. Moritz.

P.S.—The Kroll-Berlin *Tannhäuser* has fallen through after all. Schöneck has just written to me that he has broken with the director, Wallner, because the latter refused to carry out his undertaking as to the excellence of the *ensemble*.

122.

As usual, dearest friend, you have had an excellent idea. It is settled then that we go to Paris, and there have a meeting at the end of September, after the Carlsruhe performances. As before then your chief purpose is to see the Mediterranean, I advise you to go to Genoa and Marseilles, and thence to Paris. Napoleon says, " La Méditerranée est un lac français," so you may go from your Swiss lakes to the French lake for a few weeks and then come to me in Paris.

By the middle of October I must be back at Weymar, but a fortnight of Paris will be quite enough for us. Therefore this is settled.

T. will be very welcome at Weymar. He wrote to me once or twice before, and, between ourselves, I have heard several things about him which make me think that his character is not *oversolid*. But that does not matter, and may be left to Meser.

A few days ago I received a letter from Berlioz, in answer to my last, in which I had said several things about you.

I quote the following lines :—

" Our art, as we understand it, is an art of millionaires ; it requires millions. As soon as these millions are found every difficulty disappears ; every dark intellect is illumined ; moles and foxes are driven back into the earth ; the marble block becomes a god, and the public human : without these millions we remain clodhoppers after thirty years' exertion.

"And yet there is not a sovereign, not a Rothschild, who will understand this. Is it not possible that, after all, we, with our secret pretensions, should simply be stupid and insolent fools ?

"I am, like yourself, convinced of the ease with which Wagner and I should fit each other if only he would grease his wheels a little. As to the few lines of which you speak, I have never read them, and therefore feel not the slightest resentment on their account. I have fired too many pistol-shots at the legs of passers-by to be astonished at receiving a few pellets myself."

In Paris we shall continue the subject ; material and good fun will not be wanting.

At Leipzig I hope to find a few lines from you, and by the end of this month I shall write to you from Weymar when and how long I can be in Paris. If in the meantime I should have to write to you, I shall address to Zurich, as you must to Weymar.

Farewell, and be cheerful, and do not talk nonsense about what you might have lost in my eyes.

At Leipzig I shall attend to the *Lohengrin* affair ; so far I have heard nothing about it.

Your

FRANZ LISZT.

123.

Let me to-day, dear Franz, thank you by a few lines for your last letter. I cannot get on with "writing" to you any longer ; nothing occurs to me but my sorrow at your disappearance and my desire to have you again soon and for long. All else scarcely moves me, and "business" relations between us have very little charm for me. The only thing I can think of is seeing you again in the present year. Give me a rendezvous in Paris after the Carlsruhe festival. In any case I shall send my wife to Carlsruhe, so that she may bring back a taste of you.

Almost my only object in "writing" to you is to ask you to forward the enclosed letter to L. Köhler. I know neither his title, nor his address. You might also apologise to him for this very letter, which, I believe, is written in a terribly bad and confused style. The foolish man wants to hear something from me about his book, but as soon as I bend my head a little towards *theory* the nerves of my brain begin to ache violently, and I feel quite ill. I can and will theorise no longer, and he is not my friend who would lure me back to that cursed ground. *Pereant* all X. and X. if they know of nothing better than this eternal confused speculating about—art !

Here I live in a wild solitude, ice and snow around

me. The day before yesterday we roamed for half a day over glaciers. Herwegh must put up with it. I shall not release him from my net ; he must work. He swore yesterday that he had the poem for you in his head. Good luck !

Get me your medallion, you wicked man. I must have it at once. As to the rest, do with me what you like. About the sending of the parts and score to Carlsruhe I await your instructions. I assume that you received my letter from Coire.

I am almost annoyed that you have had intercourse with X. ; these people are not worth looking after. Be sure that nothing satisfactory will come of it ; we must have *whole* men or *none at all*, no half ones ; they drag us down : we shall never drag them up. I should be proud if this "man of talent" would decline to assist me altogether.

However, in this matter also you must do as you like. Before all, take care that you continue to love me, and that we see each other soon.

Farewell, dearest friend.

Your

R. W.

Many greetings from St. George.

ST. MORITZ, CANTON GRISONS, *July* 26*th*, 1853.

124.

Truly, writing is a misery, and men of our sort should not write at all. However, your *rosy paper* and your luminous letters, which looked like Spanish grandees, gave me real pleasure.

While you are at Coire, intent upon your water-cure, I sit here in Carlsbad looking at nothing but puffed-up faces, excepting one which shines on me like a bright, comforting sun. Till the 16th I must remain here, and on the 22nd I shall be back at Weymar.

By way of entertainment I enjoy Labitzki and his water-cure orchestra, Aldridge, the black Roscius, who plays beautifully Othello, Macbeth, and Fiesco; also spurious Arabs and genuine Chinese, who howl and tinkle to make one run away.

Passing through Leipzig, I saw B. His new book will appear soon, in which there is a separate chapter entitled "Criticism of R. Wagner." We must see whether he has brewed digestible stuff. At Dresden I visited the R.'s. Frau Kummer and her sister had gained my affection at Zurich, and C., who was summoned specially from Pillnitz to meet me, pleased me very well this time. On my journey back I shall again look up the R.'s, for I like to remain in communication with people who prove real friends of yours. We form a little Church of our own, and edify each other by singing your praises. Take note, dear Richard, and make up your mind to it, for it cannot be otherwise. You are now, and will be still more, the concentric focus of every high endeavour, high feeling, and honest effort in art. This is my true conviction, without pedantry and charlatanism, both of which I abhor. Do not fail to use your powerful influence with C., so that he may exert his faculties with some consistency and regularity. I spoke to him of B.'s plan of an *Art Review*. If you set him tasks, he may do good

service to the cause and himself. How about the
"leading programme" which you and H. are to sketch
together ? This is the corner-stone of the whole enterprise. Do not be deterred ; I think it necessary that
you should submit to some trouble and tedium for the
purpose. Before going to Weymar I shall have some
definite talk with B. about the matter. If you want to
communicate with me on the subject, address *Poste
restante*, Leipzig, or, better still, to the care of Y., so that
the letter arrive in Leipzig on the 19th inst. Perhaps
by that time you will have been able to settle the chief
heads of the programme of "Blätter für Gegenwart und
Zukunft der Gesammt-Kunst" and to draw the outline
of the whole scheme.

I repeat it once more, without you and your direct
and indirect influence nothing, or something much
worse than nothing, will be done. Therefore be
patient and help as and where you can.

Do not forget that E. D. expects the *Tannhäuser* and
Lohengrin scores and parts for the Carlsruhe festival
on August 15th. You are always so careful and
punctual in fulfilling your promises that I am under
no anxiety, and only tell you that they wish to
begin studying your pieces in Carlsruhe as soon as
possible.

B. will probably come to Carlsruhe, and will be at
Weymar at the end of this month. I have spoken to
Meser at Dresden and warmly recommended to him H.
as the most suitable musician to entrust with the
four-hand pianoforte arrangement of *Tannhäuser*. If
Meser should write to you about it, be good enough
to propose H. to him for this work in preference to

other arrangers and derangers. Give my best remembrances to G., and abide with me.

Your

F. L.

CARLSBAD, *August 7th*, 1853.

P.S.—Our friend Köhler has latterly been severely
attacked by several individuals who have the arrogance
to think that they stand in opposition to you, while in
reality they move in a low and *bottomless* region. As
you probably do not read similar newspapers, I tell you
of the fact, and ask you to take account of it in your
intercourse with Köhler, whom you should keep in
kindly remembrance as one of the *loyal*.

Köhler will visit you next year ; you will be satisfied
with him. I forwarded your letter to him at once.

P.S.—Try, if possible, to be back from your intended
journeys by the end of September, so that we may
meet after Carlsruhe. I hope to be quite free on
September 24th.

125.

DEAREST FRIEND,

I returned from St. Moritz a little sooner
than I had thought ; of my intention to that effect, I
believe I wrote to you before. Your last letter was
forwarded to me punctually. What pleased me most
in it was your good humour and the fact that you spent
your day at Dresden with the R.'s, of which they had
already informed me in great triumph. Reading their
accounts, I felt as if I had been there myself, and as
if that evening had only been a continuation of the
Zeltweg days. It was splendid and kind of you. As
to K. I must wait ; we shall see later on.

George promised me yesterday that he also would write to you to-day. From what he says, he is well inclined towards the matter; I shall be glad if it is taken in hand seriously, for then I shall have hope for a possible success of the enterprise even *without* me.

My dear Franz, once for all do not reckon upon me for any critico-literary enterprise; I CANNOT go in for that kind of thing. Just as some time ago it was an absolute necessity to me to express my revolution in the fields of art and of life in perfect continuity, even so, and for *that very reason*, I have at present no inclination for such manifestations, which are no longer a necessity to me. Of this you must be aware, for you know and prove by your own deeds that "quand on agit, on ne s'explique pas;" and I am at present disposed only for action, no longer for explanation. You seem to be of opinion, however, that for the sake of the cause I might conquer my inclination a little and in my own way exert myself. It is just this point which I have made clear to myself: my faculties, taken separately, are not great, and I can only be and do something good when I concentrate all those faculties on one impulse and recklessly consume them and myself for its sake. Whatever part that impulse leads me to adopt, that I am as long as necessary, be it musician, poet, conductor, author, reciter, or what not. In that manner I at one time became a speculative art philosopher. But apart from this main current I can create and do nothing except under extreme compulsion, and in that case I should do something very bad and expose the smallness of my special faculties in a deplorable manner. What you want of me, or rather, as I know very well, what X. wants of me, there is no longer any need for my doing. I have spoken about the theme in question so often and at such length that I am conscious of having done quite enough. X. and his friends and enemies have not even read my writings as they should be read in order to be understood. Otherwise it would be quite impossible that this wretched " separate art" and " universal art" should be the upshot of all my disquisitions. Honestly speaking, I am sick of discussing with stupid people things which they can never take in, because there is in them not a trace of artistic or really human stuff. If I were to take up the cudgels once more, it would be rather against these unfortunate enlightened people than against the intentionally retrograde Jesuits of litera-ture, with whom one need not trouble one's self unless one wants to talk for victory as a litterateur, which has never entered my mind. *Certainly*, MOST CER-TAINLY, *I should be very glad* to know that I had been rightly understood by many people, glad to see and to hear that clever, instructive, and enlightening things were written and laid down in a journal devoted to such an object; this, indeed, would be the reward of my sacrifices. But, good heavens! there is surely no need that *I* should write, that *I* should help, again ; these things should come to me from ANOTHER quarter. It cannot possibly suit me to write the same thing over and over again on the chance of being at last understood, besides which I should probably only puzzle people worse and worse.

Therefore if, in your opinion, the review cannot be started without me, I simply say, Very well then ; leave till I reach Geneva. From the *Carlsruhe Gazette* I see that the festival is fixed for October 3rd to 5th; to me this delay does not matter, and I hope it does not to you either. The Härtels recently forwarded to me some louis d'or on the part of Wirsing, without informing me that you had been invited to superintend *Lohengrin* at Leipzig or that you had accepted the invitation. I hope soon to get particulars from you. I suppose you received my letter at Leipzig. The lazy H. informs me that he has not yet written to you. What is one to do? I am on my way to Turin, dearest Franz, where I shall stay a little time; and if you answer at once, your next letter will find me there *Poste restante*. (In any case address Turin until further notice.) I am out of sorts, and suffer from sleeplessness. The French *visé* worries me very much. I should like so much to meet you in Paris; it would be splendid.

Greet Berlioz for me; he is a funny customer; he has not yet arrived at the point where millionaires only could be of use to him. But he is a noble fellow, and all will be right in the end.

Adieu, you best and dearest of all men; continue to love me.

Your
RICHARD.

BERNE, *August 25th*, 1853.

127.

DEAREST FRIEND,
I am back again in Zurich, unwell, low-spirited, ready to die.

---

it alone, for in that case it has no object and no value. I still have hopes of G.; he is certainly lazy, but, at any rate, I know that *he* knows what is at stake and what should be done. Moreover, his whole nature at present impels him to discharge his inner being in the direction necessary for us; if he once is in the proper swing, I hope he will persevere. It is of course understood that my advice, my views, and my opinions are always at his disposal, and in very special cases I may go to work myself; but I must first see that others commence and initiate the work.

Before all, keep that unfortunate "Universal Art" out of the title!

Enough of this!

I am in a miserable condition, and have great difficulty in persuading myself that it must go on like this, and that it would not really be more moral to put an end to this disgraceful kind of life. Solitude and disconsolate loneliness from morning till night—such are the days that follow each other and make up life. To cure my sick brain the doctor has prevailed upon me to give up taking snuff altogether; for the last six days I have not taken a single pinch, which only he can appreciate who is himself as passionate a snuff-taker as I was. Only now I begin to perceive that snuff was the solitary real enjoyment that I had occasionally, and now I give that up too. My torture is indescribable, but I shall persevere; that is settled. Therefore no more *snuff-boxes*; in future I accept only *orders of merit*.

My journey is settled in this manner: August 24th I start from here, and arrive in Turin on the 29th at the latest. You can address *Poste restante*, unless you write to me here first, from where all my letters will be forwarded to me. Genoa, Spezzia, Nice, will detain me till I hear from you for certain when and where our meeting is to be. In the *Carlsruhe Gazette* it was announced that the Musical Festival had been postponed till October; will our meeting have to be postponed too? If you cannot come to Paris, I will of course come to Basle; that is understood. As you happen to be in Leipzig, very kindly remember me to Brendel; I wish he could have visited me, and think that we should have got further in many ways. (Devrient was here when I and my wife too were absent!) Frau Steche recently wrote to me; she shall have an answer before I start. Could you lend her a copy of the *Nibelungen*? B. is not to read it out. Altogether I am very sorry that I ever had the poem printed; it is not to be pulled about like this; it still is *mine*.

Have you received any communication as to *Lohengrin* at Leipzig? Härtel has left me without an answer for ever so long. I hope I shall hear soon how the matter stands.

Farewell; ah, farewell. How I envy you your whole existence. Greet your esteemed friend from me, and arrange so that you both come to Switzerland soon; in that case something may still become of me. Adieu, dear, unique friend.

Your

R. W.

Zurich, *August 16th*, 1853.

126.

"Sancte Franzisce! ora pro nobis!"

I write to you to-day from the very first stage of my Italian journey, because, as fate would have it, I was unable to answer your last letter from Carlsbad before this. Everything else is thrown into the shade by our rendezvous in Paris, to which you have given your consent in so splendid a manner. But now you must do all in your power to assist me in making it possible. Listen.

The French minister has refused to give me his *visé* for my passport to Paris, and to-day I called on M. Salignac-Fénélon at Berne and had a long talk with him about it. Here again you must help me. Salignac after having become better acquainted with me, promised that he would write at once to his Government in Paris, setting forth that, in his opinion, I have been calumniated, that personally I have inspired him with confidence, etc. He wishes that you should talk to the French minister at Weimar about this matter, so that he too might write to Paris and put in a good word for me. Salignac thinks it would be of good effect if the Grand Duke himself would say a few words in my favour to the minister. As I have told them the true object of my journey to Paris and mentioned Berlioz as one who is to take part in our meeting, it would be well if you could let Berlioz know at once, for it is very possible that inquiries may be made of him as to the truth of my statements. Do get me this *visé* for Paris. I am too delighted to think of our meeting. I was in hopes of getting a few lines from you from Leipzig before my departure, but shall probably not receive them

At Genoa I became ill, and was terror-struck by my
solitary condition, but I was determined to do Italy, and
went on to Spezzia. My indisposition increased; enjoyment was out of the question; so I turned back to die or
to compose, one or the other; nothing else remains to me.

Here you have the whole story of my journey, *my*
" Italian journey."

I am anxious because I have had no letter from you
for so long. You received a letter from me at Leipzig;
has it annoyed you? From Berne I wrote to you
about the *visé* of my passport for France, and you were
to send your answer to Turin. If that has been done,
the letter will be forwarded to me. But why is it that
I hear nothing else of you? Has the Carlsruhe festival
been postponed, and will it be too late for you to come
to Paris? I must be content; I want to see *you,*
wherever it may be; if Zurich is too far for you, I will
come to Basle. Paris begins almost to be unpleasant to
me in my imagination; I am afraid of Berlioz. With my
bad French, I am simply lost.

I have found many silly letters here, amongst
others the enclosed from Director Engel, of Kroll's
establishment, Berlin. It seems to me as if I could
scarcely accept his proposition. May I leave the
matter to you, and will you kindly take the decision
upon yourself? In order to know what may be useful
or detrimental, one must have a local knowledge,
which I cannot possibly acquire here. Could you
through Kroll, Schäffer, and others make inquiries which
would enable you to judge of the effect of such an
undertaking as that projected by Engel? To me this
Tannhäuser on the concert platform is horrible, in spite

of the six louis d'or for each performance. Of course I cannot tell whether, apart from the absurdity of the thing, it would not be well to keep the fire alight in Berlin. It seems certain that in the *higher regions there* everything is as dull as possible, and that no decisive step in my favour will be made in that quarter. I wish you would simply say "Yes" or "No." How about Leipzig? I can get no real information from there. It is very long since I heard anything of *you*!

Alas! I am out of sorts and God-forsaken. I feel so lonely, and yet do not want to see any one. What a miserable existence! I cannot help smiling when I read in B.'s paper the articles by R. F.'s brother-in-law; the man thinks he is going thoroughly to the bottom of the thing, because he is so moderate and cautious; *he* knows very little of me. Formerly I was very sensitive to being fumbled about in this manner; at present I am quite indifferent, because I know that this kind of thing does not touch me at all. If these people would but know that I wish to be entirely happy only once, and after that should not care to exist any more! Oh for the leathern immortality of india-rubber, which these people think it necessary to attribute to one by way of reward!

Adieu, dearest and best. See that we soon possess each other again, otherwise I shall go from bad to worse.

Adieu, dear Franz.

Your

RICHARD.

ZURICH, *September* 12*th*, 1853.

128.

DEAR FRANZ,

There is a young Frenchman here who lives at
Florence, and wants to become acquainted with my
music, in which your pamphlet has interested him. His
journey is arranged chiefly with a view to hearing my
operas, and in order to reward his zeal I thought I
could not very well decline his request of a few lines to
you ; so I commend him to your kindness.

Your

RICHARD W.

ZURICH, *September* 13*th*, 1853.

129.

CARLSRUHE, *September* 19*th*, 1853.

At last, dearest, unique friend, I am again nearer
you, and in a fortnight or eighteen days we shall
meet either at Basle or Paris. As soon as I know
myself I shall send you particulars. To-day I only
ask you to send me your passport by return of post, so
that I may transact the affair with the French minister
here in case you have not yet received a definite
answer from Berne. The French minister at Weymar,
Baron de Talleyrand, is unfortunately at present in
Scotland, but I think it will require no special patron-
age to get the necessary *visé*. Send me your passport
by return of post, and I will take care of the rest.

At Dresden I stayed lately for more than a fortnight.
About Tichatschek, Fischer (now operatic stage-
manager), and the theatrical affairs there I must tell
you several things when I see you, also about matters
at Leipzig. I have settled with Rietz that I shall be

present at the final rehearsals and the first performance
of *Lohengrin*, and shall give you an accurate account of
it. When I came to Leipzig, I found a good deal of
gossip about the *Lohengrin* performance current there.
But now it has probably ceased, and you will hear
no more of it.

The opera is to be given in the course of November,
and, in my opinion, a very warm reception of your
work on the part of the public may be expected. The
fortress of Leipzig has been conquered for your name
and your cause, and even the " Wohlbekannte " informed me that he had been moved to tears by the
Lohengrin finale. If things go on in this way, Leipzig
will soon " Lohengrinise." If there should be a delay
of the performance, it will do no harm; *au contraire*, and
in that respect even the aforesaid town gossip was not
unfavourable. I shall tell you about all this at length.
The matter concerning Engel I shall settle to-morrow,
and shall write to you at once ; I am still a little
doubtful whether one ought to accept or not. Conradi,
the Capellmeister, is a friend of mine ; and if anything
comes of the matter, I shall put myself in communication
with him. He has known *Tannhäuser* ever since the
year 1849, when he was staying at Weymar. Such an
undertaking depends largely upon the manner of execution. For the present I am of opinion that we ought
to be in no hurry about giving our consent ; a concert
performance of *Tannhäuser* at Kroll's establishment
has much against it, and might probably interfere
with the stage performance which must of necessity
follow. Leave the whole matter to me. H. has a good
idea ; he thinks that if E. is so favourably inclined

towards spreading your works in Berlin, or rather towards making money by them, he might arrange a repetition of your Zurich concerts with the identical programme. But about this also there is no hurry. On certain conditions I should be prepared to go to Berlin and undertake the direction of the three Zurich concerts. I should probably employ the Male Choir Association which Wieprecht conducts, and of which I have had the honour of being honorary conductor ever since the year 1843.

More about this on an early occasion. In the meantime I think you will do well to write to E. that you cannot accustom yourself to the idea of a concert performance of your drama.

Enough for the present.

Your

F. L.

CARLSRUHE, *September 20th*, 1853.

130.

DEAREST FRANZ,

Very angry as I am with you for having left me without news so long, you shall have a rose-coloured sheet to-day in return for the excellent news of your proximity and of our early *meeting*. By return of post I was unable to answer you, because your letter had to be forwarded to me at Baden, where I stay at intervals with my wife, who is undergoing a cure there. Enclosed is the passport. Salignac-Fénélon, the French minister at Berne, has sent me no news up to date, and it will therefore be well if you can settle the matter with the minister at Carlsruhe. Even if Paris had to be given up for the present, which must entirely depend on you, it will be of importance to me to have the French *visé*, so as not to be shut out from Paris and France for the future. You may safely offer every possible guarantee, and promise that I shall not mix myself up with any political matters. I know that this will satisfy the French Government. They may, moreover, be certain that I shall not permanently stay in France, but without fail return to Switzerland. For your communications about Leipzig and Berlin I thank you cordially; as to Berlin it shall be exactly as you say.

What will happen at Carlsruhe? D. again left me recently without an answer, probably because I asked him to advance me the honorarium for *Tannhäuser*, as I had reason to be anxious about my income.

By the way, concerning the rendering of the very difficult male chorus "Im Früh'n versammelt uns der Ruf," I must ask you to choose the best singers for it.

For the *piano* passage (A major, E in the bass) it would be well if eight soloists were to sing about eight bars by themselves; the neat, elegant *piano* cannot be done by a large chorus. (This is a minor matter.)

You appear to be well and in good spirits; you are a *happy* man. From Dresden Julia wrote to me in ecstacy about you; you must have been very comfortable; a good thing I was not there and remained alone instead.

Child, I have much to tell you. If matters are to go well, you must frequently stay in Switzerland; then all will be right. About this and similar things we shall talk.

In the meantime let me have news from Carlsruhe now and then.

My real life lies always abroad.

God bless you. Take my most joyful greeting and kiss.

Your
RICHARD.

ZURICH, *September 22nd*, 1853.

131.

I have at last hit upon a way of settling your passport affair which will make it unnecessary for me to have your passport here. When all is settled, I will let you know how it has been done. I herewith return your passport and ask you to apply to Fénélon again, either by letter or personally, when probably he will not hesitate to affix his *visé* to your passport. Tell him that you intend to start for Paris on October 5th at the latest, and that we two are to meet at Basle. Concerning this meeting I ask you particularly to be at Basle on the evening of the 6th without fail. J., Pohl, and probably several others are longing to see you, and I have promised to take them to you at Basle. I should like to come again to Zurich, but am too much pressed for time. At Basle, then, either at the "Storch" or at the "Drei Könige," as you prefer. I hope that by that time you will have received your passport, and we can then at once concoct our journey to Paris.

Answer "Yes" without fail, and do not mind the somewhat tedious journey from Zurich to Basle. To-day my rehearsals begin here, and I shall again have to go to Darmstadt and Mannheim to have separate rehearsals, till we return here next Saturday for the general rehearsals. In addition to this, I have to *pay my respects* to a number of known and unknown people of all sorts.

Are not your wife and Madame Heim coming to the festival ? Let me know in case they have that intention, for at the last moment it will be difficult to get tickets.

I am obliged to you for your instruction as to the eight singers in the A major passage (E in the bass) of the *Lohengrin* chorus, and shall act upon it. Do not be angry, dearest friend, on account of my long silence and my insignificant letters. You know that my whole soul is devoted to you, because I love you sincerely, and that I always try to serve you as well as I can.

Your

FRANZ LISZT.

Sunday, September 25th, 1853.

P.S.—It would be the simplest thing if you could go to Berne yourself; but this is not absolutely necessary, and it will be sufficient if you write to his Excellency, enclosing your passport and asking him to return it to you at Zurich by October 3rd. Perhaps it would be better if you were to write, so that he may forward your letter to Paris. Consider this, and do not forget that we are to meet at Basle on the evening of October 6th.

132.

Best thanks, my dearest Franz. I have just written to M. Fénélon, enclosing my passport once more. Candidly speaking, the matter suddenly begins to annoy me very much, and I do not expect a good result. My

wish quite coincides with your plan. I fully anticipated that Basle could not be avoided altogether; it is
adapted for a meeting with the friends who have come
to Carlsruhe. The excursion to Paris after that concerns
us two alone; so our thoughts have once more been the
same.

As to the rest, I am longing to get to work at last.
My ordinary life is unbearable unless I, so to speak,
devour myself. Moreover, I cannot keep my peace, as I
particularly want to do, unless I devote myself to this
music.

After your visit, everything came to nothing with me
this summer; no other hope was fulfilled, all went
wrong, and—well, we shall see whether I get this
passport.

The day after to-morrow week, we shall meet! (I
wish it were the day after to-morrow.) Will you, or
shall I, engage the hotel? Let it be the "Drei Könige;"
they have nice rooms there and a balcony looking over
the Rhine; let us engage some of those. You are once
more in the middle of your exertions, and I must almost
envy you; I at least realise by such exertions alone
that I am alive. Rest is death to me; and if sometimes
I go in quest of it,—I mean that other rest; the beautiful,
the joyful,—I feel that in reality it must be nothing but
death, but real, noble, perfect death, not this death in
life which I die from day to day.

Adieu, dearest friend.

What a blessing that you have no double!

Au revoir soon!   Your

RICHARD W.

ZURICH, *September 29th,* 1853.

133.

DEAREST FRIEND,

It just occurs to me that in *Lohengrin* I have forgotten to mark the tempo in one place, which I discovered only when I conducted it here—I mean in the "Bridal Song" in D major, after the second solo passage of the eight women, the last eight bars before the *tempo primo*.

Here the tempo is to be considerably slower even than at the first entry of the D major; the impression must be one of solemn emotion, or else the intention is lost.

How are you?

To-day week!

Your

R. W.

September 29th, 1853.

In the "Bridal Procession" (E flat), where the first tempo reappears in the woodwind,

that woodwind ought to be doubled.

134.

I have promised the concert score of the *Lohengrin* pieces to Apt, director of the "Cäcilienverein,"

Prague; therefore kindly leave word at Carlsruhe that this score is to be sent immediately after the last concert to Apt in Prague; the parts to go back here.

Yesterday you had the general rehearsal; I am always with you.

The day after to-morrow! I say, "The day after to-morrow!"

Adieu.

Your
R. W.

ZURICH, *October 2nd*, 1853.

135.

Here I stand and stare after you; my whole being is silence; let me not seek words, even for you. Speech seems to exist only to do violence to feeling. Therefore no violence, but *silence*!

I have not much news for you from the "world." To-morrow I start for home, but shall see your children before I go. Madame Kalergy I did not find at home, and am doubtful whether I shall see her. Make my excuses to her.

From Zurich I shall write to you again. Be thanked for your blissful love! Greet the Princess and the Child! Can I write more? Ah, I am all feeling. My intellect is within my heart, but from my heart I cannot *write* to you.

Farewell, farewell, you dear beloved ones.

Your
RICHARD W.

PARIS *October 26th*, 1853.

136.

I suppose you have nothing to write to me, dear Franz, or else you would have sent me a few lines.

Your children told me that they had had a letter from you, telling them that you had quickly got to Weimar and had lived there quietly till your birthday without seeing anybody. On your birthday I made some music in Paris; I had at last to offer something to my two or three old Paris friends, one of whom you appreciated.

Erard sent me a grand pianoforte, which has filled me with a fanatical desire to perform some flights on it, even if I had still to learn fingering. So then I began to *Tannhäuser* and to *Lohengrin* on the Boulevard des Italiens as if you were with us. The poor devils could not understand why I was beside myself. However, it went better than at Madame Kalergy's, although you were present then. Why ?—Madame Kalergy I did not see again, but I hope the few lines I sent her have made my excuses. Apart from this, I received a visit from an *agent de police*, who, after I had passed my examination satisfactorily, assured me that I might stay in Paris *a whole month*. My answer that I should leave *sooner* astonished him, and he repeated that I might stop *a whole month*. The good man ! dear Paris ! The Emperor also I saw. What more can one desire ?

The day before yesterday I arrived here. Peps received me joyfully at the carriage, and in return I gave him a beautiful collar, engraved with his name, which has become sacred to me. He never leaves my side ; in the morning he comes to my bed to awake me. He is a dear, good animal.

The minster of Strassburg I saw again; my good wife stood with me in front of it. It was dull, rainy weather. The divine point of the tower we could not see; it was covered by mist. How different from that other day, the sacred Sunday before the minster!

Let it be night; the stars shine then. I look upwards and behold; for me also there shines a star.

Farewell, and greet the dear ones. To-day the *Rhinegold* was coursing through my veins; if it is to be, if it cannot be otherwise, you shall have a work of art that will give you JOY (?).

Dear, unique friend, remember your poor

RICHARD W.

137.

The " pale mariner " has once more gone across the stage here, and in his honour I yesterday occupied the conductor's seat again, after an interval of eight months.

With the *Flying Dutchman* I left the orchestra for a time at the beginning of last March, and with the same work I resume my connection with the theatre for this season.

You may assume that my passion for your tone and word-poems is the only reason why I do not give up my activity as a conductor. Small as may be the result that I can achieve, it is not, I think, altogether illusory. We have arranged a Wagner week; and the *Flying Dutchman, Tannhäuser,* and *Lohengrin* have taken firm ground and cast deep roots here. All the rest is moonshine to me with the sole exception of Berlioz's *Cellini.* For this work I retain my great predilection.

which you will not think uncalled for when you know it better.

Next week I shall have to rehearse *Tell*, and the opera will be given in a fortnight. *Tannhäuser* will follow immediately afterwards. As our new tenor, Dr. Liebert, a very willing, industrious, and gifted singer, has never sung the part, I shall go through it with him separately once or twice. In all probability the performance this year will be better than the previous ones. The *Flying Dutchman* was given yesterday, to the increased satisfaction of the public. Milde and his wife acted and sang beautifully, and I may assume that you would have witnessed the performance without grumbling, although our weak chorus is a fatal evil. Four or five new engagements have been made for the chorus, but that of course is by no means sufficient.

Immediately after my return, I proposed to Zigesar to give *Lohengrin*, with Tichatschek and Johanna, on the evening when the court visits the theatre again. (The strict mourning will last several months still, and during that time the court box remains empty and dark.) If no special impediments arise, that performance will take place. Up till then I shall conduct only your two operas, *Tell* and Dorn's *Nibelungen*.

Of my personal affairs I say nothing. The poor Princess sends her friendliest greetings. She is troubled with a large mass of correspondence of the most unpleasant kind. May God grant that next summer we enter a new stage of the *status quo*, and that our Zurich trip need not be delayed after the end of June.

Your *Rhinegold* is ready, is it not? Bestir yourself,

dearest friend. Work is the only salvation on this
earth. Sing and write, therefore, and get rid of your
brain abscess by that means. Perhaps your sleep
will become a little more reposeful in the same manner.

Kind remembrances to your wife from your

FRANZ.

October 31st, 1853.

Do you remember a Herr Friedrich Schmitt, professor of singing at Munich? Have you read his
pamphlet, and what do you think of it? Write me
two words about it. How about Tyszkiewiz? Did
you see him at Paris several times after I had left?

138.

DEAREST FRANZ,

My threat that I should once more lay you
under contribution in an impudent manner must to-day
be realised. Listen to me! I feel so hale and hearty
at my work that I may expect everything—not only the
success of my music, but better health as well—if I can
only stick to it without interruption and yield to my
splendid mood without anxiety. If I had to get up in
the morning without taking at once to my music, I
should be unhappy. This is the first day I break into
in order, if possible, to get rid once for all of this fear
which follows me like a treacherous spectre. For that
reason I must arrange my money affairs so as not to be
molested by them any longer. This I can do by selling
my theatrical royalties on *Lohengrin.* By the peculiar
character of this income I am kept in a state of strange
and most painful excitement. Although it is tolerably

certain that my two last operas will be given at all German theatres, as *Tannhäuser* has already been at most of them, the *time* when they may be asked for and paid for is so uncertain that I, being largely dependent upon this income, often get into a fatally unsettled state of mind, in which my sanguine temperament is apt to suggest to me that the royalties to be expected are nearer than they really are. By that means I overrate my immediate income, and consequently spend considerably more than I possess. By the occasional and illusory character of these theatrical royalties and by my certainly indefensible liking for a pleasanter way of life than I have led these last years, I have been placed in the position of having to pay large sums next Christmas without being able to reckon upon any income whatever with certainty. Even if the case were not as urgent as it is, this eternal waiting upon chance, this continual expectation of the postman, whether he is going to bring me an offer or a favourable answer, are so troublesome, so humiliating and disturbing to me, that I am compelled to think of a radical cure, and for that purpose I want you to assist me with the Härtels.

I propose to sell to the Härtels the copyright of the score of *Lohengrin*, including the right of selling it to theatrical managers, with the following exceptions only:—

1. The court theatres of Berlin, Vienna, and Munich, which will have to acquire the performing rights of *Lohengrin* from *me*.

2. The theatres of Weimar, Dresden, Wiesbaden, and Leipzig, which have already obtained those performing rights from me.

A list of the theatres which will have to apply to the new proprietor will be found on the enclosed sheet. It includes all those theatres which have already successfully produced *Tannhäuser* or will produce it soon, as may be safely predicted from these precedents In the case of the twenty-two theatres to which 1 have already sold *Tannhäuser* the amount of the honorarium received has been indicated; and for the correctness of these indications, as well as for the fact that I am not going to let the other fifteen theatres have it cheaper than is in each case stated, I pledge my word of honour. The aggregate income from the twenty-two and from the fifteen theatres I calculate, as the enclosure shows, at six hundred and thirty-two louis d'or; and the question is now what sum I can demand of the purchaser of *Lohengrin*, including the theatrical rights, on condition that he pays me in cash by Christmas of the present year ; that is, by December 20th, 1853.

I should prefer to apply to Messrs. Härtel in this matter—(1) because they would be the most respectable purchasers ; (2) because they are the publishers of the score and pianoforte arrangements, and are therefore interested in the success of the whole ; and (3) because this would at last give me an opportunity of coming to terms with them as to a proper honorarium for the copyright of *Lohengrin*.

If Messrs. Härtel remember in what circumstances I at that time offered them the publication of *Lohengrin*; if they call to mind that I expressly told them that I did not believe in the success of my operas, at least during my lifetime, and that therefore I looked upon their undertaking the publication simply as a sacrifice, which they made in the interest of a hopeless but respectable cause; if they bear me out in saying that I myself acknowledged the wiping out of an old debt (of the settlement of which they had, on account of my position, the very remotest chance) to be in these hopeless circumstances a sacrifice on their part, but that at the same time I expressed my conviction that in case, against all expectation, *Lohengrin* should turn out a success, and its publication a GOOD speculation, they would think of me in a generous manner—in case of all this these gentlemen will not consider it unfair or inopportune if I look upon the circumstances as changed to such an extent that I may now think of some profit for myself. In the first instance it is a fact confirmed to me by repeated observations and experiences that even before there was a sign of a further spreading of these operas by means of theatrical and concert performances the publication of my works had developed into an exceptionally good business, entirely through means of Weimar and of your efforts, dearest friend. In consequence of some concerts, and recently the incredibly successful performance at Wiesbaden, this has become more and more certain, and nothing similar has perhaps ever happened to an opera before it had been made known by the leading theatres. It has also been shown that wherever parts of it were performed the music of *Lohengrin* was much more attractive even than that of *Tannhäuser*, although the latter also occupies the theatres and the public to such a degree that it everywhere prepares the way for *Lohengrin*. It may therefore be confidently assumed that *Lohengrin*, after the example of *Tannhäuser*, will

make the round of all the theatres and secure the favour
of the public even more lastingly than the latter, which
has been the saving of more than one manager. In
such circumstances, while thanking the Messrs. Härtel
for undertaking the publication in the first instance,
I venture to remind them of a debt of honour in the
sense that they should allow me to have my share
in this success of the business. If, in accordance with
their generous turn of mind, I may expect Messrs.
Härtel to be favourably inclined towards this—
especially as at the time they undertook the matter
less for the sake of gain than of honour—the question
would only be in what manner they should assign to
me my share of the profits. Perhaps they would
be very willing to let me have a certain portion of
the money accruing from the sale of detached parts
of the opera. I remember that when, ten years
ago, I proposed to them the publication of the *Flying
Dutchman*, they offered me the profits of the sale of
the large pianoforte score after fifty or a hundred
copies had been disposed of. Lucrative as my share
might turn out in this manner, yet this kind of
income would show the same unsatisfactory and painful
features already complained of in connection with
the uncertain theatrical royalties, which therefore I
should like to sell outright. I should then prefer
a sum payable at once, and all that we need find out
is the price, fair to both parties. For that purpose I may
first mention the step which I have fixed upon taking
in order to make the copyright of *Lohengrin* much more
valuable than otherwise it would be—I mean the publication of *separate vocal and pianoforte pieces.* We all

know that the so-called *morceaux détachés* are the chief source of profit in the case of operas ; to publish such would in the case of *Lohengrin* be impossible on account of the peculiar character of the opera, in which there are no single vocal pieces that in a manner detach themselves from the context. I alone, being the composer, was able to separate a number of the most attractive vocal pieces from the whole by means of rearranging and cutting them and writing an introduction and a close to them, etc. *Nine* such pieces, short, easy, and even popular, I gave you some time ago, asking you to keep them till further order and then send them to Messrs. Härtel ; they may be published as arranged *by me.* In addition to this, I indicated to B. five numbers, arranged in a similar manner as the vocal pieces, only longer, which he is to transfer to the pianoforte as independent and melodious pieces. By that manner the bad impression of the pianoforte scores without words, arranged without my concurrence, and perfectly useless, would be obviated.

Apart from adding in this way to the value of the copyright, I have opened to my publishers an unexpected source of income by transferring to them the right of printing the librettos for the theatres. How very lucrative this generally acknowledged right is may be seen from the fact that in *one* winter six thousand copies of the libretto of *Tannhäuser* were ordered for Breslau alone. Messrs. Härtel offered to *share* the profits of the sale of librettos with me, but in this case also I prefer to take at once a lump sum, to be settled upon. After having stated in this manner what I offer to my publishers for sale, I think it appropriate to name the lump sum which I think I may ask.

The receipts from the theatres (with the exception of those specified) I have in the above calculated at six hundred and thirty-two louis d'or. This is a minimum which, no doubt, could be considerably increased. I have already announced to the theatres that they will have to pay more for *Lohengrin* than for *Tannhäuser*. Breslau, for example, would certainly have to pay at the least twenty-five louis d'or, as they did for the *Flying Dutchman*, instead of twenty; I might even insist on thirty. Apart from this, I have not mentioned *all* the theatres; I have, for example, omitted Ratisbon, Innsbruck, and others, although even the smallest theatres have attempted *Tannhäuser*; Zurich also I have not mentioned. In addition to this, I place at the disposal of the purchasers the non-German theatres abroad, such as Petersburg, Stockholm, Copenhagen, Amsterdam, etc., with the exception, however, of London and Paris. All this and everything accruing from the copyright I should cede to the Messrs. Härtel for the sum of 15,000 francs (I have calculated the theatrical receipts at a minimum of 13,000 francs), payable in full at Zurich on December 20th.

I wish very much that this or something similar could be brought about, so that I might be able to dispose of the next few years—those most important working years— and to keep them clear of all mean anxieties. If you consider, dearest Franz, that I do not offer rubbish for sale, that *in the future* this opera and *Tannhäuser alone* are likely to yield me an income—I do not wish, even in my thoughts, to soil the *Nibelungen* with Jewish calculations, so as to keep them, if possible, quite clean in this respect also—if you, finally, go through my general, but I think accurate and by no means chimerical, calculations, you will perhaps find my demand fair enough and—now I am coming to it— *support it with the Härtels.*

This I ask you fervently to do.

An opportunity will be offered to you by the impending performance of *Lohengrin* at Leipzig. No one of course can compel the Härtels to undertake the purchase, even for a smaller sum; but if any one can, it is you, and therefore I had to apply to you.

Perish all this Jewish business! To-day has been a bad, musicless day; out of doors also it is grey and misty; let us hope to-morrow will be better.

Farewell, my most unique, my dearest friend.

Your

Richard W.

Zurich, *November 16th*, 1853.

139.

Dearest Richard,

I returned last night from Leipzig with a bad cold; and the enclosed letter from Härtel, which I found here, has made my cold and my temper worse. When I went to Leipzig on December 1st, I spoke to the Härtels about your proposal, and showed them your letter, because that document explains the matter clearly and comprehensively. I have known the Härtels for years to be respectable and *comme il faut*, and therefore flattered myself that they would meet your wish in one way or another. Such, however, is unfortunately not the case; and I am in the unpleasant position of having to forward you a refusal. It is just possible that they were a little riled by your dislike of the pianoforte arrangement for four hands, which I think quite justified and natural on your part. I was unable to conceal this detail from them, because I think it of some importance for all further copyright transactions. The Härtels belong to the "moderate party of progress," and are influenced by several friends of the so-called historic school. Jahn especially is a great friend of Dr. Härtel's; and your and my friends Pohl, Ritter, Brendel, etc., are a little in their bad books.

To-morrow week (December 21st) *Lohengrin* is announced at Leipzig, but probably the first performance will be delayed till the 26th (Boxing Day). In any case I shall go over for the two last general rehearsals and for the first performance, and shall send you an accurate account. Rietz is said to be very careful with the orchestral rehearsals, taking the woodwind, the brass, and the strings separately. Altogether the *Lohengrin* performance at Leipzig has been very well prepared, and a decisive and permanent success of the work may be anticipated *with certainty*.

Berlioz has had his *revanche* for his previous appearance at the Gewandhaus by the two performances of his works which took place at the Gewandhaus December 1st and 11th, under his own direction. I was present on both occasions, and shall tell you more about it when we meet. To-day he returns to Paris, and at the end of April he is coming to Dresden, where Lüttichau has offered him the chance of conducting two concerts at the theatre. There is also some talk of a musical festival under Berlioz's direction at Brunswick next summer, where his Requiem and Te Deum are to be performed.

Tannhäuser will be given here next Sunday. I have studied the part with Liebert, and think that he will do it well. The whole finale of the second act will be given, also the new close with the reappearance of Venus, and on an early occasion I mean to restore the sixteen bars in the adagio of the finale of the second act which I believe T. had cut; that is, if you agree. It, however, always requires some prudence and caution to make similar changes here, especially as the theatre is to be conducted more than ever on economic principles, etc.

How is Herwegh? I shall write to him this week for certain. Since my return to Weymar I have been plagued in many ways; my chief business is almost in a worse state than before, but there is not as yet any definite result. Pardon me, dearest Richard, if I pass this over in silence; you know that generally it is my way if I can say nothing good. . . .

I should have liked much to send you a different answer from the Härtels; but, alas! it cannot be helped. Be of good courage, nevertheless, and work at your *Rhinegold*. Next summer I hope to visit you and to stay with you for some time. My best remembrances to your wife. The honey she sent me is splendid, and I am always rejoiced to look at it when it is put on the table in the morning with my coffee.

Farewell, dearest Richard, and write soon to

Your

F. L.

WEYMAR, *December 13th*, 1853.

Hoplit's pamphlet about the Carlsruhe Musical Festival you have probably received. At Christmas I shall send you the *Künstler* chorus, which is being autographed in full score.

140.

DEAREST FRANZ,

Two words to-day in great haste. I am angry with myself for having burdened an overpatient friend like you with this Härtel affair. Pardon me. It is all over now, and (D.V.) you will hear nothing more about this Jewish business. I am, it is true, for the moment in an awkward position, but you must not mind that. Are you out of temper ?

But you are composing. The Princess has written to me about it. You must surprise me soon !

I spin myself in like a cocoon, but I also spin something out of myself. For five years I had written no music ; now I am in Nibelheim. Mime made his complaint to-day. Unfortunately I was last month taken ill with a feverish cold, which disabled me for ten days ; otherwise the sketch would have been ready this year. At times also my somewhat cloudy situation disturbs me ; there is at present an ominous calm around me. But by the end of January I must be ready. Enough for to-day. I have many things to tell you, but my head is burning. There is something wrong with me ; and sometimes, with lightning-like rapidity, the thought flashes through me that it would be better, after all, if I died. But that has nothing to do with my writing music.

Adieu. Greet the Princess and the Child many times.
Soon more from

Your

WAGNER RICHARDTÓL.

ZURICH, *December 17th*, 1853.

P.S.—You will have another letter very soon.

141.

Many thanks, you dear bringer of Christmas
cheer. You come like a true saviour to me, and I have
placed you on my work-table, as on an altar. Thanks,
a thousand thanks, to you for coming. I was very
lonely.

If I had a sweetheart, I think I should never write
to her, and to you also I must write little—I mean writing apart from relating external events. The events I
experience within me I can write of all the less, because
I could not even tell them, so necessary is it to me to
feel or—to *act*.

I know that I shall have another letter from you soon,
because you have something to relate to me; so I am
proud, and rely upon it, and keep my peace, telling you
thereby that I love you sincerely with all my heart.

Your

R. W.

ZURICH, *December 26th*, 1853.

142.

Thursday, December 29th, 1853.

WEYMAR,—*just returned from Leipzig.*

After waiting in vain yesterday and the day before
at Leipzig for *Lohengrin*, I returned here to-day. Probably the performance will not take place for a few days;

ι at present nothing can be settled, because now Elsa, now
the King or Telramund, is ill, or because the bass
clarinet ordered from Erfurt has not arrived ; and when
it does arrive at Leipzig, it is not certain whether the
clarinet-player there will be able to play it, etc., etc.

David and Pohl had informed me Monday evening
that the general rehearsal would take place on Tuesday.
I had to conduct *Tannhäuser* here on Monday,
December 26th. This was the second performance with
Liebert as Tannhäuser; the first took place on the
preceding Sunday (December 18th), the subscription
being on both occasions suspended—an unprecedented
fact at Weymar in connection with an opera which had
reached its fifteenth performance. House crowded, so
that on the first occasion *many* people had to be refused
admission. Performance upon the whole satisfactory ;
Liebert in places excellent. The tempi were slower than
Tichatschek takes them, just as I had studied them
with Liebert ; for I had been obliged again to have five
or six rehearsals of *Tannhäuser*. Your metronomical
indications I naturally accepted as my rule, which
formerly I had not been able to do—69 for the song of
Tannhäuser, 70 or thereabouts for the D major passage
of Wolfram, etc. The impression on the whole public
was *striking* and *inspiriting*. The Mildes were called
Liebert was called, and even my nose had to show
itself at the end. In brief, the two evenings gave me
a degree of pleasure which only my fear that you,
glorious, dearest, best of friends, might be in trouble,
could impair.

But to continue. Tuesday, at 3 a.m., with the
thermometer at twenty degrees below zero, I and

Cornelius took the train in order to be at Leipzig in
time for the *Lohengrin* rehearsal at 8.30 a.m. I at
once sent word to David, who informed me that the
rehearsal would not take place, on account of the
indisposition of Herr Schott (King Henry). David soon
afterwards called on me, and gave me hopes for another
day. Yesterday they sent a telegram here to summon
the Mildes, for Brassin and Frau Meyer also had been
taken ill, but Zigesar would not permit the Mildes to
go to Leipzig, because the *Flying Dutchman* is announced
here for New Year's Day. At last this morning I am
credibly informed that some days must elapse before
Lohengrin is given at Leipzig. They promised to
let me know by telegram as soon as anything was
settled ; and if I can possibly manage, I shall again go
to Leipzig, in order to give you an account of the
performance.

In the meanwhile I have handed the nine pieces
from *Lohengrin*, which H. had recently sent me, to the
Härtels ; and you will have a letter about them together
with these lines, as Dr. Härtel assured me yesterday
that he would write to you direct and without delay.
En fin de compte: The Härtels are very trustworthy ; and
if you will permit me, I advise you to make use of their
excellent and well-deserved reputation as publishers,
because I feel convinced that later on your relations
with them will turn out very satisfactory. As you have
appointed me your humble court-counsellor, I add the
remark that you will be well advised in insisting upon
H.'s name being inserted in the title-page of the
Lohengrin pieces, for there is no rational cause for
refusing H. this satisfaction, which he has fully deserved

by his faithful and energetic adherence to you as well
as by his actual talent.

The Härtels will finally agree to this, and I have
spoken to them in that sense. Of course in similar
affairs I have to take the mild position of a mediator,
which now and then is a little troublesome. However,
so it must be; and side issues must not be allowed to
impede or endanger the principal question. If therefore
you reply to the Härtels, write to them that you
specially desire to have the name of H., as the author
of the pianoforte arrangement of your *Lohengrin* pieces,
inserted in their edition, and that if you write other
operas later on you intend to entrust H. with the
pianoforte arrangement. H. is devoted to you heart
and soul, and you may feel sure that he will do the
work to your satisfaction. However, if you like, I will
revise the arrangement and after that send it to you,
so that not a single note may remain which does not
please you and is not in accordance with the design of
the composition as well as with the requirements of
the pianoforte. On New Year's Day we shall have the
Flying Dutchman here. The two last performances of
Tannhäuser have made Weymar your official *Moniteur*
amongst theatres; and, without flattering myself, I
venture to doubt whether your works have been
performed anywhere else in an equally satisfactory
manner all round. For next year, for example, a new
hall of Castle Wartburg is being painted, also a
bridal chamber for the third act of *Lohengrin*, etc.
Several a little more expensive dresses have been
ordered, and in May Tichatschek and probably Johanna
will play Lohengrin and Ortrud.

All that is possible has been done. The impossible you will provide in the *Rhinegold*. How far have you got with it ? Shall I have the score in May, according to promise ? Go on with it bravely ! As soon as you have finished, the rest will follow.

Forget all about Philistia and Jewry, but remember cordially

Your

FRANZ.

I presume you have received the medallion which the Princess sent you. In the first week of the new year I shall send you the score of my *Künstler* chorus, which I have had autographed here. Devote a quarter of an hour to it, and tell me plainly your opinion of the composition, which of course I look upon only as a stepping-stone to other things. If you find it bad, bombastic, mistaken, tell me so without hesitation. You may be convinced that I am not in the least vain of my works ; and if I do not produce anything good and beautiful all my life, I shall none the less continue to feel genuine and cordial pleasure in the beautiful and good things which I recognize and admire in others.

Farewell, and God be with you.

END OF VOL. I.

E DUE

	PRINTED IN U.S.A.